WORKING WITH SPOKEN DISCOURSE

WORKING WITH SPOKEN DISCOURSE

DEBORAH CAMERON

Los Angeles | London | New Delhi
Singapore | Washington DC

First published 2001

Reprinted 2009(twice), 2010, 2011

SAGE Publications Ltd
1 Oliver's Yard
55 City Road
London EC1Y 1SP

SAGE Publications Inc.
2455 Teller Road
Thousand Oaks, California 91320

SAGE Publications India Pvt Ltd
B 1/I 1 Mohan Cooperative Industrial Area
Mathura Road
New Delhi 110 044

SAGE Publications Asia-Pacific Pte Ltd
33 Pekin Street #02-01
Far East Square
Singapore 048763

British Library Cataloguing in Publication data

A catalogue record for this book is
available from the British Library

ISBN 978-0-7619-5772-0 (hbk)
ISBN 978-0-7619-5773-7 (pbk)

Library of Congress catalog card number 2001131054

Typeset by Keystroke, Jacaranda Lodge, Wolverhampton.
Printed in Great Britain by CPI Antony Rowe, Chippenham, Wiltshire
Printed on paper from sustainable resources

Contents

Acknowledgements   vii

Introduction   1

I Preliminaries   5

1 What is discourse and why analyse it?   7

2 Collecting data: practical and ethical considerations   19

3 Transcribing spoken discourse   31

II Approaches   45

4 Approaches to discourse analysis: an initial orientation   47

5 Situations and events: the ethnography of speaking   53

6 Doing things with words: pragmatics   68

7 Sequence and structure: Conversation Analysis   87

8 Small differences, big difference: interactional sociolinguistics   106

9 Hidden agendas? Critical discourse analysis   123

III Applications   143

10 Working with spoken discourse in social research   145

11 Identity, difference and power: locating social relations in spoken discourse   161

12 Designing your own projects   180

Bibliography   193

Index   201

Acknowledgements

This book was written with students in mind, and my greatest debt is to my own students. I am especially indebted to Kim Atherton, Catriona Carson, Michael Higgins, Marko Kukkonen and Stuart May, all members of a discourse analysis class I taught at Strathclyde University, who encouraged me to write this text and generously permitted me to use their own projects as examples in it. Among the other students whose work I have supervised (and some of which I refer to in these pages), I am grateful in particular to Christine Callender, Christine Christie, Deborah Hills, Fiona McAlinden, Kathy O'Leary, Helen Reid-Thomas, Sylvia Shaw and Shân Wareing. I have been fortunate to encounter so much curiosity, enthusiasm and talent among the students to whom I have taught discourse analysis, and I mean it when I say that I could not have written this book without them.

The text has benefited at various stages of its composition from the attentions of several careful readers: I thank Meryl Altman, Jane Davies, Don Kulick, Donald Matheson and Kay Richardson for their intelligent and sympathetic criticism. For the errors, obstinacies and patches of ignorance that remain, I hope they will forgive me.

Introduction

This is a book about discourse analysis, and its title – *Working with Spoken Discourse* – was chosen with two points in mind. First, I wanted to emphasize the practical side of discourse analysis as well as the theory, since for many readers these will be equally relevant concerns. Many linguistics students taking a class in discourse analysis are required to undertake small-scale research projects; growing numbers of research students in a range of academic disciplines are using discourse analysis to investigate all kinds of questions. There is a place, then, for a textbook which approaches discourse analysis not only as subject matter (something readers want to know *about*), but also as method (something they want to know how to *do*).

Second, I have focused on *spoken* discourse because so many researchers with an interest in discourse analysis are dealing, specifically, with spoken language data. It is obvious that spoken discourse is of interest to students of language and linguistics; but it is also, in principle, of interest to students in other social science disciplines, who make use of qualitative research methods like participant observation, interviewing, conducting focus-group discussions, and so on. It is characteristic of these methods that the researcher interacts with research subjects and/or records their interaction with each other – and that, of course, produces data in the form of talk. Researchers then confront the question of how to analyse this kind of material in a systematic and insightful way. Whether they choose to adopt the techniques of microanalysis developed by discourse and conversation analysts, or make use of qualitative software packages to code their data, a good understanding of how spoken discourse works can only enhance their analysis.

The analysis of *written* texts is also, of course, a qualitative method used in social science research, as well as being of interest to linguists. Though speech rather than writing is my main focus here, some of the same questions arise in relation to written texts, and some of the approaches outlined here are applicable to the analysis of those texts (a case in point is critical discourse analysis, see Chapter 9). However, this book is not intended to be a comprehensive guide to the analysis of written discourse, and readers whose main interest is in writing should consult other sources. Texts that deal with written as well as spoken discourse include Biber (1988), Brown and Yule (1983) and Maybin and Mercer (1996). The forms writing takes and the uses it is put to in diverse social contexts are major topics in the 'new literacy studies' (for a selection, see Barton et al. 2000). Another relevant approach that has recently emerged, enabled by new computer technology, is 'corpus linguistics', the analysis of recurring patterns in very large samples of linguistic data. Currently, written texts make up the bulk of most large corpora; Stubbs (1996) provides a good illustration of what a discourse analyst can do with this sort of material.

Technological change does not only produce new methods for analysing discourse, it also produces new kinds of discourse. Some analysts have suggested that dividing the field according to medium (speech versus writing) is already outmoded and will become increasingly difficult to justify in the digital age of 'multimedia' texts which integrate not only spoken and written language but also graphic devices, still and moving images, and music. Here I do not address the issues raised by new technologies and new media in detail (though I do make passing reference to those forms of electronic communication which can be analysed as 'hybrids' of spoken and written discourse, such as the interaction that takes place in internet 'chat rooms'). Those issues will doubtless be important in the future development of discourse analysis. Whatever the future holds, however, I am confident that 'working with spoken discourse' will continue to occupy an important place in the study of language, communication and social life.

A NOTE ON THE STRUCTURE OF THIS BOOK, AND SOME SUGGESTIONS ABOUT HOW TO USE IT

The book is divided into three parts, called 'Preliminaries', 'Approaches' and 'Applications'. 'Preliminaries' (Part I) deals with issues that need to be addressed before analysis proper can begin: the definition of *discourse* and the goals of discourse analysis (Chapter 1); the collection of data for analysis (Chapter 2); and the process of making a written record of speech for analysis, transcription (Chapter 3). 'Approaches' (Part II) introduces, and illustrates with examples, a number of different paradigms or 'schools' of discourse analysis. This serves two purposes. On one hand, it is a way of developing the reader's knowledge *about* talk, by introducing various theories about the way it works, and some of the empirical findings that go along with those theories. On the other hand, it is intended to give readers tools they can use in doing their own analyses. The section begins with a short survey of the approaches that will be considered, sketching their similarities, differences and relationships with one another, as well as their links to other academic disciplines (Chapter 4). Then it looks in more detail at the ethnography of speaking (Chapter 5), pragmatics (Chapter 6), conversational analysis (Chapter 7), interactional sociolinguistics (Chapter 8) and critical discourse analysis (Chapter 9). Part III, 'Applications', explores how discourse analytic approaches and techniques can be used to address various problems and questions of a broadly social rather than purely linguistic kind. The part begins (Chapter 10) with a discussion of discourse analysis as a method for doing social research, showing how systematic attention to the form and the context as well as the content of talk can be helpful to researchers trying to interpret spoken language data. It continues (Chapter 11) by taking up questions of power, identity and difference, which are concerns for discourse analysts in a range of academic disciplines, and which have occasioned some debate among analysts. It ends with a chapter on designing small-scale projects (Chapter 12), which includes a number of case studies of real projects done by real students.

All chapters end with a short section headed 'Suggestions for further reading about . . . ' in which I draw attention to other useful readings on the topic under discussion (there is also a full bibliography at the end of the book). In addition, most chapters in the first two sections include an 'activity', in which readers are invited to work with a piece of data – sometimes data I provide and sometimes data they collect themselves – and then to reflect on their procedures, problems and conclusions.

This text can be used in a number of different ways, and different kinds of readers may find different reading strategies useful. For those who are taking a class in discourse analysis, it makes sense to read the three parts of the text in the order they appear. The order, both of sections and of chapters within them, is designed to help students of discourse analysis acquire knowledge and skills progressively, ending up with a reasonable overview of a field of study that is internally complex and diverse. Those who are not taking a class, but who are planning or working on a research project and are therefore most interested in discourse analysis as a method, may prefer to read more selectively. These readers – especially, perhaps, if their research is not in language/linguistics – might want to orient themselves by reading the first chapter and then skip to 'Applications' (Part III), returning later to those chapters in 'Approaches' which seem potentially useful for their own work. Other readers doing research may already know that they want to use, say, CA or critical discourse analysis, and may wish to go straight to the relevant 'Approaches' chapter.

The final chapter, on designing projects, is probably more helpful to readers who want to focus on questions about language (or 'language and something') than to other social researchers. Readers whose primary focus is not linguistic may find some of the analytic advice in Chapter 12 helpful, but their need for guidance on research design – certainly on matters like sampling and elicitation techniques – may be better met by a more general textbook on qualitative methods in social science.

A NOTE ON DATA EXAMPLES

Working with Spoken Discourse contains various data extracts intended to illustrate the workings of spoken interaction or to provide material for readers to analyse. In some cases the examples I have chosen come from the published work of other researchers. Where that is the case, I have cited the source in the text. In other cases, examples come from small-scale projects done by people who at the time were my students (I use their work with their permission; acknowledgement is made in the text). Unlike the authors of the published work I use, however, these students generally collected their data for end-of-course assignments, which are not available for readers to consult. In a few instances students carried out analysis for a Masters dissertation, which can be obtained from the relevant university library. Where that is so, I include a citation for the dissertation in the bibliography.

In a few cases, my examples are 'constructed' – in plainer words, I have made them up. Where I have done this, I have indicated it in the text. Readers may with good reason wonder why an empirical researcher would make up bits of talk. In this case, it is not because I don't have 'real' data that would illustrate the point; my constructed examples are modelled on real ones. I have, however, modified reality to save space, in cases where my real example was very lengthy or difficult to understand without a lot of contextualization.

Where an example is neither attributed to any other source nor labelled 'constructed', that means it comes from the collection of spoken discourse data that I have built up over time for research and/or teaching purposes. In line with normal procedures for the ethical treatment of research subjects (see Chapter 2), I have given fictitious names to all the speakers who feature in examples from my own collection of data, and occasionally I have modified some minor details where this was necessary to prevent the identification of specific individuals or institutions.

Readers will notice that data examples are not all displayed using the same transcription conventions. There is no single, standard system for transcribing spoken discourse; analysts have to make choices, and these may have theoretical implications (see Chapter 3). On the assumption that the researchers whose data I reproduce here considered their own choices carefully, I have refrained from altering their transcripts.

A NOTE ON LANGUAGE(S)

It is obvious that not all talk is in English; indeed, not all conversations are in any single language, since in many communities people know two or more languages and regularly engage in what linguists call 'code-switching'. In this book, however, as in most English-language texts on this subject, English serves rather consistently as a reference point for discussion. While I do make some reference to work dealing with languages other than English, I do not claim to provide a systematic comparative analysis, nor do I deal in any detail with issues relating to bilingual language-users' talk (such as language choice and code switching). All the extended data examples I discuss are in English (though they are not all in the same variety of that language), and the bibliography does not list publications in languages other than English (though it does list some that are *about* other languages). That these are limitations, I do not deny. I would encourage readers who use languages in addition to English to work on data from those languages (both when doing the activities included in this book and in their own research projects), to search out literature in and about other languages, and to test claims that depend on evidence from English against their knowledge of what happens in other languages.

Preliminaries

1 What is discourse and why analyse it?

In 1996 a spokesperson for British Telecom (BT), the UK's largest phone company, launched a campaign to improve the nation's communication skills, explaining that 'since life is in many ways a series of conversations, it makes sense to be as good as we possibly can at something we tend to take for granted' (quoted in the *Guardian*, 30 December 1996). Analysts of spoken discourse do not usually share BT's goal of making people 'better' at talking: they begin from the assumption that people are, with few exceptions, highly skilled users of spoken language. But most would probably agree that 'life is in many ways a series of conversations', and that talking is 'something we tend to take for granted'. When linguists and other social scientists analyse spoken discourse, their aim is to make explicit what normally gets taken for granted; it is also to show what talking accomplishes in people's lives and in society at large.

The reference to 'linguists and other social scientists' in the last paragraph is meant to underline the important point that working with spoken discourse is an interdisciplinary enterprise: among those who may be engaged in it are anthropologists, linguists, philosophers, psychologists, sociologists, students of the media or education or the law. A commonly used academic label for what these various people are doing, and one which I will use myself throughout this book, is *discourse analysis*. But while it is useful in many contexts to have this generic label available, it does need to be remembered that 'discourse analysis' is an umbrella term, allowing for considerable variation in subject matter and approach. For instance, I should make clear straight away that discourse analysis is not exclusively concerned with *spoken* discourse: in principle it can deal with socially situated language-use in any channel or medium. Discourse analysts may work with written data, or data from sign languages of the deaf, and some analysts work with textual graphics and images as well (e.g. Kress and van Leeuwen 1996).

There is also a distinction to be made between analysing discourse as an end in itself and analysing it as a means to some other end. Some discourse analysts – including many of those whose disciplinary affiliation is to linguistics – are primarily concerned to describe the complex structures and mechanisms of socially situated language-use. They ask questions like 'how does turn-taking work in conversation?', or 'does the form of a question affect the form of the answer?' or 'why do people misunderstand one another?'. They study talk because they want to know about talk. But some linguists, and many researchers who are not linguists, are more interested in the idea that 'life is in many ways a series of conversations', which implies that people's talk can be a source of evidence about other aspects of their lives. Though they may not be studying discourse as an end in itself, many sociologists and social psychologists, or researchers in education, in cultural studies and media studies, adopt methods which produce discourse data. Interviews, focus group discussions and ethnographic studies using participant observation all involve verbal interaction between a researcher and research subjects, and/or between research subjects themselves. At least some of the analysis carried out by researchers who choose these methods will involve listening to talk, transcribing it, and reflecting on its meaning and significance.

As we will see in more detail later on, there are many different varieties of discourse analysis, and there is a certain amount of argument about their relative merits. My aim in this book is to be as inclusive as possible: though I write as a linguist myself, I have tried to design my account of what discourse analysis is, and does, to be helpful to readers across a range of academic disciplines. That means trying to cover the spectrum of approaches they are likely to encounter, making clear what the similarities and differences are, and bringing out the distinctive contributions made by different approaches.

As the title *Working with Spoken Discourse* suggests, this book will not be concerned with *all* forms of discourse, but only with *spoken* discourse. In the Introduction I gave one reason for this choice: talk forms the data many social researchers turn to discourse analysis to help them interpret, and they are often unsure how to approach this data in a suitably 'analytic' way. Arguably, this is less true of written discourse. Anyone who has been educated in a highly literate society will have developed, not only the ability to read and write, but also some ability to think analytically *about* written texts. For instance, many school students have had some experience of learning how to do 'close reading' of literary texts: they have had their attention drawn to the structure of a poem or to the existence of competing interpretations of its meaning. By contrast it is much less likely that they have ever been taught to approach ordinary talk – or any kind of spoken language – in the same systematic way. Similarly, most people acquire in the course of their schooling an extensive metalanguage ('language about language') with which to describe the structures of writing: terms like *letter, comma, sentence* and *paragraph* belong to this metalanguage. They rarely possess a parallel metalinguistic apparatus for discussing the structures of spoken language: as we will see in more detail in Chapter 3, most people do not realize the extent of the differences between writing and speech.

The above reference to metalanguage reminds us that issues of terminology and definition tend to loom large in all academic enterprises; discourse analysis is no exception. I have already used several different terms – *conversation, talk* and [spoken] *discourse* – for what might appear to be much the same thing. Do all these terms, however, really mean the same thing? The question would be unlikely to arise in the context of an ordinary, non-academic exchange, but an important part of being 'analytical' is being able to reflect on and ask questions about the conceptual frameworks and vocabulary we take for granted in everyday life. So at this point I want to look more closely at some of the key terms that are relevant to discourse analysis, beginning with the apparently straightforward term *conversation*.

CONVERSATION, TALK, DISCOURSE

ACTIVITY

(Note: this activity is more interesting to do in a group, and it is especially interesting if the group includes speakers of more than one language.)

As quickly as possible, list all the words you can think of that are used to describe different kinds of talk in each of the languages/varieties you know. Now examine your list more closely.

- How would you define each of the terms you have listed (for the benefit of someone learning the language, for example)? Is each one distinct from all the rest or is there overlap? Is there any disagreement in the group about the definition of certain terms?
- What dimensions of contrast (e.g. formal v. informal, serious v. non-serious) seem to be important in distinguishing different kinds of talk?
- If different languages/varieties are represented in your list, do they all make similar distinctions?
- How many of the kinds of talk you have listed could you also describe as 'conversation'? If that term applies better to some cases than others, why do you think that is? If it is inapplicable in some cases, what makes it inapplicable?

In ordinary usage, *conversation* usually refers to spoken rather than written language. I say 'usually' because recently an interesting exception has become noticeable: people who regularly interact with others via the internet, for instance in 'chat rooms', sometimes refer to what they are doing as 'talking' or to their exchanges as 'conversations', though the medium is actually written language. The term 'chat room' makes an explicit parallel with a certain kind of informal conversation, namely *chat*. If we are being analytical, these usages might prompt some questions. Are *interactivity* (the fact that on-line exchange can involve a relatively rapid 'back and forth' between participants) and *spontaneity* (the fact that contributions to chat-room exchanges are typically composed without much planning or editing) more salient characteristics of what we call 'conversation' than the channel or medium of interaction? Is the actual language people produce in chat rooms more similar to face-to-face speech than other kinds of written language?

We (that is, English speakers, though the same thing is true for speakers of many other languages too) have quite a large vocabulary for distinguishing different kinds of talk. We can describe interactions in terms of their tone, level of formality and subject-matter using terms like *argument, blether, chat, discussion, gossip*. We can describe spoken language events in terms of their setting, context or purpose using terms like *interview, debate* and *seminar*. Is *conversation* just a generic term that subsumes all the others, or does it cover only some of the possibilities? Is a seminar a 'conversation'? Is the talk I have with my doctor when I visit her surgery 'conversation' in the same way the talk I have with her if I run into her at the supermarket is 'conversation'? The activity on p. 9 is intended to encourage you to think about your own understanding of what 'conversation' is, and more generally what different kinds of talk are recognized by language-users in the community or communities you belong to.

One point the activity might illustrate is that *conversation* in English has both 'generic' and more 'specific' uses. It is generic in the sense that we can use it to describe a relatively broad range of different kinds of spoken interaction. More specifically, though, it seems most 'natural' to apply it to interaction which is characterized by informality, spontaneity and egalitarian relationships between the participants (if your boss asks you to come and have a 'conversation' about your punctuality, you tend to suspect euphemism, or irony). Certainly, for me as an English-speaker it seems more natural to use the word *conversation* in connection with 'chat' or 'gossip' than for a seminar or a medical consultation. Each of these has features of conversation, but intuitively I feel it is not the prototypical case.

In this book I want to consider many kinds of spoken interaction, and to examine the similarities and differences among them. Therefore, when I discuss spoken interaction in a generic sense I will use two other words in preference to *conversation*: one is *talk* and the other is *discourse*. Just to complicate matters, one of these terms is more generic, or at least more inclusive, than the other. *Talk*, to state the obvious, refers only to spoken language-use, whereas *discourse*, as I have noted already, can refer to language-use in any channel or medium. But that is not the only difference between the two terms. *Discourse* is evidently a more 'technical' term than *talk*. And like a lot of technical terms, it is also 'contested' – that is, it has generated a lot of debate among scholars about what it means and how it should be used. In fact, the term *discourse* is notorious for the arguments surrounding it and the confusion it can cause. A major source of potential confusion is that the meaning of the term tends to vary quite significantly depending on the academic discipline and the theoretical preferences of the person who uses it. The range of meanings *discourse* can have in academic discussion is an issue that needs to be clarified sooner rather than later. So before I go any further: what is *discourse*?

LANGUAGE 'ABOVE THE SENTENCE' AND LANGUAGE 'IN USE'

The most straightforward definition of *discourse* is the one often found in textbooks for students of linguistics: 'language above the sentence'. Of course, that is not at all straightforward unless you understand some basic assumptions in linguistics, so let me spell them out.

Linguists treat language as a 'system of systems', with each system having its own characteristic forms of structure or organization. For instance, the sound system of a language (its phonology) does not have the same kinds of units, or the same rules for combining them, as the grammatical system of that language. As your units get larger (e.g. words are larger than sounds and sentences are larger than words), you metaphorically move 'up' from one level of organization to the next.

If discourse analysis deals with 'language *above* the sentence', this means it looks for patterns (structure, organization) in units which are larger, more extended, than one sentence.

One of the earliest discourse analysts, the linguist Zellig Harris (1952), posed the question: how do we tell whether a sequence of sentences is a *text*[1] – that is, the sentences relate to one another and collectively form some larger whole – as opposed to just a random collection of unrelated bits? The answer to that question, Harris thought, would make clear what kind of structure exists 'above the sentence'. Texts would have this structure, whereas random collections of sentences would not.

Plainly, language-users do routinely interpret sequences longer than a sentence as texts in which the parts combine to form a larger whole. Consider the following example, a simple text produced by a child, which is discussed in a famous article by the conversation analyst Harvey Sacks (1972).

> The baby cried.
> The mommy picked it up.

One obvious instance of 'structure above the sentence' in this example is the pronoun *it*, which is *anaphoric* (referring back). It comes in the second sentence but it refers to something mentioned in the first: 'the baby'. A reader or hearer automatically takes it that the 'it' which the mommy picked up must be the baby, and not some previously unmentioned object like a rattle or a banknote. The pronoun is a *cohesive* device, tying the two sentences together, and cohesion is a property of texts.

But there is more to say about what makes this sequence work as a text. For instance, it is natural to read it as a *narrative*, in which the sequence of events in the text mirrors the sequence of events in the reality being reported: the baby cried *and then* the mommy picked it up. Indeed, in this case we are likely to infer not merely sequence but causality: the mommy picked up the baby *because* it cried. The way we process the text as a narrative implies that we are following a general procedure for dealing with structure 'above the sentence': where A and B are sentences, we assume that A followed by B means 'A *and then* B' or 'A *and consequently* B'.

But there is a problem with Zellig Harris's proposal about distinguishing texts like the child's story from random collections of sentences which are not texts: we seem to have a strong tendency to apply the principles just described to any sequence we are confronted with, however bizarre. Michael Stubbs (1983: 93) quotes a radio announcer who once said:

> Later, an item about vasectomy and the results of the do-it-yourself competition.

Why does this raise a smile? The default assumption is that the parts of the announcement on either side of the conjunction *and* relate to one another in the same way as the two parts of the baby/mommy sequence, and so we reason that the announcer must be referring to a do-it-yourself vasectomy competition. However, I am confident that most of us immediately go on to reject this interpretation. We recognize that the announcer did not intend the structural relationship that is implicit in the organization of his discourse. But this recognition does not come from pondering the details of the announcer's language, and deciding that, contrary to our initial assumption, his utterance has no structure. Rather, we realize that the scenario we have conjured up by applying the usual procedure is implausible and ridiculous: no one would organize, or enter, a competition in which men performed vasectomies on themselves. In other words, we take account not simply of the linguistic properties of the announcement, but also (and in this case more significantly) of what we know about the world.

Real-world knowledge is also relevant to the interpretation of the baby/ mommy text. There is no purely structural reason why we have to take it that the mommy who picked the baby up is the baby's own mother, since the child does not specify that by using a possessive pronoun, referring only to '*the* mommy'. Nevertheless I would bet that most readers did make that assumption. The text follows a familiar script whereby babies cry and are picked up by their mothers to stop them crying. It is imaginable that a crying baby might be picked up by a total stranger who was, however, the mother of some other baby; but that would not be many people's first guess.

I am suggesting, then, that we make sense of discourse partly by making guesses based on knowledge about the world. If that is accepted, then arguably the definition of discourse as 'language above the sentence', and of discourse analysis as a search for structure at a level higher than sentence structure, is not adequate. That definition suggests that single sentences and texts have a similar kind of organization: the difference is one of *scale*. But is that really the case? To be grammatical, a sentence must contain certain constituents in a certain order: it is conformity to structural rules that makes the difference between grammatical sentences and 'word salad' (like *stood boy the on up chair a* – the asterisk is a linguist's convention for denoting ungrammatical sequences). But our ability to decide whether and how discourse makes sense appears to involve much more than quasi-grammatical generalizations about what can go with or follow what.

It might also be asked whether the characteristic features picked out by discourse analysts have much to do with the size of the units being analysed – the fact that they are larger than a sentence.[2] Henry Widdowson (1995) has pointed out that a 'text' can in fact be smaller than a sentence. He observes for instance that the legend LADIES on the door of a public lavatory is a text, as is the letter P which is used in Britain to indicate a space for parking cars. A single word or letter cannot have 'structure above the sentence'. So what makes these examples texts? Widdowson's answer is that in the contexts he is concerned with, each of them is intended to convey a complete message. Of course, what we take that message to be does depend on the context, and once again, its interpretation relies on real-world knowledge that is not contained in the text itself. Looking up the word *ladies* in a dictionary would not, on its own, make clear what message it conveys when written on a door. (Someone who spoke English but was unfamiliar with the concept and etiquette of public lavatories might think it meant 'there are ladies behind this door'.) A great deal of general knowledge and contextual information has to be brought to bear on even the most banal texts we encounter if those texts are to serve their communicative purpose. A distinctive feature of discourse analysis, as opposed to the study of syntax (sentence structure), is its overt concern with what and how language communicates when it is used purposefully in particular instances and contexts, and how the phenomena we find in 'real language' (implicitly contrasted to the idealized, made-up example sentences most often discussed by analysts of syntax) can be explained with reference to the communicative purposes of the text or the interaction. From this standpoint a better definition of *discourse* than 'language above the sentence' might be 'language in use': language used to do something and mean something, language produced and interpreted in a real-world context.

Deborah Schiffrin (1994) suggests that the two definitions of *discourse* I have just outlined correspond, roughly speaking, to two important currents or tendencies in twentieth-century linguistics. One is *formalism* or *structuralism*: an interest in the abstract form and structure of language. The other is *functionalism*: an interest in what language is used to do. But Schiffrin goes on to point out that treating this as an absolute distinction would be an oversimplification. Because its meaning is so dependent on context, discourse is not amenable to 'pure' formalist analysis. Conversely, functionalists have always been concerned with form as well as function. They are interested in how the two are connected, suggesting that language has a certain kind of formal organization because of the purposes it is designed to serve.

Most discourse analysts who locate themselves within the academic discipline of linguistics are concerned with both form and function, though the balance between these concerns may vary. But not all discourse analysts are linguists, and not all would define their goals in terms of improving our understanding of language as such. Many social scientists (including, in fact, some linguists) are more interested in discourse as a source of evidence or insight about social life and social relations. Their questions are not like Zellig Harris's, primarily about the way language works. Rather they use discourse analysis as a qualitative research method for investigating social phenomena: sexual harassment, attitudes to the monarchy and youth subcultures are among the topics that have been investigated in this way.[3] But investigators doing this kind of work often adopt a definition of the term *discourse* which differs from the ones we have examined so far. That alternative definition is now sufficiently influential across disciplines to merit more detailed consideration.

POWER, KNOWLEDGE AND PRACTICE: DISCOURSE(S) AND THE CONSTRUCTION OF SOCIAL REALITY

I mentioned above that discourse analysis is an increasingly popular qualitative research method in social science. The word *qualitative* in this context contrasts with *quantitative.* Discourse analysis is an alternative to using standardized instruments like questionnaires, which yield statistical data. A researcher who wants to find out using quantitative methods what people do in their leisure time might ask a sample of subjects to fill in the same questionnaire and then produce a statistical digest of their responses (e.g. '50% of women under 35 reported shopping was their main leisure activity'). A researcher who decides to use discourse analysis as a method would be more likely to spend time talking in depth to a sample of the people s/he is interested in, encouraging them to explore the subject in their own way and in their own words. The researcher would record subjects' talk, transcribe it and analyse it – not in order to make statistical generalizations, but in order to point out recurring themes in the way people talk about leisure activities.

This method is sometimes criticized on the grounds that it will not tell us accurately what people *really* do in their leisure time. The criticism is not without validity, but a discourse analyst might point out that it could equally be made of the questionnaire/statistical analysis approach. When people answer a researcher's questions, whether in a face-to-face interview or by completing a written form, they are constructing a certain representation of themselves for the researcher's benefit: they may be telling the researcher what they think s/he wants to hear or what they would like her/him to believe. This is another version of the process of self-construction that goes on in ordinary talk, which is always produced with an eye to the situation and the person(s) to whom it is addressed. Arguably it is an unavoidable element of all communicative acts: people simply do not answer questions, in any situation, without first making some assessment of who is asking and why. (As a simple illustration of this point, recall the last time a doctor or nurse asked you how many units of alcohol you consume in a week. Was your answer affected by your assumptions about what use the nurse or doctor planned to make of the information? Was your answer accurate and truthful? Would you have given just the same answer to your mother, your best friend, or a prospective employer? What is your attitude to the questions I am asking now – for instance, if you don't drink alcohol, are you offended by my apparent assumption that all my readers do? Would that affect your response to me, if this were a conversation?)

Researchers who favour discourse analysis over supposedly more 'objective' methods argue that paying attention, not merely to *what* people say but to *how* they say it, gives additional insight into the way people understand things. It is less about collecting facts than about studying interpretive processes. Such researchers may also argue that analysing 'real' talk does a better job than standardized instruments of capturing the messiness of real life, and to that extent could be seen as more rather than less 'accurate'. Giving people a multiple-choice questionnaire obliges them to choose one option from a set constructed by someone else: they check box A, and that makes them look as if they are committed to A while rejecting B and C. Yet when people talk it often becomes clear that matters are more complex than that: they don't dismiss B and C out of hand, and they have their doubts about A. Standardized instruments produce an impression of certainty and consistency which is, arguably, misleading. Another advantage that might be claimed for discourse analysis is that it generates data by getting people to engage, or observing them while they engage, in an activity – talking – which is normal and familiar to them, rather than asking them to undertake an unusual or artificial task. Life may or may not be 'in many ways a series of conversations', but it is in no way a series of box-checking exercises.

Social researchers who do discourse analysis often want to make the point that even when we talk 'in our own words', these words may not actually be 'ours' at all, in the sense that they are not original or unique to any one individual. As one analyst, Jay Lemke, has put this point:

> We speak with the voices of our communities, and to the extent that we have individual voices, we fashion them out of the social voices already available to us, appropriating the words of others to speak a word of our own. (1995: 24–5)

Within any community there is a finite range of things it is conventional or intelligible to say about any given concern. When people talk about shopping, or drugs, or the royal family, what they say will be drawn from the community's repertoire of things it is possible to say rather than representing some unique perspective on the topic. This is not to suggest that people never say anything novel or unexpected, or that they do not have ideas of their own. But language-using is an *intersubjective* rather than purely subjective process: a 'voice' that is wholly individual runs the risk of being incomprehensible. Hence Lemke's point that individuals' ways of talking are formed using resources that are shared with others in their communities. Discourse analysis can be seen as a method for investigating the 'social voices' available to the people whose talk analysts collect.

Many social researchers today would argue that people's understandings of the world are not merely expressed in their discourse but actually shaped by the ways of using language which people have available to them. Another way of putting this is to say that reality is 'discursively constructed', made and remade as people talk about things using the 'discourses' they have access to. Evidently, the word *discourse* in this formulation is not being used in the way linguists typically use it, to mean 'language above the sentence' or 'language in use'. An obvious difference is that the linguist's *discourse* has no plural, whereas social theorists often talk about *discourses*. This plural usage reflects the influence of the philosopher and cultural historian Michel Foucault, who defined *discourses* as 'practices which systematically form the objects of which they speak' (Foucault 1972: 49).

To see what Foucault meant, let us consider the case of 'drugs'. The word *drugs* might seem to name a pre-existing 'real-world' category (of substances that affect the mind and body in certain ways). But if we think about the way the word is most often used, it becomes evident that it does not simply denote *all* substances that have certain effects: depending on context, it denotes either those which are medicinal, or those which are used non-medicinally and are also illegal. Caffeine, nicotine and alcohol are clearly mood-altering substances, but if we hear a report on 'drugs' we do not immediately think of coffee, cigarettes and beer. We certainly do not think of coffee-bean importers as drug traffickers or of tobacconists as drug dealers. What this suggests is that our category of 'drugs' (in the non-medicinal sense) has been formed through a particular set of *practices*: legislation (making some substances illegal), policing (trying to prevent breaches of the law and to catch people who do break it), the practices of the courts (where stories are told about why people have broken the law and decisions are made about how to deal with them), of social and charitable agencies (which try to reduce the harm caused by drugs), schools (which practise 'drugs education') and the media (which report on 'the problem of drugs'). Buying, selling and using illegal substances are also practices relevant to the understanding of 'drugs' as a category, though fewer people are involved in these practices compared with the numbers exposed to education or media reporting.

With so many practices and agencies involved, not surprisingly there are multiple 'discourses' on drugs. We may be working with the same category, but we can discuss it in different ways. For instance, there is a 'law and order' discourse in which drug-use is discussed as a crime, committed by people who are 'bad'. An alternative discourse is 'medical': people who use drugs are sick, and need treatment rather than punishment. There is a 'social' discourse in which drug-taking arises from deprivation and hopelessness. In contrast to these negative ways of talking, there is also a discourse in which drug-using is defined as a recreational activity, enjoyed without ill effects by the majority of those who engage in it. Another positive discourse suggests that using drugs may help people attain greater spiritual awareness.

Each of these ways of talking about 'drugs' has a history, but in some practices (and many discussions) they are not kept distinct. Drugs education, for instance, typically aims to persuade young people that they should not use drugs (it is unhealthy, illegal and dangerous), but some programmes also discuss the idea that drug-use is pleasurable, on the grounds that the appeal of drugs must be acknowledged if young people are to take warnings about the dangers seriously. Some programmes assume that many or most people will experiment with drugs, and aim to teach them how to minimize the risks involved. So drugs education may mix, in various proportions, elements of the 'law and order', 'medical' and 'recreational' discourses. Together, the various ways of discussing drugs and the practices that go along with them form a network of concepts and beliefs that set the agenda for debate and define what we perceive as reality on this subject. This is what theorists mean when they say that reality is 'discursively constructed'.

It might be asked what the sense of the word *discourse* that I have been discussing has to do, specifically, with *language*. Recall Foucault's definition, quoted above: although he calls discourses 'practices', he goes on to say that they 'form the objects of which they *speak*'. The link between practice and speaking (or more generally, language-use) lies in Foucault's concept of 'power/knowledge'. In the modern age, Foucault points out, a great deal of power and social control is exercised not by brute physical force or even by economic coercion, but by the activities of 'experts' who are licensed to define, describe and classify things and people. Definition, description and classification are practices, but they are essentially practices carried out using language. Words can be powerful: the institutional authority to categorize people is frequently inseparable from the authority to do things to them. Thus for instance, experts define mental health and mental illness, and on the basis of their definitions, individuals can be classified as mentally ill and detained in psychiatric institutions. Experts produce definitions of good or adequate 'parenting', and parents who do not meet the minimum standard may have their children taken away from them. Experts elaborate a concept of 'intelligence' and devise ways of measuring it (such as IQ tests); this may have real-world consequences for individuals' education and employment prospects.

I have explained the sense of *discourse* that comes from the work of Foucault because this usage of the term is now quite common, and students of discourse analysis in a variety of disciplines are likely to encounter it. However, it should not be supposed that all social researchers who adopt discourse analysis as a method are committed to the ideas of Foucault, or those of any other theorist. Some sociologists and social psychologists use *discourse* rather as some linguists do, to mean 'language in use'. There are varying views on whether and to what extent social reality is 'discursively constructed': you do not have to believe in the discursive construction of reality to regard what people say as a source of insight *about* reality.

As I pointed out earlier, though, any researcher who sets out to investigate some aspect of reality by studying discourse will end up with data in the form of *language*. And it is easy to underestimate the complexity of those data. As practised users of at least one language, researchers may be tempted to assume that it requires no special expertise to interpret linguistic data – that this is simply an extension of our ordinary, everyday behaviour as participants in verbal interaction. But that is at best only partly true. Being able to do something yourself is not the same as being able to analyse it from the outside. Discourse is not pure content, not just a window on someone's mental or social world; it has to be considered *as discourse*, that is, as a form of language with certain characteristics which are dictated by the way language and communication work. It is not only linguists who can benefit by paying attention to the 'how' as well as the 'what', the form as well as the content of people's discourse. Conversely, linguists have something to gain by attending to other social scientists' insights into what discourse does, or what social actors do with it.

SUMMARY

This chapter has been concerned with the meaning of the term *discourse* and the goals or purposes of analysing it. The view of discourse analysis taken here and throughout this book is a 'holistic' one, which acknowledges that discourse analysis is several things at once. It is a method for doing social research; it is a body of empirical knowledge about how talk and text are organized; it is the home of various theories about the nature and workings of human communication, and also of theories about the construction and reproduction of social reality. It is both about language and about life.

Part I continues, though, not with these grand abstractions, but with some concrete, practical considerations. The first requirement for any kind of discourse analysis is a body of data to analyse. In the next chapter we will look at the options and problems involved in collecting spoken discourse data.

SUGGESTIONS FOR FURTHER READING ABOUT 'DISCOURSE'

A book whose purpose is to 'unpack' the complex term *discourse* is Sara Mills's *Discourse* (1997). A shorter survey of various tendencies in contemporary discourse analysis is provided by the editors' Introduction to *The Discourse Reader* (Jaworski and Coupland 1999). This volume also includes an edited extract from Michel Foucault's *The History of Sexuality*, 'The incitement to discourse', which gives something of the flavour of what Foucault and his followers mean by the term. For a more traditionally 'linguistic' perspective on discourse and discourse analysis, a good source is the second chapter of Deborah Schiffrin's textbook *Approaches to Discourse* (1994), which is titled 'Definitions of discourse'. Teun van Dijk's edited two-volume *Discourse Studies: A Multidisciplinary Introduction* (1997) is a useful reference source for both linguists and others.

NOTES

1   In the next few paragraphs the word *text* occurs several times, and readers may find themselves wondering if it is just a synonym for *discourse*. In fact that is a disputed question. Some writers use the two terms more or less interchangeably (this is how I am using them in this section); some refer to spoken *discourse* but written *text* (i.e. the difference is one of medium); others (e.g. Widdowson 1995) make a more theoretical distinction. Briefly, Widdowson argues that *text* is the linguistic object (e.g. the words on a page in a book, or the transcript of a conversation) whereas *discourse* is the process of interaction/ interpretation that produces meaning from language. In speech discourse comes first, and produces a text; in writing text comes first, and readers produce discourse from it.

2   As will be discussed in more detail below (Chapter 3), the sentence is in any case essentially a unit of *written* rather than spoken language.

3   For readers who want to follow up any of these examples, Kitzinger and Thomas (1995) is a discourse analytic study of sexual harassment; Billig (1992) is a study of discourse about the (British) monarchy; and Widdicombe and Wooffitt (1995) is a study of youth subcultures using the method of Conversation Analysis.

2 Collecting data: practical and ethical considerations

This chapter and the next are about the practicalities and the ethics of studying spoken discourse. If you are going to analyse any kind of discourse, you need material ('data') to work on. But whereas most written materials (e.g. samples of news reporting, or girls' magazines, or even unpublished texts like student essays) are relatively straightforward to collect, collecting talk and getting it into an analysable form presents more of a challenge.

Spoken language data for discourse analysis consist in the first instance of recordings (audio or video) of people talking; the next part of the process is to construct a transcript, a representation of talk in written/graphic form which will serve as the main input to analysis. (Transcription is the subject of the next chapter.) To begin with I am going to assume that readers intend to collect their own data. There are alternatives to this, which I will discuss later on; but collecting data is one of the skills an analyst of talk generally needs to develop, and it raises issues that every analyst needs at least to have thought about.

WHAT KIND OF DATA?

There is no single prototype of 'good' data. Your aims as a researcher should determine both the kind of data you set out to get and the methods you use to collect it. If you are a social scientist whose research is about something other than talk itself, you will probably adopt one of the methods that are standardly used in your discipline, such as observation or participant observation (where the researcher is actually involved in what is going on, not just watching), interviewing or conducting focus group discussions. Most of these methods involve interaction between researcher and subjects, often of a fairly structured kind (the researcher asks questions on a predetermined topic, and the subjects respond). Thus the researcher ends up with a certain kind of talk to analyse – a corpus of interviews or discussions, for instance.

In other cases, however, the purpose of collecting spoken language data is to find out how some aspect of talk itself works. How do people know when it's their turn to speak? How do they change the subject? How long is a 'normal' silence? How do people 'repair' breakdowns in conversation? If these are the kinds of questions you are hoping to answer, interviewing may not be the best method for collecting data, because the conventions of the interview as a particular sort of 'speech event' (see Chapters 5 and 10) discourage certain kinds of potentially relevant behaviour – interview subjects rarely initiate or change topics, for instance. Rather than taking the role of an interviewer, therefore, the researcher may prefer the role of observer, bystander or eavesdropper.

This sounds simple: people are talking all around us all the time. All we have to do is get them to do it in such a way that we can record it. But in fact this is a complicated business. A great deal of everyday spoken interaction, of the kind we are constantly participating in or eavesdropping on, happens in circumstances where good-quality recording (or sometimes any recording) would be impossible, inconvenient or unethical. There is also the question of how a researcher's presence may affect other people's behaviour. Researchers of talk face what the sociolinguist William Labov (1972a) called 'the Observer's Paradox': ideally, we want to observe how people behave when they are not being observed.

One issue that comes up in relation to the Observer's Paradox is whether researchers should ever 'set up' a situation to generate talk for research purposes. A method sometimes used in psychology, for instance, is to invite a group of people into an office or a lab and request them to talk to each other (the researcher may or may not specify what they talk about). Some analysts of talk are critical of this proceeding, on the grounds that what we ought ideally to be looking at is 'natural' or 'naturally occurring' talk: talk that would have happened anyway, whether or not a researcher was around to record it. On this view, talk that takes place only because a researcher arranged for it to do so is not merely affected by observation, it is entirely an artefact of observation. It is not 'natural' data, and therefore it cannot be good data.

Arguments about what is or is not 'natural' raise complicated issues. I do not think anyone has shown convincingly that the talking research subjects do in a lab is a different thing in every respect from their 'normal' talk. Conversely, it is widely acknowledged that the act of recording talk, whether in a lab or somewhere else, has the potential to affect participants' behaviour and make the talk something different from what it would have been otherwise. All talk is shaped by the context in which it is produced, and where talk is being observed and recorded that becomes part of the context. It could be argued that a lab is itself a social setting, and 'taking part in a research project' is a recognizable social activity, just like 'chatting with friends'. When researchers study laboratory interactions, then, they are studying an aspect of their informants' 'communicative competence' (their knowledge of how to behave appropriately in a certain set of conversational circumstances). What is misguided is to suppose that the lab situation can 'stand in' for any/every other situation in which people talk.

Many writers about spoken discourse make a distinction between 'ordinary' talk – what happens in casual contexts with family and friends – and 'institutional talk' – what we do when we interact as, or with, professionals, as in teacher–student and doctor–patient interactions. Institutional talk is perfectly 'natural' in the sense discussed above – it is not just manufactured for research purposes – but there has been a tendency to treat 'ordinary' talk as more fundamental, and thus privileged.

The author of a widely used textbook says for instance that 'ordinary' conversation is 'the matrix of language acquisition . . . the central or most basic kind of language usage' (Levinson 1983: 284–5). The editors of a volume about institutional talk, Paul Drew and John Heritage, suggest that the study of this kind of talk is really the study of how it deviates from 'ordinary' talk: 'the basic forms of mundane talk constitute a kind of benchmark against which other more formal or "institutional" types of interaction are recognised and experienced' (1992: 19). The editor of a book about broadcast talk, Paddy Scannell, notes that 'Two-way talk, in which participants have equal discursive rights, is only one form of talk, *though it should be thought of as the primary and prototypical form*' (1991: 2, my emphasis).

I think assertions like these can be questioned for some of the same reasons I have already questioned the dismissal of laboratory interactions as 'unnatural' and therefore worthless. If you accept that all talk is shaped by its context, then arguably it does not make sense to take one context as more 'basic' than another, nor to consider some kinds of talk as more 'ordinary' than others. The distinctive discourse found in, say, a classroom or a law court is, in that context, ordinary. It would be decidedly out of the ordinary if participants in courtroom discourse started behaving as if they were chatting to friends around the kitchen table. If this strategy were used in a courtroom it would be interesting, precisely, as a kind of special effect.

One might also ask whether the comments I quoted from Levinson and Scannell tend to idealize so-called 'ordinary' talk, presenting it as more different from 'institutional talk' – for instance, freer and less subject to the effects of power and inequality – than it actually is. Scannell suggests that ordinary talk is egalitarian ('participants have equal discursive rights'). Drew and Heritage define it as 'casual conversation between peers' (1992: 19). Yet feminists in particular have been critical of the assumption that power inequalities are only relevant to institutional or 'public' talk (for a discussion of the 'public/private' issue, see McElhinny 1997). Feminist researchers (such as DeFrancisco 1991; Fishman 1983; Ochs and Taylor 1995) have pointed out that within households and families – which are typically treated as prime locations for 'ordinary' talk – women and men are not necessarily peers in the sense of having 'equal discursive rights'; nor are adults and children.

Cultural differences also need to be acknowledged. Levinson's observation that ordinary talk is 'the matrix for language acquisition' is accurate insofar as children across cultures normally do acquire spoken language in non-institutional settings. But these settings are not all the same, and in particular, they do not all resemble the western nuclear family with its child-centred parenting practices. In western adult–child interactions, children are often both permitted and encouraged to take an equal part in talk or even dominate the floor. Samoan mothers studied by Elinor Ochs (1988), however, did not treat their children as conversational equals, and engaged far less than American mothers in the kind of interaction where participants may alternate freely. (For other examples of varying language socialization practices across cultures and communities, see Heath 1983; Kulick 1992; Schieffelin 1990.)

In sum, I am suggesting that discourse analysts should be cautious about privileging any particular kind of data as axiomatically the most desirable kind of data, and cautious also in our assumptions about what makes talk 'natural' or 'ordinary'. How formal or hierarchical talk is in a given case should be treated as a question for empirical investigation; if researchers have too many preconceptions about what they are going to find, the danger is that they will not attend closely enough to the subtleties of talk in a specific situation.

ETHICAL QUESTIONS: INFORMED CONSENT AND PRIVACY

I have already noted that whenever you observe and record talk, the fact that you are doing so will become part of the context in which talk is occurring – assuming the participants know what you are doing. That raises the question: should you tell them? Might the easiest way to deal with the Observer's Paradox be to conceal the fact that observation is going on?

It should perhaps be pointed out that concealment is not as easy as it might sound. Many a researcher has carefully concealed recording equipment and found herself with an unintelligible tape. But the main problem is ethical. In her book *Women Talk* (1996), the linguist Jennifer Coates describes how she recorded a group of her friends surreptitiously over a period of more than a year. The group met regularly at one another's houses; when it was Coates's turn to be host she would get her teenage son to come into the room, ostensibly to look for a tape, and as he pretended to do this he would unobtrusively turn on the tape recorder. Eventually, Coates decided to tell her friends what she had been doing. To her surprise and horror, they felt exploited, betrayed and very angry.

The people we are closest to are often, ironically, the people we feel least compunction about exploiting – or perhaps we do not see it as exploitation, since we are confident of their goodwill towards us and their desire to help us. But Jennifer Coates's story shows that the consequences of presuming too much can be dire, not just for the informants but also for the researcher. In Coates's case it is clear that her relationship with the group was damaged, and that this caused her considerable distress. She tells her story to underline the point that if you want to record people talking you must get their consent. It is not worth risking your relationships for a research project or a good mark in a course, and it is not right to violate people's trust, whether or not you are caught doing it. My own experience, and my students', suggests that few people refuse consent: indeed, I have long found it amazing what students can get people to agree to by uttering the magic words 'it's for college'. What made Jennifer Coates's friends angry was not so much that she had recorded them as that she had deceived them. It should always be remembered that you can deceive by omission: from the informant's perspective there is not much difference between lying about your intentions and concealing them by saying nothing.

How much is it necessary to tell people? There may be a case for vagueness about exactly what aspect of their talk you are planning to focus on: if you tell people, for instance, 'I'm interested in how much you swear', there is a chance that the knowledge will affect their behaviour in such a way as to frustrate your goals. But you should be straightforward about what is going to happen to the material your informants provide. Not everyone is familiar with the conventions of academic research, and if people do not understand the implications of consenting to something, they cannot be said to have given *informed* consent.

Probably the most important implication of recording people's talk is that 'private' conversations, by being recorded, transcribed and analysed, become to some extent 'public', accessible to people other than the original participants. Professional researchers have to explain to informants that transcripts of their conversations may appear in published work, which could in theory be read by a very large audience. Student assignments are less 'public', but even they will be seen by other people besides their author – they will be marked by tutors, read by examiners, and to that extent the talk they analyse will not remain a 'private' matter between the researcher and his or her informants.

Some people feel better about making their conversations public if you offer to take steps to minimize the invasion of their privacy. For instance, something that understandably bothers people (including students, who often live in small and close-knit communities) is the possibility that individual speakers and people mentioned in their talk will be recognizable to those reading the transcript, with potentially embarrassing consequences. The usual solution is to give people – both the informants themselves and anyone else they speak about – pseudonyms in the transcript and in your own analytic comments.

If the chances of someone being recognized seem remote, here's a cautionary tale. A researcher I know slightly, a sociologist working in Ireland, once sent me the draft of an article that was going to be published in a journal. It contained a lot of personal details about some Irish women's lives, and to protect their privacy the researcher had given them invented names – except in one single sentence, where a woman she had been calling 'Mary' suddenly turned into 'Catherine' (I am using pseudonyms here myself, by the way). When I read the name 'Catherine' and put it together with the personal details given about 'Mary', I realized I knew who Catherine was. She had emigrated to New York, and I had once met her there. I also knew various things about her from conversations among American friends of mine whose circle she belonged to. I had no idea that she knew the researcher whose article I was reading, and if the researcher had not forgotten to change her name to 'Mary' in that one sentence I would never have been sure about her identity, however familiar some of the details seemed. When I drew the researcher's attention to the lapse and said I had recognized 'Catherine/Mary', not surprisingly she was astonished. What is the likelihood of someone living in New York and participating in a sociology project about Irish women being known to a British linguist working (as I then was) in Glasgow? In fact, the odds are not as bad as you might imagine. Since this incident I have been very careful about using pseudonyms, especially when – as quite often happens – people are talked about in very personal and/or unflattering terms.

Another modification you can offer to make is to delete some portions of the tape or leave them untranscribed. I have sometimes asked people: 'is there anything you said that you'd feel very uncomfortable about other people hearing?' Other researchers have found themselves with recordings that actually incriminated their informants, who had talked about upcoming drug deals or burglaries, and have thought it judicious to erase the tape. I have occasionally collected talk that touched on clandestine sexual activities or drug use, but the only tape informants ever asked me to erase in their presence was completely innocuous, as far as I could tell. Once a group of informants agreed to my using transcripts of their talk but requested me never to play the tape itself in public – an odd request, since what is embarrassing on tape is usually equally so on paper, and I do not think these informants feared their voices being recognized. Even if informants' requests do not entirely make sense to me, however, I think it is their privilege to place whatever restrictions they deem appropriate on my use of material they have provided. If their conditions are so exacting as to make the data useless to me, I cut my losses and start again. It is rare for informants' scruples to have such a drastic effect, however. Depending what your aim in collecting data is, it may not make much difference if occasional chunks of talk are left out of the analysis.

What I have said so far implies a situation where the researcher is present and in control of the recording. In my experience, students most often record conversations they are actually involved in (e.g. with family, friends or people they share accommodation with), since this is the most convenient option, and also makes transcription easier. But you do not necessarily have to be there to collect your data in person. After she gave up surreptitious recording, Jennifer Coates turned to a different method, asking volunteers to record themselves and their friends in conversation, and then send her the tapes. Many other researchers have used the same approach; it is especially useful when you are trying to investigate the behaviour of a group you do not belong to and cannot easily get into. Coates, for instance, was interested in the talk of adolescent girls as well as adult women, but she felt her presence as an adult in a group of adolescents would have inhibited their talk. Similarly, a student of mine, Michael Higgins, wanted to analyse the talk of his mother and her friends, who had been holding a weekly 'knitting bee' for 25 years. Even if Michael were not, as he is, a young man (whereas the knitting bee is an all-female affair and its members are a generation older), his presence in this long-established group of friends would have altered the very balance he was trying to investigate. He therefore chose to set up the recorder in advance, and then absent himself from the actual proceedings.

The absence of a human observer may reduce the distorting effects of observation, but it does not entirely circumvent the Observer's Paradox, since the tape recorder itself reminds people they are being observed (it is not uncommon for informants to treat it as a participant in the conversation, and talk to it directly!). But in any case, it needs to be remembered that there is only so much a conscientious researcher can do about the Observer's Paradox: it is finally insoluble except by means that are unethical (i.e. recording without informants' knowledge and consent). While it is important to be aware of the issue, it is counterproductive to fixate on it to the exclusion of all else.

Some ideas for research on talk involve recording in an institutional setting, like a workplace, a school classroom or a court of law. The ethical requirements for recording in institutions are usually quite formal, and may take a long time to negotiate. In a school, for instance, you may have to get the written consent of the head teacher, the class teacher, and the parents of every child you propose to record. Even stricter protocols govern research in institutions like hospitals, clinics, police stations and courts, because of the need to protect people's privacy in situations where they are particularly vulnerable. In general I would say it is not worthwhile for students, other than those undertaking a large-scale research project (e.g. a PhD), to consider doing research in institutions of this sort, unless their contacts and credentials are unusually good (e.g. they work or used to work in the institution concerned, and have the support of someone in authority there).

It is possible that in future, *all* research that involves tape recording people may be subject to formal written consent procedures, imposed not by the informants or their institutions, but by the investigators' institutions, universities. For some readers this may already be the reality. Concern to formalize procedures, to limit institutions' liability and to clarify issues of 'intellectual property' (who owns or is entitled to benefit economically from knowledge) is becoming ever stronger in today's academic climate. In some social science disciplines, like psychology, it has long been standard practice to have a committee approve proposals for research on human subjects, and for informants to sign consent forms before they take part in research. In linguistic discourse analysis there are some practical reasons for resistance to this. It is one thing to say to people, 'sign this form so I can record you talking in my lab', and another thing to go into your kitchen and ask the assembled company to sign consent forms before they start chatting – the danger is that this will destroy any atmosphere conducive to 'chat'. But while that may be an argument for having different procedures for research on some kinds of naturally occurring talk, it cannot be an argument for having lower ethical standards than other researchers. Barbara Johnstone (2000: 43–7) reproduces some informed consent documents that have actually been used by researchers working on talk; these models might not be equally applicable to every project, but even if there are good reasons not to use them, discourse analysts must find other ways to ensure we get our informants' consent to recording.

OTHER DATA SOURCES

There are some kinds of spoken data which you do not have to record (or ask informants to record) because they already exist and are in the public domain. An obvious example is talk that is broadcast on radio or television. Here the issue of privacy is less problematic, since broadcast talk is designed for public hearing. Even the non-professionals whose talk is broadcast, like callers to radio phone-in programmes, clearly expect and indeed want their talk to be heard by large numbers of people. (As a student once said to me about the people who appear on *Oprah*-style television talk shows, 'they're invading their own privacy!') Remember, though, that broadcast material is a form of intellectual property, just as printed material is: its use for educational and research purposes may be subject to conditions and restrictions.

The broadcast media may seem like a very convenient source for all kinds of spoken data, but they should be approached with some caution. Broadcast talk has special characteristics which arise from the nature of the medium and the relationship it produces between speakers and (different sets of) addressees. Readers who have followed me this far will appreciate that I am *not* arguing broadcast talk is 'unnatural' and thus unworthy of analysis: like other kinds of talk it is shaped by its context. What I am saying is that re-recording media talk should not be treated as a *substitute* for collecting other kinds of talk: a radio or television discussion is not the same thing as a discussion that is not designed to be broadcast.

There are some media genres which include or consist of conversation that allegedly is *not* shaped by the requirements of broadcasting: a case in point is the 'fly on the wall' documentary, which supposedly just records people going about their normal business. One early example of this genre, the BBC series *The Family*, which followed the everyday life of one family in Reading, provided data for an extended study of how conversation works in families (Kreckel 1981). In this case the researcher did treat the family's conversations as ordinary talk that just happened to be broadcast. Today, though, I think this would be less defensible. Practices of documentary production and editing have changed, while at the same time partici-pants have become extremely familiar with the conventions of the genre: this enables them to produce a kind of talk that is clearly shaped by and for the presence of the camera. Again, that does not make for uninteresting data: on the contrary, it is very interesting that so many people now know, from extensive experience watching television and using camcorders, how to talk on camera. But it is only if you are specifically interested in 'performed to camera' talk that you should use it as your preferred data source. Media discourse should not be treated as if it were unmediated, just as discourse produced in experimental settings in response to instructions from a researcher should not be treated as if it were spontaneous conversation.

The new medium of the internet is another potential source of data, in two ways. First, communication on the net – on discussion lists, bulletin boards, chat rooms, MUDs and MOOs (virtual spaces where people play fantasy games and create imaginary social worlds) – is an object of considerable interest to discourse analysts, who point out that although the medium is writing, it has many 'speech-like' features. Using this kind of data is, however, problematic in terms of both privacy and intellectual property issues. I once posted a query to a list where I had been 'lurking' (reading other people's messages but not sending my own) in which I asked whether I could reproduce people's posts (messages) in a book I was then writing, as evidence of attitudes to non-sexist and 'politically correct' language. I wanted to know whether they regarded posting to the internet as equivalent to calling in on a radio phone-in programme or writing a letter to a newspaper – in other words, as a 'public' act. The replies I received showed no consensus on the issue: some thought posting was indeed a form of public communication, others compared it to writing a circular letter to a select group of friends and relations. I decided not to use the material; but there are many scholarly articles which quote large chunks of internet-derived data, including intemperate and bigoted 'flames' which I cannot imagine the authors consented to have reproduced.

A student of mine, Marko Kukkonen, carried out research on 'Internet Relay Chat' (IRC), a kind of 'synchronous' computer-mediated communication (interactants are on-line at the same time, though distant from one another in space). He used a program that enables you to print out the 'log' of an IRC session, and he did not seek consent from participants, arguing that all regular IRC-users are aware of the existence of the program he used, and know, therefore, that their interaction is not like private conversation. Marko also pointed out that IRC-users must log on using a nickname that conceals their real identity: this both reduces the risk that they will be personally compromised by the reproduction of their messages, and makes it impracticable to secure their formal consent (participants come and go continuously, and the researcher has no idea who they are or where to contact them).

Researching internet discourse raises novel ethical problems, and at present there is no professional consensus on how to deal with them. But the net can be a source of data in another, less ethically complicated way. There are sites where a user can download linguistic data that has been collected (ethically, one trusts) by other researchers. A collection of linguistic data is known as a *corpus* (Latin for 'body'; the plural is *corpora*), and the availability of more and more corpora on-line (though it should be noted that users may have to pay to access them) is an important recent development. On-line corpora are typically searchable – that is, with the help of appropriate software you can pick out something you are interested in, like pausing, or simultaneous speech, or the word *so*, and find every instance of it in the corpus. Computers make this task quick and easy.

One obvious drawback with getting spoken language data from an on-line corpus is that typically you only get the written transcript. (Sometimes you can get sound, but it is more likely to be isolated syllables or words than whole chunks of conversation.) However, the transcript may include additional information by way of 'tagging', where the original analyst has coded the data, using symbols to indicate things like pitch, stress and volume. If you know the relevant symbol you can search for the phenomenon it codes.

Whether this kind of data is useful depends on what you want to investigate. Potentially, there is an enormous advantage in having access to corpora far larger than you could collect and transcribe yourself: it is especially advantageous if you want a lot of examples of a very well-defined feature, or if you want to check how common something is statistically. Another of my students, Catriona Carson, carried out a study of the item *oh* used to mark the beginning of reported speech. She had collected some data of her own, but she wanted to check whether the patterns she had found in her data would appear in a much larger sample. On the internet she found a corpus of transcribed talk produced by adolescents in London (a contrast to her own data, which came from adults in Glasgow). She searched the corpus for cases where *oh* followed a quotative verb (a verb introducing reported speech, as in 'she says/she goes/she's like'). For this purpose, transcript was quite good enough: the target feature was both common and well-defined, and Catriona was not interested in the details of its phonetic realization. The examples in the corpus showed the same pattern that Catriona had uncovered in her own data. She had thus obtained impressive supporting evidence for her analysis without having to do any more recording and transcribing.

People studying in Higher Education institutions (and some schools) usually have access to the internet, and are well-placed to learn how to use it effectively for research purposes. Since hands-on training is the most effective kind, I will not attempt to instruct readers further in the location and use of on-line materials, but they are certainly of interest to students of discourse analysis.

HOW MUCH DATA?

How much data is enough? It is a question that faces every researcher, and the simple if rather unhelpful answer is 'it depends'. It depends on your goals, your resources, and the kinds of claims you are hoping to be able to make.

Social scientists whose data come from interviewing people about, say, their experiences of unemployment or their views about sex education will have made a methodological decision about *sampling*: how many and what kind of people will be interviewed. The amount of data they end up with is determined by the size of the sample and the length of the interviews. The quantity of talk they analyse, measured in hours of tape-time, is less important than the number and distribution of interview subjects.

By contrast, linguists studying conversation in its own right and for its own sake have different choices. Some highly respected researchers have worked on very small and specific data samples: the linguist Deborah Tannen, for instance, is famous for an extremely detailed study of the talk which took place at a single Thanksgiving dinner (Tannen 1984). Jennifer Coates's study *Women Talk: Conversation Between Women Friends* (1996) is based on a larger sample of data from several different groups of women friends, reflecting the fact that Coates was interested in similarities and differences among women of different ages and backgrounds. Even with this larger sample, Coates does not feel able to claim that the patterns she finds in her data are typical of women friends' talk generally; but she is on firmer ground claiming that certain patterns are common than she would be if all her data came from one group.

Sometimes a researcher may be interested in a very particular kind of spoken exchange, like the encounter that takes place when you buy something in a shop or ask a stranger to tell you the time. The focus of research may be even narrower: for instance, one might choose to study what address term, if any, is used in the course of an encounter between a service employee and a customer. In such a case, where the relevant piece of data is a single item or short, self-contained exchange and the aim is to make generalizations about how the item is used or the exchange is conducted, the ideal must be to collect as many examples as possible: as many as you can handle given the time you have available for recording, transcription and analysis.

A factor that affects how many different encounters you may have to record is how frequently the variable you are interested in occurs in talk. For instance, there is a well known article called 'On questions following questions in service encounters' (Merritt 1976). Questions following questions in service encounters (for example 'can I have a pint of Guinness?' 'Are you 18?') are not exactly rare, but nor do they occur in every service encounter: a researcher will need to record quite a large number of encounters to get a reasonable number in which questions follow questions. By contrast, if you are researching something like hesitations, or minimal responses like 'mhm', 'yeah', you can be confident that they will occur very frequently in any exchange you record. It will not take long to collect a respectable number of examples. Intermediate between the extremes of 'hesitation' and 'questions following questions' is a variable like Catriona Carson's *oh* introducing reported speech. *Oh* itself is very common, and when Catriona was just exploring the range of functions it fulfilled in conversation she was able to get a lot of mileage from a fairly small sample of data (a single conversation). Once she narrowed her focus to one specific use of *oh*, however, she needed more data to get a sufficiently large number of examples. This illustrates that often you get a clear idea of whether your data sample is adequate only when you have begun to analyse it (when it may or may not be possible to go back and record more data). One way in which analysts know they have enough data for the purpose at hand is when they realize that analysis is not turning up anything new, but only additional examples of patterns they have already identified. While in principle it might seem desirable to have as many examples as possible, in practice you have to draw the line somewhere, bearing in mind that the collection of data is only the beginning of a lengthy process which includes transcription (a time-consuming activity, as we will see in the next chapter) as well as the actual analysis.

SUMMARY

It is impossible to present a set of invariant rules about data collection (how much data, what kind of data, obtained through what method or in what situation), because choices have to be made in the light of the investigator's goals. Though some writers give the impression of regarding talk that is 'ordinary' and 'naturally occurring' as the most valuable kind of data for spoken discourse analysis, it may be argued that no kind of talk should be treated as, in Paddy Scannell's phrase, 'the primary and prototypical case'. Rather, all kinds of talk are shaped by the context in which they occur. Insightful analysis of any kind of talk entails paying close attention to this contextual shaping. It also involves being aware of the impact observation may have on the situation being observed, and thinking carefully about this both in the design of a project (for instance, should you do your recording in person?) and in your subsequent interpretation of the data.

Recording people's talk raises ethical issues. It is said that 'talk is cheap', but anyone who allows you to record their talk and turn it into an object of analysis is showing great generosity; they are giving you something of themselves, and trusting you not to abuse that gift. Without such generosity, the field of study this book is about could not exist. Treating those who make our work possible in an ethical, responsible and sensitive way is the least we owe them. As we will see in the chapters that follow, our obligations to data providers do not end when their talk is safely on tape: they are also a relevant consideration when we transcribe, analyse and publicly present spoken discourse material. Transcription is the next topic to which I will turn.

SUGGESTIONS FOR FURTHER READING ABOUT COLLECTING SPOKEN DATA

Data collection, surprisingly, is rarely discussed at any length in textbooks on discourse analysis. Deborah Schiffrin (1994: 420–1) includes an appendix on the subject, but it is only a little over a page long. More attention is given to the issue in texts for students of variationist sociolinguistics (who analyse accent and dialect variation using quantitative methods), such as Lesley Milroy's *Observing and Analysing Natural Language* (1987), and Barbara Johnstone's *Qualitative Methods in Sociolinguistics* (2000), which does encompass discourse analysis as well as variationist work, and which includes a useful chapter on legal and ethical issues. Nessa Wolfson's article 'Speech events and natural speech' (1976) discusses some of the things that can go wrong in sociolinguistic interviews conducted 'by the book'. Another useful source of information about how researchers go about collecting spoken discourse data is the sections of their books or articles where they describe their methods, often in a quasi-narrative form: Jennifer Coates's *Women Talk* (1996) is a case in point. For non-linguists, there are several texts on qualitative methods in social research that discuss data collection (though the focus is not always on language as such). Examples include Hammersley and Atkinson (1995) and Silverman (1997). Researchers' relationships with their subjects are the topic of *Researching Language: Issues of Power and Method* (Cameron et al. 1992).

Transcribing spoken discourse

Without a *transcript* – a written/graphic representation – talk is impossible to analyse systematically. This might seem strange: why should it be necessary to transfer spoken language data to another medium before you can say anything analytic about it? I want to defer answering that question until you have had an opportunity to consider the business of transcribing in a concrete, practical way. So, on p. 32 is a practical activity, a problem-solving task that will work best if it is done without preconceived ideas about the 'best' outcome (the point is not to produce a perfect transcript but to experience and reflect on the challenges involved in transcribing). You will find this exercise most illuminating if you complete all parts of it *before* reading any further in this chapter.

WHY TRANSCRIBE?

I began this chapter by asking why we have to transcribe speech before we can analyse it. After spending some time working with a piece of data as you attempted to make a transcript of it, you should now be in a better position to consider this question.

Speech cannot be processed in the same way as writing: hearing and reading are different. It is in the nature of speech to be 'evanescent': it consists of sound waves in the air, and sound begins to fade away as soon as it is produced. If I say 'hello Rory', by the time I get to *Rory* it is no longer possible to hear *hello*. My hearer must therefore process my utterance as it happens, in 'real time'. Recording the utterance does not change this. It makes it possible for the hearer to rewind and do the same real-time processing an infinite number of times, but on no occasion will *hello* and *Rory* be present simultaneously. If I write down 'hello Rory', however, the whole thing can be in the reader's field of vision at the same time, and marks on paper do not disappear as the eye passes over them. This makes it possible to deal with writing in ways we cannot deal with speech. You can go backwards and forwards in a conversation more quickly and easily by scanning a written transcript than by rewinding and replaying a tape. Writing also reduces the load on memory. Though you have doubtless listened to your two minutes of tape so many times that you are heartily sick of it, it is doubtful that you could reproduce it unaided with total accuracy, nor answer questions like 'how many times does the item *oh* occur?'. Your transcript functions as a permanent record of what you heard in a form that allows you to perform analytic operations like counting the *ohs*.

ACTIVITY

1 Preparation

Record between 10 and 15 minutes of conversation, involving no more than three participants (one of whom may be you). *Secure their consent to recording before you start.* Choose a relatively informal setting (e.g. your own home, or a communal space in a residence hall) where it is normal for talking to occur. To get reasonable recording quality, use a space where people will be fairly close to the microphone and where background noise is at a minimum.

2 The task

Listen to your tape right through. Now select and transcribe (write down) approximately two minutes of what is on the tape (keep the rest for possible use in later activities). You do not have to choose the first two minutes; ideally you should begin at a point when the participants are 'warmed up' and at ease with the recorder, selecting a sequence of talk in which all participants are contributing.

A transcription is supposed to be a full and faithful written/graphic representation of spoken material. So in making one, the question you must ask is: 'what do I have to write down to make this a full and faithful representation?' Obviously you should write down the words participants uttered, but what other information is it necessary to include, and how should you represent that information on the page? There is no standard system for transcribing talk, and for the purposes of this exercise you may use or invent any conventions you like for representing speech in writing (e.g. you may use non-alphabetic symbols and vary the arrangement of your text in space). *Do not*, however, attempt to transcribe the whole sequence phonetically!

3 Questions (to be answered when you have made a transcript)

- What have you included in your transcript apart from the words?
- What features of talk were hardest to capture in transcription, and why?
- Transcribing talk is meant to make you notice things about it that are not usually evident. When you look at your transcript, what do you find especially striking, odd or unexpected?
- In what ways, if any, does your transcript look different from the sort of written-down speech you have encountered in other contexts (e.g. dialogue in novels, comic strips or play scripts?)
- How far do you think your transcript really is a 'full and faithful' representation of the contents of your tape?

4 Follow-up activity (to be done in groups of 3 or 4 people)

Show one another the transcripts you have made. Do they look similar or different? Compare your answers to the questions in (3). Have you noticed the same problems/come up with the same solutions?

Transcribing is a way to bring into focus the characteristics of spoken discourse, which are surprisingly obscure to most people, familiar as they are with the written form. As a number of historians and theorists of literacy have pointed out (e.g. Olsen 1994), one of the effects of the invention of writing was to make people conscious of linguistic structure per se; writing is not a direct representation of speech so much as a model of language more generally. This model exerts a strong influence on our perceptions of what language is or ought to be like. As a simple example, ask yourself: did you put spaces between the words in your transcript? If the answer is 'yes', was this a choice you deliberated about or just something you did automatically? In speech there is not necessarily any gap between the production of adjacent words, but because of the practice of inserting spaces in writing (a practice which is not as old as writing itself, incidentally), we find it 'natural' to represent spoken discourse as a series of individual words. I am not, in fact, suggesting that transcribed talk should dispense with spaces between words; this might be more faithful to the original but it would also make the transcript unnecessarily difficult to read, which is also a relevant consideration (see further below). Rather I am suggesting that although in principle you had a choice, in practice the possibility of not using spaces probably did not occur to you. It takes a real effort *not* to hear spoken language in terms of the written model.

I imagine many readers, answering the questions in 3 above, will have been struck by the extent to which real talk differs from what are meant to be 'realistic' representations of it, such as fictional dialogue. Among the words my own students have frequently used about the real thing are 'repetitive', 'inarticulate' and 'incoherent'. What they are alluding to is the presence, in any sample of casual, unplanned spoken discourse, of a significant number of false starts, hesitations, repeated words or phrases, and 'fillers' like *well, y'know, like, sort of.* Even the most 'realistic' made-up dialogue contains far less of this sort of thing. But that does not mean that real conversation is 'incoherent' or that ordinary speakers are 'inarticulate'. Rather it suggests, once again, that most of us usually operate with notions of 'coherence' and 'articulacy' that are drawn from our experiences of more formal and planned kinds of discourse, especially writing. This is a bias that needs to be unlearned. Analysts of talk must begin from the assumption that if communication is not breaking down in a given instance then participants must be able to make sense of it, no matter how 'incoherent' it might seem; and that if certain features recur in spoken language data, they must serve some purpose, however obscure we find it. Doing transcription helps you to adopt a more enquiring attitude to spoken language by continually drawing your attention to its particular characteristics.

If 'incoherent' and 'inarticulate' are harsh and hasty judgements, 'repetitive' does describe a lot of unplanned talk, and this will be evident in a 'full and faithful' transcription. I have a tape I sometimes use to teach transcription that begins:

Ali: and she didn't she didn't like Katie she didn't ge[t on with Katie at all   ]
Beth: [no she didn't get on with] Katie
[the brackets mark sequences spoken simultaneously]

One of the commonest errors made by inexperienced transcribers is to miss repetitions like 'she didn't she didn't'. We tend to mentally edit them out, and that tendency is compounded when we are writing, since normally when people reduce speech to writing (e.g. a stenographer makes a record of courtroom testimony or a secretary takes dictation) it is part of the task to get rid of such extraneous 'noise'. It adds nothing informative to the written message, and looks peculiar or distracting on the page.

In talk, however, repetition has useful functions. Some of these have to do with the real-time processing requirements we have already noted. Since speakers have to produce their contributions in real time, with minimal planning, it is not surprising that they often make false starts and repeat themselves. Repetition can be a way of 'buying time' to plan the next chunk. It is also useful to the hearer. Since s/he has to process utterances in real time, a certain amount of pausing and repetition increases the chance that s/he will be able to take in the information before it disappears. Casual speech is typically very *redundant*: a sizeable portion of speech may contain rather little actual information. In the passage reproduced above, for instance, the information exchanged by the speakers boils down to a single proposition, 'she didn't like Katie'. In writing, this degree of redundancy would not be necessary (though it might have a *stylistic* function – as indeed it also does in the 'Katie' example, where repetition of the basic point emphasizes the strength of the subject's antipathy to Katie). But if repetition is 'there' in a piece of spoken discourse, it should not be edited out in transcription.

Another error made by inexperienced transcribers is to try to organize what they hear into the normal structure for a passage of written prose, namely a series of sentences. I imagine some readers will have made use in their transcripts of punctuation marks like commas, full stops and question marks. It is fine to use these symbols to stand for something that is in the data. Some systems of transcription used by discourse analysts use question marks, for example, to indicate that the preceding sequence has rising intonation (i.e. the pitch goes up at the end). A sequence thus marked may or may not have the syntax or meaning of a question: that is irrelevant, since the symbol ? is used simply as a convention for representing a rise in pitch. But if punctuation marks are used in the normal way, as we use them in writing, there is a danger of imposing on spoken discourse a kind of structure it does not actually have.

It would be possible to organize the opening of the 'Katie' conversation into a series of sentences, marking the boundaries with full stops and using other punctuation to subdivide the sentences. The result might look like a play script, as follows:

> Ali: And she – she didn't like Katie.
> Beth: No, she didn't get on with Katie.
> Ali: She didn't get on with Katie at all.

The trouble with this approach is that when you listen to the tape (the reader will have to trust me here, but your own tapes will probably contain comparable examples), there is nothing 'there' that corresponds to the punctuation marks I have inserted. The speakers do not necessarily pause where I have put commas and dashes, for instance, and they have not necessarily finished speaking at the points where I have put a full stop. By punctuating it I have made the transcript easy to read, but it is not a faithful representation of my data.

When we speak we use pausing and, especially, intonation (pitch and stress) to 'chunk' our talk into units. These units may well coincide with grammatical constructs such as a clause, but they do not have to; generally what the boundaries signal is the structure the speaker wishes to impose on the *information* s/he is giving. Thus in the passage about Katie, what seem in the transcript above to be two contributions from Ali are actually a single information unit. I make that judgement not merely because they contain only one piece of information, though that happens to be the case, but more importantly because they are realized as one continuous sequence of talk, without a pause and with a single intonation contour. Part of Ali's contribution is spoken simultaneously with part of Beth's – not because Beth thinks Ali has finished when she has not, but because Beth wants to reinforce what Ali is saying. In casual conversation it is very common to find people speaking simultaneously – often, as in this case, saying much the same thing – without this being perceived as chaotic or impolite. A transcript needs to show this going on, and using standard writing conventions like commas and full stops may obscure it by making conversation look like a succession of distinct, self-contained clauses, when really it does not sound like that. In a moment we will consider how best to represent what you can hear on the tape.

Before that, though, it is worth pointing out that some things in other people's talk are difficult to hear accurately. The conversation about Katie continues with a story about Katie's problems finding a place to live; first, the speaker reports, she looked after a friend's house on 'Hurst Street', then she moved to 'Aston Street'. These are streets in East Oxford where the participants in this conversation lived at the time. When I use the tape with students who do not live in Oxford or know its geography, they often cannot hear 'Hurst' and 'Aston' well enough to transcribe these words accurately. This is interesting, because it suggests that there is more to transcription than careful listening or a 'good ear'. There is also the issue of contextual knowledge. Whereas written language is designed to communicate with someone who does not share the writer's immediate context, and writing therefore tends to be relatively explicit, casual conversation is typically very dependent on the participants' shared knowledge. The processing of talk is facilitated by the ability of participants to predict or guess what others are likely to be saying. And this is also true of transcription: if the transcriber lacks crucial background knowledge that is available to informants, s/he will find it far more difficult to understand certain parts of their talk. Most transcriptions made by professional analysts contain at least a few sequences which the transcriber has marked with a conventional symbol like an empty bracket [ ] or a series of crosses xxx, indicating a chunk of talk s/he eventually gave up on because s/he found it indecipherable. In the transcription activity I suggested you work on talk in which you were a participant to minimize this problem, but you need to be aware of it: accurate transcription requires a grasp of the immediate context as well as the ability to listen.

There are two main reasons for drawing attention to the issue of speech/writing differences in the context of discussing transcription. On one hand, transcribers of spoken discourse need to try consciously to avoid editing out typical speech features like repetition or imposing writing features like sentence boundaries. On the other hand, they need to consider what conventions they might need to adopt in order to represent spoken language faithfully in writing. Let us turn to that issue now.

NOT JUST WORDS: REPRESENTING SPEECH

Apart from the words uttered, what needs to be represented in a transcript? One obvious thing, if you are transcribing interactive rather than monologic talk, is to make clear who is speaking and how the contributions of different speakers articulate with one another. For instance, does one person speak immediately after another, or does s/he start before the last speaker has finished, or is there a gap between the two?

It is possible to exploit the graphic possibilities of page layout to show what is going on in talk. Some analysts use a notation that works like a musical score. In a score there is a line or 'stave' for each instrument or voice; each line runs horizontally from left to right, while to find the line for a particular part, you move up and down the page. A conductor or listener can look at the score and see, at any moment, who should be playing or singing what. When an instrument is not actually playing, its line still appears, but nothing is written on it. A transcription of talk, similarly, may allot each speaker a line. When the speaker is not speaking the line has no words written on it; when more than one speaker is speaking this is represented by a careful arrangement of the words on different lines. Here is an example from my own data:

Ed:	that [guy
Bryan:	[it's like a speedo he wears a speedo to class (.) he's got incredibly
	———————————————————————————————— 1
Ed:	it's worse = you know like those shorts women
Bryan:	skinny legs you know=
	———————————————————————————————— 2
Ed:	volleyball players wear?
Bryan:	3

An alternative – which can also be easier to read if speakers are taking relatively long turns – is to use conventions like slashes or brackets rather than layout to show where speakers start or stop speaking. In the extract above, I use some symbols of this kind in addition to the 'score' layout. I use brackets to show overlapping speech and = to indicate 'latching', where one speaker follows another without overlap or pausing. Some analysts find symbols are sufficient on their own to show what is going on. This is how my transcript looks when laid out using only symbols (I have used slashes instead of brackets to show the onset of simultaneous speech, and I have also numbered the turns rather than the lines of the 'score').

1	Ed:	that //guy
2	Bryan:	//it's like a speedo he wears a speedo to class (.) he's got incredibly skinny legs
3	Ed:	it's worse=
4	Bryan:	=you know
5	Ed:	you know like those shorts women volleyball players wear?

Some talk does consist of long sequences produced by a single speaker. A common example is *narrative* talk: if one speaker begins to tell a story, typically others will allow them to hold the floor for longer than normal periods. Their talk is still interactive in the sense that listeners are present and their presence matters: they may interject short remarks and minimal responses, for instance. But even if no one else says anything, when you transcribe a narrative monologue there are arguments for not just presenting it as a single undifferentiated chunk of speech. The linguist Ronald Macaulay has collected many long narratives told by Scottish speakers, and he lays out his transcripts like this:

they're nae oot to hae thoosands or millions
they're nae wanting big cars
they're wanting a car but nae necessarily a big car or necessarily a big hoose

In this case, each line contains one clause.[1] Alternatively, the story could have been divided into chunks on the basis of its information structure as signalled by the intonation. Either way, the justification for dividing it up is that it makes it easier to see how a monologue is structured internally: to notice, for instance, the repetition and parallelism which are typical of verbal art, including oral narratives.

Anyone who works with talk needs to bear in mind that meaning may lie in prosodic and paralinguistic features as much as in words (again, this is a point many people do not fully appreciate because of their tendency to treat writing as the prototype of all language). These features have to do with pitch, stress, rhythm, pace, loudness, voice quality, and so on, and there are ways of representing them which are used quite often by analysts. (Some of the conventions described below are used, for instance, in Gail Jefferson's transcription system for conversation analysis (CA), described in detail by Atkinson and Heritage (1999 [1984]), where they come under the heading of 'characteristics of speech delivery'.) For example, underlining or capitalization may be used to mark syllables that receive emphatic stress (more stress than you would normally expect them to receive) or which are markedly louder than the surrounding talk. Colons may be used to indicate syllables that are lengthened (e.g. *oh::*). Arrows pointing up or down are sometimes used to mark a stretch of speech spoken at a noticeably higher or lower pitch than the surrounding discourse. Pauses are commonly marked, and often timed, either with a stopwatch or by the more impressionistic method of clapping the hands rhythmically. Typically the duration of pausing is shown in tenths of a second, thus (0.4). Transcribers often mark stretches where a speaker's voice quality changes for effect (e.g. they deliver a chunk of discourse in a whisper). This can be done by enclosing a verbal description of the speaker's behaviour in some sort of bracket {whisper} at either end of the relevant sequence, or by writing it above the line if you are using 'score' notation (where a composer would put instructions about phrasing or dynamics). Researchers need to be attentive to features of this sort, but they also need to think about whether the time and effort it takes to transcribe them in detail will be time well spent in any particular case. It is worth bearing in mind that you can always go back and transcribe in more detail later on; your primary data is not the transcript but the tape.

So far I have assumed that you are transcribing audiotape, as specified in the activity with which this chapter began. The aim, then, is to represent what you can hear: who is speaking, when they start and stop speaking relative to other people, how they structure their contributions using intonation and pausing, whether there are noticeable changes in their voice pitch, voice quality, rhythm, loudness, whether they laugh, make animal noises or put on funny voices. This is a lot of information, and you will want to be selective about what you mark in the transcript and what degree of detail you go into. But it is of course the case that participants in face-to-face interaction have even more information than the audiotape contains. They can look at each other, move, gesture, touch things (and people). This inaudible behaviour is not necessarily unimportant to the workings of their talk.

With that in mind, some researchers of talk record videotape. Joan Swann (1988), for instance, used video recordings in a study of classroom interaction where the focus of the research was why boys tended to speak in class more than girls did. This pattern seemed to hold whether the teacher selected pupils to speak by asking them to raise their hands or allowed them simply to butt in, and the researchers suspected that it might be related to where teachers directed their gaze at the point when pupils were given the opportunity to speak. They found that, indeed, teachers in their study tended to make eye contact with boys at the crucial moment; at the same time, girls tended to avoid eye contact with the teacher, even when they knew the answer (and put their hands up to indicate that). Clearly, nonverbal aspects of communication cannot be investigated systematically unless visual as well as verbal information is recorded and transcribed. This is a complex undertaking, however: the transcriber must not only find conventional ways to represent participants' bodily movements and the direction of their gaze,[2] s/he must also articulate the visual with the verbal information, showing for example how the timing of a speaker's movements relates to the timing of their own or others' utterances. This kind of detailed information is not always directly relevant to a researcher's question, and if it is not relevant then there is nothing (except extra work) to be gained by using the more comprehensive recording technique.

Since I have raised the subject of extra work, let me consider, finally in this section, the issue of knowing when to stop. It is a serious issue because in fact there is never a point when your transcript becomes the definitive, 'full and faithful' representation of your data: the difference of medium prevents that ideal from ever being completely realized. In an exchange on this subject in the journal *Discourse & Society*, Celia Kitzinger (1998) complained about researchers apparently changing their transcripts so that different versions of the same data appeared in earlier and later articles. Two other researchers, Jennifer Coates and Joanna Thornborrow (1999) replied to Kitzinger, admitting that they had sometimes altered transcripts because when they listened to the tapes again, they noticed mistakes and omissions in their old transcriptions. Professionals, then, do not necessarily get it right first time. Students, other than PhD students, usually have a limited time to work on their data: for them it is important to keep expectations reasonable, and to develop the ability to judge when the transcript is good enough for the purpose at hand.

It is worth remembering that too much detail can be as unsatisfactory as too little. There is a trade-off between accuracy and detail on one hand, and clarity and readability on the other. In some systems, particularly those designed for searchable computerized corpora, transcripts can be very inaccessible because of both the amount of detail and the fact that so much information is represented by arbitrary symbols like $ and #. Compilers do of course provide a 'key' explaining what the symbols mean, as should anyone who uses any kind of transcription conventions, but it is typically too long and complicated to be remembered easily. However, it may be said in these compilers' defence that they have followed the principle of adopting an approach to transcription that reflects the purposes for which data has been collected. If the corpus is meant to provide as much information as possible to as many users as possible, the difficulty of reading an extremely dense transcript may be a price worth paying. The same principle should be observed by students working on a smaller scale: what it is worth including in a transcript depends on what you want to do with that transcript afterwards. There is no virtue in transcribing in great detail features you will never examine again. The activity at the beginning of this chapter was an artificial exercise, since I gave no indication of the purpose for which data was to be collected and transcribed. When you embark on a project of your own devising, the question 'what is this for' will already have been answered (by you), and the answer should determine both what data you collect and what sort of transcript you make.

Whatever conventions you choose, though, expect transcription to take a long time (some people become *slower* as they become more experienced, because they become more attentive listeners and find more to listen to). I know researchers who take several hours, or even a whole working day, to transcribe a few minutes of spoken discourse. By contrast, the beginning students to whom I have given the 'Katie' tape (which lasts less than two minutes) report taking anything between 45 and 120 minutes to transcribe it – typically, as they later realize, somewhat partially and inaccurately. The time it takes to transcribe accurately is something that has to be factored into decisions about how much data to collect, as I noted in Chapter 2. Since, as we have seen, spoken data is not usable for analytic purposes until it is transcribed, there is no point collecting a volume of data so large that you do not have time to transcribe more than a fraction of it.

TRANSCRIPTION AS THEORY

The previous section focused on what might be called 'technical' aspects of transcription, but transcribing raises issues that are not just technical. In a classic article called 'Transcription as theory', Elinor Ochs (1999 [1979]) pointed out that apparently 'technical' decisions about transcription conventions may embody covert theoretical assumptions. Ochs is known for her work on adult–child talk in different cultures. In this field, there is a convention of transcribing the adult's speech in one column and the child's in another. Ochs notes that although it is not an explicit rule, most English-speaking analysts choose to place the adult column on the left and the child column on the right. English is read from left to right, so this choice tends to give the impression that the adult leads and the child follows. In Ochs's view that is not necessarily the case, but the practice of putting adult speech on the left may prevent analysts from considering the possibility that the child is leading the adult. In talk between adults and very young children the links between utterances are often much less clear than in adult talk; the young child's one- or two-word utterances may be very inexplicit, and so open to a number of interpretations. Ochs's point is that unreflective choices about transcription may compound the difficulty of interpreting this kind of talk, and lead to questionable interpretations.

Another aspect of transcription that has prompted discussion is the question of how words are spelled. Some analysts attempt to use nonstandard spellings to represent the way connected speech sounds: this is true, for instance, of many practitioners of Conversation Analysis (CA). Here is an example of the kind of thing that often occurs in a CA transcript:

> H: Hwaryuhh=
> N: =Fi:ne how'r you
>
> > *[= latching, : lengthened vowel]*

The spelling 'hwaryuhh' represents the fact that H, like most people speaking casually, does not realize 'how are you' as three distinct words, and the vowel in 'you' is reduced (from [u] to schwa). Some critics have suggested that this impressionistic representation of speech is rather 'betwixt and between' – it is, precisely, impressionistic rather than telling us unambiguously what sound was uttered by the speaker. For linguists, the best way to represent speech sounds is to use the unambiguous

International Phonetic Alphabet (IPA) rather than tinkering with English spellings. But apart from the fact that many analysts of talk are not linguists and do not know the IPA, there is rarely any need for such precise and detailed phonetic information in the context of doing discourse or conversation analysis. All the use of IPA would do – and arguably, all the CA approach does – is make transcripts harder to read. Admittedly there are features of talk that do require a quasi-phonetic transcription, because they are not words and do not have standard spellings; one example is minimal response tokens like *mm, mhm*. There may also be an argument for representing prosodic and paralinguistic features (see above), but the conventions used to do this do not normally involve deviating from the ordinary spellings of words.

Apart from inconsistency and difficulty, there is another reason for being cautious about nonstandard spellings. How does it make your informants look if you use nonstandard spelling to represent their speech? 'Hwaryuhh' is somewhat reminiscent of the sort of spelling used in comic strips, where the speakers are caricatures and their speech is supposed to be funny. Our informants, however, are real people; not everything they say is funny and we need to take care *not* to caricature them.

The issue of spelling is especially pertinent where the informants whose speech is to be transcribed are speakers of a nonstandard variety such as Scots or Black English. Though standard English spelling is not a very exact representation of any kind of English pronunciation, its status as the default way of writing means it tends to bring to mind a 'standard' pronunciation (educated, belonging to no particular region) as opposed to anything else. So if you are working with a markedly non-standard or localized variety you may not want to transcribe it in a way that makes it look indistinguishable from standard English, thus misrepresenting your informants; but on the other hand you will not want to reinforce stereotypes of nonstandard speakers as illiterate buffoons.

The dialectologist Dennis Preston has called this problem 'The Li'l Abner Syndrome' (Preston 1985). Li'l Abner is a character in a long-running US comic strip, who represents the stereotype southern 'hillbilly'. His speech is represented in 'eye dialect', where standard spelling is manipulated to evoke the speaker's pronunciation (as with 'li'l' for 'little'). There is a long tradition in English of eye dialect being used by, for instance, novelists and journalists. Sometimes it is used to claim authenticity for a speaker or a character, but often it is used for comic effect. In Britain the speakers who are mocked using this device are usually working class and/or provincial (the cartoon Scots who cry: 'hoots, mon!' or the chirpy cockneys assailing one another with 'wotcha, me old cock!'). In the US they are mainly southerners or African Americans. Dennis Preston points out that many folklorists, perhaps unwittingly, have carried over the conventions of eye dialect into their own renderings of vernacular speech. But when this sort of spelling is used in an academic context, it may retain the racist or snobbish connotations it has acquired in a tradition of stereotypical 'humorous' writing – a reason, Preston suggests, to avoid eye dialect. Another objection to eye dialect is more theoretical: it tends to make nonstandard speakers appear more different than they really are from standard speakers. For example, representations of African American Vernacular English (AAVE) may use spellings like 'sump'm' for *something* and 'yella' for *yellow*. But if these spellings are phonetically accurate for African Americans, they are also accurate for many white speakers in informal contexts. Why should the spelling reflect the pronunciation in one case and not the other?

Ronald Macaulay, who has worked extensively on the speech of working class Scots, suggests in an article about the representation of dialect in writing (Macaulay 1991), that there is no reason to represent *predictable* features of pronunciation in nonstandard spelling; it is only worth deviating from the standard spellings where variation has meaning effects. Here is Macaulay's transcript of an extract from a story told by a man from Aberdeen:

> he comes from Kilwinning this fellow
> and we were on the golf course out there
> and the rain started to come down
> I just says to him
> 'lucks like we'll get weet'
> he said
> 'what a way to spick man'
> he says
> 'you mean
> you'll get wat'

This story is actually about language differences between people from different parts of Scotland (Aberdeen in the north east and Kilwinning in the south west), so there is an obvious reason to put the reported speech of the two men in a form that brings out the differences in their pronunciation (e.g. 'weet' versus 'wat' for standard English *wet*). But Macaulay makes no special attempt to represent the Aberdonian accent the narrator uses throughout.

Elsewhere in the same piece of data, Macaulay does use nonstandard spelling in the narration, as opposed to confining it to reported speech. The speaker is talking about people he knows in the area:

> they're nae oot to hae thoosands or millions
> they're nae wanting big cars
> they're wanting a car but nae necessarily a big car or necessarily a big hoose

Once again, if you were listening to it this sequence would sound 'Aberdonian' throughout, but in his transcript Macaulay spells most words in the customary way. In a few cases he deviates from the standard spelling, but this is not just a random sprinkling of local colour. He writes 'thoosands' and 'hoose' because Scots speakers may alternate between English and Scots variants of the relevant vowel, and this is a meaningful choice. Macaulay wants to show that the speaker in this extract is asserting his identity as a Scot. His spellings of *nae* and *hae* are also motivated by the fact that these are not just Scots pronunciations of *not* and *have*, they are actually Scots *words*. Rather than making up his own spellings for them, Macaulay uses the spellings that are traditional in written Scots.

Preston and Macaulay are concerned about stereotyping informants by consistently using nonstandard spellings to represent their speech, and the point is worth considering carefully. However, it can be argued that the meaning of this practice is changing, as writing in dialect has stopped being something done mostly by patronizing outsiders and started being something done by insiders. African American writers like A.J. Verdelle, London Jamaicans like Linton Kwesi Johnson and Scots like Irvine Welsh and Tom Leonard use nonstandard varieties for serious literary purposes, not just comic relief: such writers have both rehabilitated eye dialect and made certain spelling conventions familiar to a larger audience. Working in Scotland during the 1990s, I noticed that over time my students had progressively less difficulty deciding how to spell words when they transcribed the speech of informants from their own local communities, and they did not seem to regard the results as embarrassing or disrespectful. Michael Higgins, whose study of his mother's knitting bee I mentioned in Chapter 2, found it natural to use nonstandard spelling in his transcript. The issue is one on which there are conflicting opinions, and if you are dealing with data in a nonstandard variety you will have to make your own mind up.

SUMMARY

There is no 'standard' way to transcribe talk. Analysts may use a variety of conventions for just about every aspect of transcription, including how to lay out talk on the page, how to represent prosodic, paralinguistic and nonverbal features, and whether to use nonstandard spelling to give a more realistic impression of the speaker's pronunciation. Since talk itself is varied, and is collected by researchers for various purposes, it is no bad thing that there are choices about transcription rather than a 'one size fits all' prescription. But various issues need to be considered if an analyst is to make informed choices.

Transcription is not just a tedious, mechanical process that has to be got out of the way before the more 'interesting' part – analysing and interpreting your data – can begin. Despite the fact that I have included it in the 'Preliminaries' section, transcribing is effectively the first stage of analysis and interpretation: some would say it is the part of the process in which the analyst's engagement with the details of talk is most intense, as s/he works at hearing them accurately and experiments with different ways of representing them. Thinking through the issues transcription raises will make you not just a better and sharper transcriber, but more generally, a better analyst of talk.

SUGGESTIONS FOR FURTHER READING ABOUT TRANSCRIPTION

Discussions of transcription in discourse textbooks often take the form of presenting one or more sets of conventions that students can use as models in their own work. Deborah Schiffrin's appendix on transcription (1994: 422–33) reproduces three – the coding system suggested by DuBois, the conventions developed by Gail Jefferson for conversation analysis (CA) and those used by Deborah Tannen in her book *Talking Voices* (1989). Jefferson's system is widely used, and a full presentation of it by Atkinson and Heritage is reprinted in Jaworski and Coupland (1999). The actual business of transcribing using this system is also discussed in some detail in the relevant chapter of Hutchby and Wooffitt's textbook on CA (1998: 73–92). For more theoretical discussion about the principles and problems of transcription, Ochs's 'Transcription as theory' (also reprinted in Jaworski and Coupland 1999) is recommended; on the specific issue of transcribing dialect, see Preston (1985) and Macaulay (1991). Roger and Bull's collection *Conversation* (1988) includes a whole section on transcription procedures, one chapter in which (Kelly and Local 1988) discusses the issue of phonetic detail in transcription.

NOTES

1 'Clause' here means a stretch of talk that contains a subject + finite verb (e.g. '*they [a]re wanting* a car'), together with conjoined stretches which do not have their own subject or finite verb (e.g. '*but nae necessarily a big car*').
2 Kay Richardson (pers. comm.) reminds me to warn readers that if you want full, clear and consistent information on things like gaze direction you have to videotape your own data with that in mind, and not assume you can substitute tapes of television broadcasts, films, etc. In a film or television recording what you see is what the director and editor have decided you should see. The number and angle of cameras, decisions about who should be in shot at any given moment, etc., produce a selective representation of what is happening, and this representation may not be appropriate for the analyst's purposes.

II Approaches

| 4 | Approaches to discourse analysis: an initial orientation |

Each of the chapters in Part II deals with one approach to the analysis of talk. Chapter 5 deals with the **ethnography of speaking**, Chapter 6 with **pragmatics**, Chapter 7 with **conversation analysis** or 'CA' as it is often called for short, Chapter 8 with **interactional sociolinguistics** and Chapter 9 with **critical discourse analysis** (sometimes abbreviated to **CDA**). It might be asked why I have chosen just these approaches, and put them in just this order. More generally, readers may feel the need for an overall map of the terrain, locating different approaches in relation to one another. In fact, it is difficult to draw a detailed map without getting bogged down in arguments and excursions into intellectual history which are peripheral to this book's purpose (readers who want this sort of detail should look at some of Chapter 1's suggested further readings). But I do want to offer readers, if not a map, then some sort of initial orientation to help them find their way around the territory of discourse analysis, and that is the purpose of this short chapter.

I will take as my starting point the *interdisciplinary* nature of discourse analysis. It now has an academic life of its own – there are, for instance, scholarly journals specifically devoted to it – but if we look back at its history, it is clear that many of its questions and conceptual frameworks were borrowed in the first place from longer-established academic disciplines, such as anthropology, philosophy, sociology and linguistics. The influence of these intellectual traditions is still discernible, not least in the way teachers and textbook writers (myself included) divide up the field when they present it to students. It may be helpful to the reader, therefore, to make some observations about what, broadly speaking, discourse analysis has taken from the various disciplines that helped to form it.

From **anthropology**, discourse analysis takes a concern with the embedding of language and language-use in a wider sociocultural context. Anthropologists study the diversity of human cultures, often using the method of participant observation (observing a community while participating as much as possible in its activities oneself) to produce a kind of description that is known as *ethnography*. A researcher undertaking ethnographic work in any community must try to understand that community's culture – its ways of acting in the world and making sense of the world – in the way community members understand it themselves. Speaking is both a way of acting in the world and a means for making sense of it, and language has thus been one of the aspects of culture that anthropologists have paid attention to.

Ethnography of speaking is an approach to talk informed by the principles and practices of anthropology. It focuses specifically and systematically on language-using as a cultural practice, one which is intricately related to other cultural practices and beliefs within a particular society. It has a strong interest, also, in how the cultural practice of language-using may be done differently, and understood differently, in different societies.

From **philosophy**, discourse analysis takes a concern with the way language acquires meaning when it is used. The so-called 'problem of meaning' has been a traditional concern for the philosophy of language, and discourse analysis has drawn in particular on the tradition known as 'ordinary language' philosophy (the philosophical study of ordinary language as opposed to symbolic 'languages' such as formal logic). Ordinary language philosophers such as J.L. Austin, John Searle and H. Paul Grice drew attention to a feature that seems to be characteristic of human linguistic communication, that we can 'mean more than we say' (or less than we say, or something different from what we say). To interpret utterances in discourse, we have to be able to do more than just decode the meaning of the words: we have to work out how the speaker intends us to take the utterance. If someone utters, for instance, 'I'm addicted to soap operas', is this an idle remark, a confession, or a hint that someone should switch on the TV? All these are possibilities: in any given circumstances our decision on which of the alternatives it is intended to be will depend not only on what is said and how, but on all sorts of contextual factors as well.

The approach to discourse analysis that has developed from the tradition of ordinary language philosophy is known as **pragmatics**. (This use of the term *pragmatics* is commonest in English-speaking academic communities. In Europe, the term is often used generically for all kinds of discourse analysis, and sometimes it also encompasses what elsewhere would be called 'sociolinguistics'. Here I use the term in the 'English' way.) Pragmatics concerns itself with the principles language-users employ to determine the meaning behind words – how we get from what is said to what is meant. Many pragmaticists are interested in the possibility that certain principles of utterance interpretation are universal, not specific to a particular culture but characteristic of all linguistic communication. The question of what, if anything, is universal and what is culturally particular has generated some debate between the more 'philosophical' pragmaticists and the more 'anthropological' ethnographers, as we will see.

From **sociology**, discourse analysis takes a concern to account for the orderliness of social interaction. The question of how social order in general is produced and reproduced is traditionally a central concern of sociology. One particular approach to this general sociological question – the approach known as *ethnomethodology*, and associated in particular with the theorist Harold Garfinkel – gave rise to the way of analysing talk that is now known as **Conversation Analysis** (CA). The central idea of ethnomethodology is that social actors are not just 'dopes' following externally imposed rules, but are always actively creating order through their own behaviour. Some researchers became particularly interested in conversation as an example of the kind of mundane, everyday behaviour in which participants jointly create order. We are not conscious of having particular procedures for conducting conversations, but our conversations rarely degenerate into the kind of chaos that might be expected if we did not have procedures of any kind. CA is, among other things, an enquiry into the nature of the procedures conversationalists follow to produce the orderliness of ordinary talk.

From **linguistics**, discourse analysis takes a concern with the structure of language and the distribution of linguistic forms (i.e. where particular bits of language are and are not found). Linguists studying phonology (sound patterns) or syntax (sentence structure) look for formal regularities and patterns which can be described in general statements like 'In English the sound [h] only appears at the beginning of a syllable', or 'the normal order of grammatical constituents in English is SVO (subject, verb, object)'. As I mentioned in Chapter 1, in the 1950s the linguist Zellig Harris proposed to extend this kind of analysis to language 'above the sentence'. Interest in the formal and structural properties of spoken interaction remains prominent in some traditions of discourse analysis. For instance, in the 1970s a group of linguists studying classroom interaction elaborated a model of 'exchange structure', pointing out that when teachers ask questions in the classroom, the resulting exchanges typically have a three-part structure which the analysts termed 'elicitation–response–feedback'. The teacher asks a question, a pupil produces a response, and the teacher takes another turn in which s/he makes clear whether the pupil's response is acceptable (see Sinclair and Coulthard 1975). This contrasts with what happens in ordinary conversation, where asking a question typically initiates a two-part exchange, 'question–answer'.

A rather different example of a 'structural' approach to discourse is found in the work of the sociolinguist William Labov, best known for his pioneering work on language variation and change. Labov has also made important contributions to discourse analysis, proposing an influential model of the structure of spoken narrative (Labov and Waletzsky 1967) and co-writing a study of therapeutic discourse in which the analysis sets out to discover structural regularities beneath the (sometimes chaotic-looking) surface of talk between therapists and their clients (Labov and Fanshel 1977). An observation once made by Labov provides a good summary of this version of the 'structural' approach: 'the fundamental problem of discourse analysis', he asserted, 'is to show how one utterance follows another in a rational, rule-governed manner' (Labov 1972a: 299).

Regularities are not only found, however, in the way utterances are put together. They are also observed in the choices speakers make between different ways of doing a particular interactional job, such as addressing someone respectfully, or marking something as a question rather than a statement, or indicating which bit of an utterance is particularly important and which is just background information, or showing that they are highly engaged with what someone else is saying. If we consider the last of these functions, for example – demonstrating engagement with another speaker – one person might do it by gazing at the speaker in rapt silence, while another might do it by talking along with the speaker, making approving comments or even finishing the speaker's utterance for them. The existence of variation in matters like this is somewhat reminiscent of the variation we find in the pronunciation of particular sounds (e.g. the final nasal consonant in a word like *talking*, which is sometimes pronounced *talkin'*). This sort of phonological variation has been studied under the rubric of sociolinguistics, which has found that it is not just random but 'socially conditioned' (it correlates in a regular fashion with the speaker's social position and with aspects of the situation in which s/he is speaking). Variation in the performance of *interactional* tasks is the province of **interactional sociolinguistics**. Interactional sociolinguists do not usually use the same (statistical) methods as sociolinguists who study phonological variation, but they do make a similar assumption, that variation is socially/contextually conditioned rather than random. Interactional sociolinguistics, then, can be viewed as another kind of 'structural' approach with roots in linguistics, because it is concerned with the distribution of particular features in talk (where in talk you find them, and whose talk you find which ones in). At the same time the approach has roots in anthropology too: people's different ways of doing things interactionally may be analysed in relation to their cultural beliefs, assumptions and values.

There is also an approach to discourse analysis, known as **Critical Discourse Analysis**, which borrows its conceptual and analytic apparatus from both structural linguistics and the intellectual enterprise sometimes known as **critical theory**. Critical theory is not an academic discipline in the same sense as anthropology or sociology. It is better thought of as a set of interests and theoretical commitments that have influenced groups of academics in a number of disciplines. The disciplines where critical theory has had or is now acquiring a degree of influence are a diverse collection, ranging across the humanities (e.g. literary studies, philosophy) and social sciences (e.g. geography, sociology and psychology). Important reference points for critical theory across disciplines include the work of literary/cultural theorists such as Julia Kristeva, Roland Barthes and Edward Said, psychoanalysts like Jacques Lacan, philosophers like Jacques Derrida, historians of ideas like Michel Foucault, and feminist or 'queer' theorists like Judith Butler.

As readers may be aware, the critical theorists just listed are often characterized as 'post-structuralists' or 'postmodernists'. I will not detour here into the complicated and much argued-about question of what those terms 'really mean', but what they imply at the most general level is a critical attitude to traditional ways of thinking and talking about reality, subjectivity (that is, the condition of being a person or 'subject') and knowledge. Does what we call 'reality' have any independent existence apart from our perceptions and representations of it? Do people have stable, fixed identities (e.g. as men or women), and is there such a thing as 'human nature'? Can knowledge be completely objective, disinterested and 'true'? Post-structuralist/postmodernist theory answers these questions in the negative. Theorists who adopt a critical perspective are sometimes caricatured as denying that there is 'any such thing as truth' or 'any such thing as gender/race/sexuality', but it would be more accurate to say that they regard such phenomena as *constructed* rather than 'natural'. Here it should be remembered that something which is constructed is nevertheless part of reality rather than merely an illusion we could dispense with at will. The building I work in and the amount I get paid at the end of the month are clearly not the results of any natural process, but that does not mean I can change them simply by choosing to think about them in a different way!

Critical theory is the source of the usage of the word *discourse* which I discussed in the latter part of Chapter 1. One thing that critical theorists (or post-structuralists/postmodernists) have in common is the idea I introduced during that earlier discussion, that reality (including such aspects of it as power and gender relations) is constructed in and through discourse – through acts and practices of speaking and writing. Critical discourse analysis is an approach that focuses on *how* this is done by analysing actual examples closely, and, importantly, by paying attention not only to their content but also to their form. CDA makes use of the insight derived from traditional, structure-oriented linguistics and sociolinguistics, that meaning is about contrast. When someone expresses an idea in form X (using these particular words and this particular grammatical structure), it is significant that they are *not* expressing the idea in form Y or Z, though Y and Z would also have been possibilities. CDA looks for the ideological significance of the choices speakers and writers make, and for significant patterns in the distribution of their choices.

The account I have given of discourse analysis and its relation to various academic disciplines is oversimplified in certain ways. It would be inaccurate, for instance, to say that anthropology has contributed nothing to the discussion of meaning, that sociologists have paid no attention to culture, that questions of structure have only been addressed by linguists, or that philosophically oriented pragmaticists have no interest in power. The themes I have picked out in my account – culture, meaning, order, structure, power – are likely to crop up in all the approaches I will describe in this section. What distinguishes the approaches from each other is the balance of differing concerns, and the analytic procedures that follow from taking any particular concern as central. For example, if your main concern is with what participants in a conversation are doing to produce the orderliness of their talk (a typical question in CA), you will focus on the talk itself and be less concerned to describe the whole social or cultural milieu in which that talk is taking place. If, by contrast, you are mainly concerned with the way a certain speech event fits into a whole network of cultural beliefs and practices (a typical concern for ethnographers of speaking), you will spend more time describing things that are external to the talk itself: who the speakers are, where they are, what beliefs and customs are important in their lives.

It would also be inaccurate to suppose that anyone who uses an ethnography of speaking approach must be an anthropologist, that anyone who does pragmatics is a philosopher, and so on. These approaches have historical roots in particular academic disciplines, but they have not remained hermetically sealed within those disciplines. On the contrary, they have influenced and mixed with one another to produce a field – discourse analysis – that cannot be claimed as the 'property' of any single discipline. CA, for instance, is an approach with a distinctive identity, but not everything that is distinctive about it can be traced back to its roots in ethnomethodological sociology. It is also quite strikingly a 'structuralist' approach that makes general statements about the distribution of linguistic features, and in this respect it has much in common with approaches that originated in structural linguistics. While some individual scholars adhere quite strictly to one approach, others feel free to draw on a broader range. Labov and Fanshel's (1977) study of therapeutic discourse, for instance, which I cited above as an example of the 'structural' approach, also makes use of the concept of a 'speech act' which comes from pragmatics. There is, then, a degree of artificiality about what I have just done and what I will continue to do in the rest of this section, namely separate out a series of approaches that are often, in practice, much less clearly demarcated and separated than this proceeding makes them appear.

As well as choosing to define and discuss a particular set of approaches, I have chosen to put them in a particular order (though the chapters do not necessarily have to be read in that order). The logic behind the ordering of Chapters 5–8 is about moving from a kind of analysis that looks at the 'big picture' to one which focuses on the most minute details. I begin with an approach – the ethnography of speaking – in which the main unit of analysis is the 'speech event'. Examples of speech events would be things like 'job interview' or 'seminar', and an ethnographer analyses these events with reference to the whole social context in which they occur. This is a 'big picture' approach. Then I move on to pragmatics, which tries to formulate quite general principles people use in producing and interpreting talk. Pragmatics too is essentially a 'big picture' approach, though in a different way from ethnography of speaking. I then turn to two approaches – CA and interactional sociolinguistics – in which analysis tends to concentrate on small details that recur in talk, like overlaps, silences, utterances of *yeah* or *well* or *y'know*. The chapter on critical discourse analysis (CDA) does not entirely fit the logic just outlined. As noted above, CDA *mixes* a microanalytic approach with a 'big picture' approach, the big picture in this case being framed in terms of social or 'critical' theory. I have placed CDA at the end of this part because it is an approach to discourse analysis that deliberately tries to bring together the two main senses of the term *discourse* (the linguistic sense and the critical theory sense) that I discussed in Chapter 1. The chapter on CDA thus forms a bridge to the final, 'Applications' part of the book, whose primary concern is with the uses of discourse analysis in research on various social phenomena.

Each of the approaches I deal with in Part II has both its own internal complexities and a complex set of relationships with the others. On the principle that showing is better than telling, at this point I will stop making general, abstract observations and get down to the concrete business of showing what different approaches enable the analyst to do.

SUGGESTIONS FOR FURTHER READING ABOUT APPROACHES TO DISCOURSE ANALYSIS

Each of the chapters in Part II gives suggestions for further reading about a particular approach. Other textbooks in which a variety of approaches are discussed include Stephen Levinson's *Pragmatics* (1983), which in spite of the name is not just about 'philosophical' approaches, and Deborah Schiffrin's *Approaches To Discourse* (1994). A critical assessment of selected approaches (including pragmatics and CA), which brings out the similarities and differences between them, is Talbot Taylor and Deborah Cameron's *Analysing Conversation* (1987).

In this chapter I will consider the approach to working with talk that is known as 'ethnography of speaking'. An alternative term is 'ethnography of communication', which does not presuppose that the medium of communication is exclusively spoken language. It is worth bearing in mind that few instances of communication rely *exclusively* on speech or indeed language. In face-to-face conversation, for example, the fact that participants can see one another and are located in a shared environment can be exploited for communicative purposes (e.g. by staring, pointing, brandishing objects). In written texts, communication is accomplished through layout, images and graphics as well as words. The ethnographic approach is one in which attention is paid to the interdependence of language-using and other activities. Any given instance of language use is analysed as part of a whole social situation; more generally, ways of using and understanding language are analysed in relation to the wider culture in which they occur. Of course, it is recognized in other approaches that language-using does not go on in isolation from everything else; precisely because that point is fundamental for any analysis of language in use, I have chosen to begin with an approach where it is explicitly and systematically addressed.

WHAT IS THE ETHNOGRAPHY OF SPEAKING?

The term *ethnography* belongs to the specialist vocabulary of anthropology; it refers to the investigation of culture(s) using a particular methodology, that of *participant observation*.[1] Typically, anthropologists go and live with the people they wish to study for an extended period of time. They learn about the community's way of life both through observational techniques (e.g. recording things that happen, interviewing people) and through participating as much as possible in community activities themselves. They are simultaneously 'inside' the culture, immersed in its day-to-day life, and 'outside' it, trying to understand the way its members think and act, and reflecting on their own progress towards that goal.

Participant observation is also used by researchers who are not anthropologists, but who are working in fields like sociology, cultural studies or sociolinguistics. For example, a sociologist studying youth subcultures (punks, goths, skinheads, etc.) might decide that instead of just interviewing young people individually or in groups about their subcultural practices, they should seek out one or more groups prepared to let a researcher spend time with them regularly: join in their activities, record their conversation, and of course talk to them about what they do and why. This resembles the methods used in anthropological fieldwork, and is therefore labelled 'ethnography'. However, there is some dispute about whether the label is always appropriate, given that unlike anthropologists, sociological researchers do not usually live among their subjects for long periods of time. Is hanging out with people for a few hours every week, while otherwise following your normal routine, sufficient to constitute 'participation' in their way of life? Can it produce the depth of understanding that ethnographic methods aim for?

Occasionally a project may prompt the opposite criticism, that the researcher is too much a participant and not enough of an observer. For instance one researcher, Sarah Thornton, describes doing ethnography in an advertising agency (Thornton 1999). Her strategy was actually to get a job in an agency; she was accepted as an insider because by all the relevant institutional criteria she *was* an insider – indeed, she gave those around her no indication that she was doing research at all. If we asked Sarah Thornton to justify calling this 'ethnography', she might reply that the world of advertising was as unfamiliar to her when she joined it as an African village would be to someone starting a research project in anthropology. Like any ethnographer in the field she had to go through the process of figuring out what it took to be a competent member of the culture, and she documented that process in the same systematic way. Then again, a critic might observe that because Sarah Thornton did not present herself to her colleagues and clients as an ethnographer, but simply as a new advertising executive, there were things an ethnographer ought to do that she could not do. It is awkward for someone in Thornton's position to ask too many questions about things they are already supposed to know, or to ask people to explain and justify what count within the culture as common sense beliefs. Although ethnographers too may find this sort of probing awkward on occasion, it is easier for them precisely because their position is ambiguous, simultaneously 'inside' and 'outside' the culture.

It is arguable that the terms *ethnography* and *participant observation* have come to be overused in social science, and it is clear that some of what is called 'ethnographic' research does not meet the standards set by 'classical' anthropology. At the same time, there are obvious family resemblances among the various enterprises that claim the label 'ethnography'. They tend to involve ongoing regular contact and some degree of participation by the researcher in the (sub)culture being studied; research is done in a naturalistic setting (not in a lab or an office); and – perhaps the most important distinguishing feature of ethnographic approaches – the aim is not just to collect 'objective' factual data about the group's way of life, but to understand that way of life as group members understand it themselves.

Language is a relevant consideration in all ethnographic research, since participant observation inevitably involves, among other things, talking to the people you are studying and observing their talk among themselves, which is to say, it produces at least some data in the form of spoken discourse. I will return to the implications of that later on. However, the main subject of this chapter is the ethnography of speaking, which as its name suggests is the application of ethnographic methods specifically to language-using: it does not just use language as a tool for finding out about other things, but makes it an object of ethnographic interest in its own right. One textbook writer, Stephen Levinson (1983: 279), has defined the ethnography of speaking as 'the cross-cultural study of language usage'. This definition recalls the subject-matter of anthropology, which is concerned with the diversity of human cultures. But ethnography of speaking also takes some of its concepts and assumptions from linguistics, and this is the next point I will elaborate on.

Linguists are familiar with the distinction, introduced by Noam Chomsky in the 1960s, between linguistic *competence* and *performance*. Performance is what language-users *do*, but competence is what they must *know* in order to be able to do it. This is not, however, conscious knowledge which a linguist could investigate simply by asking language-users to explain what they are doing. Rather it involves abstract rules and generalizations that people are not aware they 'know'. (For instance, in the sentence *Simon says Rory hurt himself*, English speakers can be counted on to recognize that *himself* must refer to *Rory* and not *Simon*. This recognition depends on 'knowing' the general rule that reflexive pronouns in English can only be indexed to noun phrases in the same clause. But how many people are aware of any such rule?) Since Chomsky proposed the competence/performance distinction, it has been the orthodox view that what linguists need to focus on is not just people's surface linguistic behaviour but their underlying 'competence', the knowledge that enables them to produce an infinite number of grammatical sentences.

As we saw in Chapter 1, discourse analysis is the study of 'language in use', which means that in Chomsky's terms, it is concerned with 'performance'. However, 'competence' in the sense of 'underlying knowledge' has a place in some analysts' thinking as well. In the 1970s the anthropologist and linguist Dell Hymes pointed out that a 'competent' language-user needs to know more than just a set of rules for forming grammatical sentences; s/he also needs to know how to use language in a contextually appropriate way. It is not by chance that people regularly produce the 'right' kind of utterance at the right time to the right person. Just like the use of reflexive pronouns, this communicationally appropriate behaviour must depend on knowing certain rules (though these may operate, like grammatical rules, below the level of conscious awareness). Hymes proposed an analogue for Chomsky's 'linguistic competence', which he called *communicative competence* (Hymes 1972a). Linguistic competence is about rules of grammar; communicative competence is about rules of *speaking*. The ethnography of speaking developed as a way of investigating the rules of speaking that are operative in particular language-using communities.

If one is investigating rules of grammar, the objects of analysis will be grammatical units such as sentence, clause, phrase. What, though, are the relevant units for an investigation of rules of speaking? Hymes proposed three, and like sentences, clauses and phrases in grammar they are hierarchically ordered.

The highest-level unit is the *speech situation*, the social context in which speaking takes place. Speech situations provide occasions for the use of language, but they are not purely linguistic. For example, a family meal might be analysed as a speech situation, but other activities feature in it besides talking (e.g. eating, drinking, serving food and drink, feeding infants, kicking people under the table, etc.) and the overall proceedings clearly are not governed *only* by rules of speaking.

The next unit down from the speech situation is the *speech event*. Speech events are constituted by the use of language: they involve activities which could not occur except in and through language, such as 'argument', 'gossip', 'storytelling'. Typically, community members have metalinguistic labels for recurring speech events; they say things like 'I went over to Jeannie's for a *chat*', 'today's *lecture* was really boring', 'the bus was late and Mrs Smith gave me a good *telling off*', 'how did your *interview* go?'. It will be apparent that more than one speech event might occur within the same speech situation: 'chat', 'argument' and 'telling-off', for instance, are not uncommonly observed to occur in the course of a single family meal. By contrast, 'institutional' events like 'lecture' or 'interview' are more likely to occur within situations that have been set up expressly for the purpose.

The 'lowest' level unit of analysis in this framework is the *speech act* (in a sense similar but not identical to the sense we will encounter in Chapter 6). Speech acts are things like 'greeting', 'apologizing', 'insulting', 'asking/answering a question'. They are not speech events in themselves, and in many cases (e.g. 'greeting') they can figure in many different kinds of events; but the distinctiveness of a particular speech event is partly a question of which acts are performed and in what order.

While all three levels are analytically relevant, the most important is the mid-level one, the speech event, since it is essentially the event to which 'rules of speaking' apply. Hymes proposed that speech events have a set of 'components', characteristics which the analyst needs to look at in order to produce a satisfactory description of any particular speech event. In the work of Hymes and others we find various lists in which the components are named and ordered in slightly different ways, but the listing most often used to introduce this descriptive framework is a mnemonic device that labels each component with one of the letters of the word *speaking*.

S *setting*: where the speech event is located in time and space

P *participants*: who takes part in the speech event, and in what role (e.g. speaker, addressee, audience, eavesdropper)

E *ends*: what the purpose of the speech event is, and what its outcome is meant to be

A *act sequence*: what speech acts make up the speech event, and what order they are performed in

K *key*: the tone or manner of performance (serious or joking, sincere or ironic, etc.)

I *instrumentalities*: what channel or medium of communication is used (e.g. speaking, signing, writing, drumming, whistling) and what language/variety is selected from the participants' repertoire

N *norms of interaction*: what the rules are for producing and interpreting speech acts

G *genres*: what 'type' does a speech event belong to, and what other pre-existing conventional forms of speech are drawn on or 'cited' in producing appropriate contributions to talk (e.g. do people quote from mythology or poetry or scripture?)[2]

This set of components is sometimes referred to as the 'SPEAKING grid', and its purpose is to help analysts put their observations in some kind of order. Someone observing a culture to which s/he is an outsider is likely, at least initially, to observe various things – including unfamiliar speech events – whose significance s/he does not fully understand. In this situation it can be useful to have some kind of pre-existing descriptive framework to put your observations in. Without such a framework you may miss important things, or interpret things in terms of categories that are used by your own society rather than the one you are observing. Hymes's grid is meant to be both comprehensive and applicable to any community's ways of speaking.

It should be remembered, however, that ethnography can also be done in the observer's own culture. Here the potential problem is not that the observer will have no idea what is going on, nor that s/he might interpret it in terms of 'outside' cultural assumptions. Rather the potential problem is that the observer, *because* s/he is already an insider, will take things for granted instead of seeing them clearly and describing them explicitly. Insider-observers have to put some distance between themselves and the phenomena they are observing; they have to notice what normally passes unnoticed. Once again, it may help them to do this if they come to the task with a systematic framework for making observations.

I find it more helpful to regard Hymes's model for analysing speech events as an aid to being systematic than to treat the model as a sort of recipe ('to make an analysis of the speech event, take these ingredients and add to the pot in this order'). I agree with Deborah Schiffrin (1994), who talks about using the grid as a 'heuristic', that is, an exploratory device. I emphasize this point for two main reasons. First, it is not always easy to apply the framework in a straightforward way to data; if you find it is hard, then it may be more fruitful to think about why the categories don't fit than to try to force your data into them. Secondly, ethnography (of speaking or anything else) does not have to stop at *description*. Certainly, an ethnographer will want to address such 'descriptive' questions as 'what speech events occur in such-and-such a community?' and 'what are the components of speech events X, Y and Z?' But s/he will also be interested in explaining *why* particular events occur and why they have particular characteristics.

These 'why' questions are really about the social or cultural significance of speaking in a particular way. Why, for example, do people in the culture I belong to gossip, or engage in lengthy rounds of joke-telling? Just listing the components of the relevant speech event – describing what you have to do to be a competent gossiper or joke-teller – does not explain what the point of it is. Explaining the significance of a particular speech event involves relating its characteristics to a broader range of cultural beliefs, practices and values – both those relating directly and specifically to language and those relating to other things, such as the culture's view of what a 'good person' is, or its attitudes towards emotion or conflict. Much of the interest and value of the ethnographic approach lies in its ability to make these connections, and it is limiting to view the approach narrowly in terms of a particular model for describing speech events.

I will illustrate what I mean by 'making connections' further below. First, though, let us return to the question of how Hymes's framework can be applied to actual examples of spoken discourse. For this purpose I will present an extract from some data, recorded by Christine Callender in the 1980s at a Pentecostal meeting, and later transcribed and analysed by her (though I have modified the transcript slightly here).

A PENTECOSTAL MEETING IN SOUTH LONDON

The data below come from a meeting held at the C. Temple, whose members have come together to engage in a form of Christian worship. The Temple is located in a working class area of south London and its congregation is drawn from the local African Caribbean community. The researcher was herself a member of that community with ties to C. Temple.

The form of Christianity practised at C. Temple is known as 'Pentecostalism'. Pentecost is the event described in the New Testament when the Holy Spirit (the third 'person' of the Christian Holy Trinity) descended to inspire Jesus's followers, who began to 'speak in tongues', i.e. produce utterances in languages they did not know. Pentecostal worship is similarly understood to be inspired by the Holy Spirit. The meeting involves various activities which are common in church services, for instance preaching, reading from the Bible, prayer, singing, testimony given by individual members of the congregation, administrative announcements, etc., but the overall style is distinctive. Most strikingly, members of the congregation do not speak only at designated points in the proceedings, but may intervene throughout 'as the spirit moves them'.

ACTIVITY

Read through the data extract below and consider the following questions. You should bear in mind that although some answers may be better than others, there is not necessarily one 'correct' answer. You should also remember that in a 'real' analysis you would have resources in addition to this transcript (e.g. you would know what the meeting actually looks and sounds like, and you would have the opportunity to ask insiders how they understand what is happening).

1 How would you analyse this in terms of the 'situation/event/act' framework? Does this extract contain one speech event or several? If more than one, where would you locate the boundaries and why?
2 Now go through the 'components' of the speech event using the SPEAKING framework. What can you say about each component on the basis of the transcript? Note any problems you encounter applying the categories to this extract. Also note anything you find interesting that does not seem to come under any of the headings.

Complete this activity *before* you read the discussion that follows the data extract.

Transcription conventions: P = Pastor, E = Elder (a senior member of the congregation), T = Testifier (a person who has been called on to 'bear witness' in front of the congregation), M = Member, C = Congregation (acting as a body), // = turn 'latched' to preceding or following turn (shown on line above/below), [ ] = speech that is simultaneous with bracketed sequence on line above/below, xxxx = applause, (.) short pause

E: I'm going to call brother Tony Tracey and if he would come and speak to us for just ten minutes. Come on Tony come and say what the Lord will have you to say to us//
M: //Amen//
M: //Praise him
_____1

E: Oh glory to God a young man that love the Lord let us praise the Lord for him
_____2

M: Praise God praise God glory praise the Lord
_____3

T: Hallelujah Lord Jesus//   //Hallelujah Lord Jesus//
M: //Praise him//   //Praise the Lord
_____4

T: Thank you Lord Jesus//   //Hallelujah hallelujah [Lord Jesus]
M: //Praise//   [Hallelujah]   5

T: [Hallelujah] thank you Lord Jesus Hallelujah
M: [Hallelujah]
M: [Praise him]
_____6

T: Praise the Lord everybody//
C: //Praise the Lord   7

T: The brotherhood has asked me to speak to you for a few minutes (.)
    Now don't get scared of me I'm not the preacher. Just got a little word I want to give to you //
M: //[praise him]
M: //[praise the] Lord
_____8

T: What I want to talk about is the word repentance//
E: //yes
_____9

T: And what we've got to understand here is that the Bible is wrapped up in principles and the word principle in the Bible is used as law as to Psalms 19 verse 1 says the law of the Lord is perfect//   //converting the soul//
E: //yes//
M: //Amen Hallelujah
_____10

continued . . .

(*several minutes of Biblical commentary omitted*)

T: Now the word repentance means to have a change of heart a change of mind a
     change of direction uhm if you've ever seen soldiers walking their walking left
     right left right about turn (.) he turns//

M: //yes

_____11

T: that's repentance when you turn from what you're doing//

M: //[yes prai]se the [Lord]

M: //[Amen]

M: [alright]

C: xxxxxxxx

_____12

T: Before I got saved I was//   [*laugh*] I was no good yes thank you pastor I was

P: //no good

_____13

T: no good//   //I smoked I swore I commit fornication

M: //praise the Lord//

_____14

T: you named it I done it//   //but until I fully repented of my sins

M: //yes//

_____15

T: then God dealt with me in a mighty way//   //and I truly give him thanks for that

M: //yes//   16

(*testimony continues*)

Groups I have discussed this extract with in the past usually agree that the speech
situation is that of a religious gathering, where people have assembled to worship
their God, but they are sometimes unsure whether the meeting itself constitutes one
speech event or whether meetings contain a series of separate events (e.g. prayer,
preaching, testifying). This issue is difficult to resolve on the evidence presented
above. One relevant question to ask would be whether or not the same rules of
speaking seem to apply throughout the meeting (which might support an analysis
of it as one event), or whether different rules are followed in, say, 'prayer' sequences
and 'testifying' sequences. That question cannot be answered using such a short
extract from the data, since the extract does not cover the whole range of things that
can happen at a Pentecostal meeting.

Most readers of this transcript define what is happening in it as an instance of
'testifying' (a judgement they are prompted to make by the label the analyst has given
to the main speaker, 'Testifier'. 'Testifying' is in fact a genre category used by insiders,
as the researcher discovered by talking to them, but it is worth pointing out that in
the extract itself, no one uses the word *testify*). Whether this example of testifying is
a discrete speech event or whether it is only one part of a longer one, readers usually
note that it can itself be subdivided into relatively distinct parts or stages. The Elder

calls the Testifier (1–3); and the Testifier engages in an exchange of 'hallelujahs' and 'praise the Lords' with members of the congregation (4–7) before he moves into his actual testimony. Should these segments be labelled 'acts' and if so what would we want to call those acts? Can any of them be subdivided into still smaller units? How predictable is the order in which acts occur? It is possible to give a number of more or less convincing answers to these questions, which suggests (among other things) that analysing the structure of speech events is not like analysing sentence structure. For instance, the ordering of acts is less a matter of grammar-like rules and more a matter of following the overall logic of the event: thus for obvious logical (and not specifically linguistic) reasons, the act of calling someone to testify occurs before the actual testimony. One question that might be raised is whether the exchange between testifier and members that occurs just before the testimony proper (4–7) is an 'obligatory' or an 'optional' constituent: could the testifier have gone straight into the remarks at line 8, or is testimony always preceded by these formulae? Obviously, to answer a question like this, which calls for a generalization, it is necessary to look at a number of cases rather than just one.

What can be said about the 'components', that is, *setting, participants, ends, act sequence, key, instrumentalities, norms* and *genres*? I will mention only a few of the observations that people have made in discussions of this extract. Under *setting*, it is often mentioned that this event takes place in a special place (the Temple) and at a special time (the sabbath). In fact, an insider might point out that these are not necessary components of the event – members might equally worship on a Tuesday night in someone's living room. Religious ceremonies are often performed in a special place, but at the same time, engaging in religious worship tends to imbue whatever the spatiotemporal setting is with a kind of psychological 'specialness'. How much of the meaning of the event derives from the setting is something one might want to investigate further by trying to find out how insiders perceive this. A somewhat similar question about insiders' perceptions arises under the *participants* heading: whether God (in any or all of his three persons) should be counted as a participant. In an utterance like 'thank you Lord Jesus', Jesus figures linguistically as the direct addressee (though it is evident that the speaker is also addressing the congregation). We might ask, then, if the congregation understands God as being present.

Probably the most interesting question about the extract, and the meeting as a whole, comes under the heading of *norms of interaction*. It is striking that members of the congregation frequently intervene in the proceedings, and that whoever is the main participant holding the floor at the time (in this extract mainly the testifier) apparently 'makes space' for them to do so. This is suggested, for instance, by the high incidence of 'latching' between turns (i.e. changes of speaker occur with no overlap or perceptible gap). If interventions occurred in a totally random, unpredictable way, we might expect to find simultaneous speech rather than latching. When more than one member intervenes at the same point, their contributions often do overlap (e.g. 6, 12), but there is far less overlap between the testifier and the members who intervene in his discourse. So what rules are people following? When is intervention permitted or expected? What 'cues' the member to utter something like 'hallelujah', and the testifier to expect this?

When Christine Callender asked insiders this question, the answer she got was that people did not control this aspect of their behaviour; if they spoke it was because they were moved to do so by the Holy Spirit. She noted this belief as one important underlying reason for members behaving as they did: the frequency and intensity of their contributions reflects the value they ascribe to the workings of the spirit. Interventions signal that the spirit is at work among participants, and this is one criterion for a 'good' meeting. However, by looking at a large amount of data, Callender was able to discern patterns in the placement of interventions – they certainly were not, as members seemed to be claiming, random. I do not have space to reproduce her analysis (see Callender and Cameron 1990), but it relates the norms of interaction governing interventions by members both to beliefs held by Pentecostalists specifically (such as their veneration of scripture, which means that direct quotations from the Bible are particularly likely to elicit supporting interventions, as at 10), and to the ways of speaking which are part of their cultural heritage as people of the African diaspora. For instance, lines 4–5 show the 'call and response' structure which has been noted as a feature of many kinds of oral performance in Black communities.

Callender's analysis raises an important point. Ethnography of speaking aims to discover how people understand their own communicative practices rather than imposing the analyst's own cultural frame. However, this does *not* mean just presenting local understandings without further comment. As we have seen, members of C. Temple represented their contributions to the discourse of the meeting as 'the spirit moving them' to speak. As far as they were concerned there were no 'rules' governing when they intervened or what they said. Callender however saw clear patterns, which she described in addition to explaining how insiders represented what was happening. The view that people speak because the spirit moves them is part of what you have to know *explicitly* to function as a competent member of the congregation, and is therefore an important part of the analysis. But in addition, whoever speaks must possess *implicit*, 'practical' knowledge, in virtue of which they are able to behave appropriately, shouting or clapping at the right points and not the wrong ones. For the insider it serves no particular purpose to make this knowledge explicit (in this case, indeed, making it explicit would threaten to undermine the 'official' view that speech in Pentecostal meetings is inspired directly by a supernatural force), but making the implicit explicit is an important part of an analyst's job. What people tell you about their linguistic practices is not all there may be to say about them; it is part of the input to analysis rather than the output. This point is also illustrated in the next example I discuss.

THE *KROS* IN A PAPUA NEW GUINEA VILLAGE

I take this example from the work of the linguistic anthropologist Don Kulick (1992, 1993, 1998). Kulick did fieldwork in a small and remote village, Gapun, in Papua New Guinea, where he observed and recorded examples of a speech event for which villagers used the label *kros* (a Tok Pisin word related to English 'cross', i.e. 'angry'). Here is Kulick's initial description of the *kros*:

Kroses in Gapun are public displays of anger. They can and do occur any time during the day and night, but the time most likely for one to break out is in the late afternoon and early evening, when villagers arrive home tired, hungry and exhausted after a hard day's work in the rainforest working sago or hunting. As men stroll off to their waterholes to wash and as women begin preparations for the evening meal, chopping firewood and ordering their daughters to fetch water, it is not uncommon to hear a high, indignant voice suddenly rising above the playful screams of children and the barking of the village dogs. The voice will often begin in low, loud, dissatisfied mutters, but it rises quickly and peaks in harsh crescendos. It becomes rapid, piston-like, unrelenting – so fast that the words become slurred and distorted to the point where it sometimes takes the villagers a while to work out what is being said. As the voice grows in volume and rancor, villagers stop what they are doing, cock their ears and listen. '*Husat i kros?*' ('who's angry/having a *kros*'?) somebody will ask, eliciting a quick identification from anyone who has heard, a hissed admonition to 'listen to the talk' (*harim tok*) and a counterquestion addressed to no one in particular: '*Em kros long wanem?*' ('what's s/he *kros* about?'). (1993: 513)

As well as setting the scene and providing some background information about the community whose practices are being analysed, this passage also gives us an idea of Kulick's grounds for treating the *kros* as a speech event – to wit, that the villagers themselves recognize it as such. Rather than asking 'what on earth is happening here?', witnesses ask who, on this occasion, is producing the behaviour and for what particular reason. This suggests they find the behaviour itself familiar, and readily categorizable as someone being *kros*.

This first description explains what kind of behaviour prompts recognition on the part of community members that a *kros* is underway, but on its own it does not tell us in detail what sort of a speech event a *kros* is, or in what way it is distinct from other instances of people getting angry, in this community or any other. Kulick goes on to clarify this by explaining the rules people in Gapun follow when having a *kros* or being witness to one. *Kros*es are fundamentally abusive monologues involving obscene insults and threats directed by one person against another, often at considerable length. As Kulick notes, 'they are structured by precise conventions to which all villagers adhere for as long as they want the conflict to remain a shouting match [as opposed to a physical fight]' (1993: 514). One such convention is that the person who starts the shouting is physically separated from the person or people their complaints are directed against. The *kros*er usually shouts from inside their own house, or very near it, where they cannot be seen by others. The person being shouted at does not reply directly: they have the option of beginning their own *kros*, in which they abuse the abuser, but this has to be structured as an overlapping monologue rather than an attempt at dialogue. Trying to engage a *kros*er directly in dialogue is seen as a breach of their right to display their own anger, and this has the potential to provoke physical confrontation. The *kros* is a form of self-display, whose intended audience is not just the target of abuse (they do not even have to be there for it to happen) but the whole village community. It never results in the conflict being resolved then and there; it simply stops when the speaker feels s/he has said all s/he wishes to say. Later on, the conflict may be addressed in another forum, but the immediate purpose of having a *kros* is to display one's grievances publicly rather than get them addressed.

We could use the information provided by Kulick to 'fill in' Hymes's SPEAKING grid.[3] Under *setting* we would place the information that a *kros* is initiated from inside or near to one's own house, while the target and audience are located at some distance. Under *participants* we would note that a *kros* is essentially monologic, performed by one speaker (though related *kroses* can go on simultaneously). Others within earshot are constituted as listeners, though in practice they do sometimes comment on what is said by addressing the speaker directly – something the speaker may construe as a violation of their rights, known as 'giving back mouth'. Under *ends* we would observe that the purpose of the *kros* is to display grievances publicly, and when it finishes the grievances are not resolved. Under *act sequence* we might list a number of things that speakers having a *kros* typically do, such as insult, accuse and threaten the objects of their anger while at the same time complaining that they themselves are unreasonably put-upon. One speaker whose *kros* Kulick analyses in detail says, for instance (in Kulick's colloquial English translation, 1993: 528–9), 'fucking rubbish bastard you!' (insult); 'you black prick, all these years you've sat by your fire doing nothing' (insult plus accusation); and 'I'm gonna slice him up with this machete' (threat). She complains: 'I look after you all for nothing every day. Hard work, work that makes me pain ah ah doing it, getting burned by the cooking fire. My skin blisters at the fire. The fire burns my hands.' Similar moves are repeated many times. Under *key* we would observe that the tone or manner of a *kros* is strongly emotional, and more specifically, angry: linguistically this is marked by, for instance, the use of hyperbolic and obscene expressions (see the examples above).

At this point we come to *instrumentalities*, the use of different channels and forms of speech from the community's repertoire, and *norms*, how the *kros* is interpreted in relation to more general cultural beliefs. It is here that Kulick's analysis goes beyond just describing the characteristics of the *kros* as a speech event and does more complex interpretive or argumentative work. Interesting though his data are, Kulick does not present them simply for the sake of describing an 'exotic' speech event. Rather he uses the phenomenon of the *kros* to illuminate broader questions about the social/linguistic situation in Gapun.

One of the points Kulick makes is that the *kros* is associated with women speakers. Some men do have *kroses*, but the general consensus in Gapun is that they are characteristic of women, who are stereotyped negatively as 'disruptive, divisive, begrudging, anti-social and emotionally excessive' (Kulick 1993: 512). The *kros* is also opposed to many of the social and cultural values that people in the village overtly endorse. For instance, it involves the expression of anger, which is seen as dangerous, and obscene language, which offends against religious norms (in recent decades the villagers have adopted the Christian religion). Kulick (1998) contrasts the *kros* to the talk men produce in the men's house, which downplays anger or conflict and emphasizes consensus; men in this forum are sometimes explicitly critical of people (mainly of women) who quarrel and fight.

There is another, not unconnected difference between the *kros* and the talk that goes on at men's meetings. Adults in Gapun have two distinct languages in their repertoire: the local language Taiap, and the language used for wider communication across Papua New Guinea, Tok Pisin. Both languages may be used in a *kros*, but Taiap usually predominates, whereas in men's house meetings Tok Pisin predominates. Like the *kros* itself, Taiap is associated with women and with pre-modern/pre-christian tradition; Tok Pisin is associated with modernity and with men. And Taiap is progressively losing ground to Tok Pisin in a process of language shift. In 1991, Kulick reports, no one under the age of 14 had an active knowledge of Taiap. He sees the shift as a consequence of the different symbolic value accorded to the two languages. Villagers will say that they value Taiap, and regret that children no longer use it; but the actual division of labour between Taiap and Tok Pisin, exemplified by the prominence of Taiap in a kind of speech (the *kros*) that is overtly disapproved of, in practice sends a different message. Kulick's discussion of the *kros* is thus part of a wider argument about language shift in Gapun: it helps to explain why Taiap is likely to become extinct.

THE USES OF ETHNOGRAPHY IN DISCOURSE ANALYSIS

The two speech events I have used as examples here may tend to reinforce a perception of the ethnography of speaking as prototypically an exercise in describing the 'exotic' and the ritualized. Though the Pentecostal meeting and the *kros* are both regular occurrences in their respective settings, they are distinguished from the mundane exchanges of everyday life, being public performances which have clear boundaries and well-defined conventions, and which are also characterized by a particularly high degree of expressive intensity. It might be asked whether the ethnography of speaking is equally applicable to the more mundane genres that occupy most time for most language-users – domestic chat or workplace 'water cooler talk', village gossip, arguments in pubs. In fact, such cases have been discussed in published work with an ethnographic or anthropological orientation (e.g. Harding 1975; Ochs and Taylor 1995). If I have neglected them in this chapter it is because I wish to present a range of examples in this section as a whole, and genres like 'chat' and 'gossip' will feature more prominently in later chapters.

Ethnography in general does not have to be about only unfamiliar cultures, or institutions like schools and churches, or ritual practices. As I said at the beginning of this chapter, in recent years more and more social scientists have turned to some version of participant observation as a research method for investigating a huge range of cultural practices among all kinds of social groups, from punks to advertising executives to TV soap opera viewers. That leads me to the last question I want to consider: whether the ethnography of speaking provides any useful insights or analytic tools for social researchers who are investigating something other than language per se, using either participant observation methods or other methods that elicit spoken discourse data (e.g. interviewing). My answer to this question goes back to the observation I made in the introduction, that discourse is not just a straightforward window on research subjects' social or mental world. If social researchers treat getting their subjects to talk simply as a means for getting to know 'how things are' for those people, they are missing an important point. In effect they are using subjects' speech as a source of evidence about their culture, but forgetting that speaking is itself a part of that culture with norms and conventions of its own. There is, then, much to be said for researchers who engage in talk with their subjects, or record subjects' talk among themselves, explicitly asking themselves a few 'ethnography of speaking'-type questions about the data they obtain as a result. What speech event or genre does it represent? What norms of interaction are operative? How might that affect the interpretation of what is being said?

An obvious case where these questions apply is that of the interview. *Interview* is plainly a recognized category of speech event in many societies where social researchers conduct interviews, and equally clearly there are specific interactional norms to which people orient in interviews. For example, interviewees are very likely to treat interviewers' questions, by contrast to questions posed in the course of some other speech event like a conversation, as 'trying to catch them out'. The interview is a kind of contest, in which the participants may be seen to have differing interests (put crudely, 'you want to make me look bad, and I must try to make myself look good'). This norm may operate differently depending on the setting and purpose of an interview. Politicians being interviewed by journalists, and job candidates being interviewed by selectors, are particularly aware that the interviewer may be trying to reveal their weaknesses and/or elicit 'damaging' admissions from them, and they work hard to counter that. Celebrities being interviewed for something like *Hello!* or *People* magazine can afford to be a bit less cautious, though they are still likely to pay some attention to the way they present themselves. Research subjects being interviewed by an academic are between these extremes, but they are certainly not without preconceptions about what an 'interview' involves, and researchers need to treat these preconceptions as potentially relevant for the analysis of interview data (which implies of course that they must reflect explicitly on what their subjects' preconceptions are).

The issues I am raising here are ones I will return to again in later chapters (especially Chapter 10): the overall point is that discourse data have to be treated as *discourse* as well as just *data*. The ethnography of speaking makes some important contributions to thinking about talk as a culturally embedded activity. The primary purpose of analysis may not be to produce a description of speech situations, speech events and speech acts, but nevertheless a sophisticated analysis must give some consideration to what people are doing, and what they think they are doing, when they speak.

SUGGESTIONS FOR FURTHER READING ABOUT THE ETHNOGRAPHY OF SPEAKING

There are several textbooks that deal in detail with the ethnography of speaking, notably Duranti (1997), Saville-Troike (1989) and Schiffrin (1994). Influential statements by Dell Hymes can be found in, for example, Hymes (1972a, 1972b). However, the best way to appreciate what this approach is about is probably to read something that applies it to a particular case. A selection of examples, dealing with a wide range of cultural settings, can be found in Bauman and Sherzer's edited collection *Explorations in the Ethnography of Speaking* (1974); an interesting later collection is Silverstein and Urban's *Natural Histories of Discourse* (1996). Among the specific topics that have interested many researchers since the 1970s are the social-ization of children into their culture's ways of speaking (e.g. Ochs and Schieffelin 1983); the relationship between gender and ways of speaking (discussed by several contributors to Philips et al. 1987); bilingualism and language shift (Gal 1979; Kulick 1992; Woolard 1989); and the 'language ideologies' (roughly, beliefs about language) held in various societies (Schieffelin et al. 1998).[4] It is not uncommon for social researchers to combine ethnographic (in the broad sense) field research methods with a CA approach to the analysis of their data – examples include Goodwin (1990), and Widdicombe and Wooffitt (1995; and see also Moerman 1988). On the social scientific interview as a cultural/linguistic phenomenon, see Briggs (1986). Finally, although literacy practices lie outside the scope of this book, it is worth noting that there is an ethnographic literature on them which relates reading and writing to other aspects of cultural/linguistic practice (e.g. Barton and Ivanič 1991; Barton et al. 2000; Heath 1983).

NOTES

1   It also refers to the description/analysis an ethnographer produces on the basis of having done participant observation in a particular culture.
2   The term *genre* is most familiar in literary studies, where it denotes classes of texts (e.g. 'novel', 'lyric poem', 'tragedy'), and it is used in complicated ways in discourse analysis. The gloss given here is intended to acknowledge that speech events might both 'have' a genre themselves (e.g. 'interview', 'gossip') and be composed of elements of other genres (e.g. people might repeat proverbs in the course of gossiping). One frequently cited discussion of 'speech genres' which foregrounds the generically mixed or 'intertextual' character of many actual speech events is that of the (basically literary) theorist Mikhail Bakhtin, originally written early this century in Russian. An abridged version of the English translation is reprinted in Jaworski and Coupland's *Discourse Reader* as 'The problem of speech genres' (Bakhtin 1999 [1935]).
3   As they read the following discussion, readers who are familiar with William Labov's classic paper 'Rules for ritual insults' (1997[1972]) may find it an interesting exercise to compare the practices Labov describes with the *kros* as described by Kulick. Though both have 'ritual' elements and both involve 'insults', an important difference between the two cases is in the *key* (in the *kros* there is real conflict and insults are intended seriously, whereas the case discussed by Labov is a mock-conflict, a game, and giving real offence is a breach of the 'rules'). Comparing the two cases also highlights the differences between Labov's sociolinguistic approach and Kulick's anthropological one. Labov is far more concerned with the formal linguistic properties of appropriate insults, while Kulick focuses more on questions of context and meaning.
4   Here I select the topics I consider most likely to be of interest to people working with spoken discourse across disciplines. One prominent concern in the cross-cultural study of language use which I do not mention in this context is with the genres of oral performance which are accorded the status of art. There is a large literature on this subject, much of it coming under the heading of 'poetics' rather than discourse analysis (though the boundaries are not entirely clear-cut). See for instance Bauman and Briggs (1990), and for a survey/introduction aimed at readers who are linguists, Fabb (1997).

6 Doing things with words: pragmatics

The word *pragmatic* is derived from the Greek *pragma*, meaning 'deed'; in everyday usage *pragmatic* means something like 'practical' or 'realistic'. The 'technical' usage examined in this chapter is not unrelated: *pragmatics* is the field of enquiry that deals with how language can be used to do things and mean things in real-world situations.

In the real world it seems people frequently disregard the common-sense maxim 'say what you mean and mean what you say'. I stand at a bus stop in freezing rain and a stranger addresses me: 'lovely day, isn't it?' 'Gorgeous', I reply. Another stranger comes up and says: 'have you got a light?'. I hand him a cigarette lighter. If I were operating on the principle 'what is said is what is meant' I could have responded to the first stranger's remark by saying 'no, it's horrible' and to the second stranger's request by answering simply 'yes'. But such behaviour is the province of characters in television sitcoms about aliens from outer space. The characters involved in the bus stop scenario, by contrast, are well used to the idea that when people talk, the words they actually utter may bear a complicated relationship to what they mean.

As I noted in Chapter 4, pragmatics has roots in the philosophy of language; it has also been of interest to cognitive scientists who seek to model the complex operations involved in processing and interpreting utterances. People who come at the subject from a philosophical or cognitivist angle, however, have different priorities from those who want to use pragmatics as an approach to analysing real-life examples of interactive spoken discourse. For the latter group, which is also the one addressed by this book, possibly the most helpful definition of pragmatics is offered by Jenny Thomas (1995), who defines it as the study of 'meaning in interaction'. Thomas notes that pragmatics has typically been characterized as the study of either 'speaker meaning' (what speakers intend by an utterance) or 'utterance interpretation' (what hearers make of an utterance). She comments, however, that both these definitions tend to focus attention on what goes on in individuals' heads rather than on the social and collaborative aspects of meaning-making; whereas in her view

> meaning is not something which is inherent in the words alone, nor is it produced by the speaker alone, nor by the hearer alone. Making meaning is a dynamic process, involving the negotiation of meaning between speaker and hearer, the context of utterance (physical, social and linguistic) and the meaning potential of an utterance. (Thomas 1995: 22)

This is a view which fits well with the preoccupations of discourse analysts. Discourse is the site for the dynamic process of meaning-making (or meaning negotiation) that Thomas describes here, and analysts of discourse need tools for making sense of that process.

In this chapter we will look at the tools provided by pragmatic approaches, with particular reference to the concept of a *speech act* and the concept of a *pragmatic principle*. The discussion below is by no means a full survey of the field of pragmatics; rather I discuss it selectively with the needs of discourse analysis in mind (for more extended treatments see the suggestions for further reading at the end of the chapter).

SPEAKING AS DOING

The basic idea behind the notion of a 'speech act' is that when we say something we are always also *doing* something. The title of this chapter, 'Doing things with words', alludes to the title of a short but extremely influential early work – *How To Do Things With Words* – in which this point was made by the philosopher J.L. Austin (1962).[1] Austin identified a class of utterances which he called 'performatives', because they perform a particular action in and of themselves. A simple example is the utterance 'I apologize'. To utter this is actually to make an apology. Similarly, when you utter 'I promise I'll do X tomorrow' you have made a promise.

Austin's 'performative' utterances have some peculiarities. For instance, they only 'work' in the first person and the present tense. A person who utters 'I apologized yesterday' or 'Michael is now apologizing' is not making an apology. Another peculiarity is that utterances of this kind cannot be true or false. If someone tells me 'Michael apologized' I can respond 'no he didn't', but if they say 'I apologize' I cannot respond 'no you don't', since the utterance itself constitutes an apology. What I can do, of course, is cast doubt on the status of the apology – is the person who apologizes truly sorry? Did they do anything that calls for an apology in the first place? Austin suggested that while performatives cannot be true or false, they can be more or less 'happy' (later theorists have preferred a Latin-derived word, *felicitous*, for the same idea). The performance of an act will be felicitous only where certain conditions are met – a point to which we must return later on.

Austin began by distinguishing utterances which are 'performative' from other (proposition-making) utterances, which he labelled 'constative'. But he went on to question that distinction, suggesting that every utterance can be analysed as the performance of some act by the speaker. Consider the utterance 'it's raining'. Unlike 'I apologize' this contains a proposition which may be true or false. But to understand it fully, the hearer must determine not only the propositional meaning of the utterance, but also decide how it is supposed to be taken and what the speaker intends to accomplish by uttering it. Is it meant, for instance, simply as a factual assertion about the world, or could it be functioning as an indirect request to the addressee to hand the speaker her umbrella? In recognition of the fact that utterances can *both* make propositions *and* perform actions, Austin proposed a three-part framework for classifying 'speech acts' (actions performed using language). *Locution* is the actual words a speaker utters. *Illocution* is the 'force' of the utterance, what it is meant to be taken as (e.g. assertion, request, apology, promise). *Perlocution* is the effect on the hearer (e.g. if s/he hears 'it's raining' as having the force of a request for an umbrella, s/he supplies the speaker with an umbrella).

The part of this framework that has been most important in subsequent discussion is the 'illocution' part, with much attention focusing on the question of how we decide on the illocutionary force of a given utterance. The distinguishing characteristic of the type of utterance Austin originally classified as 'performative' is not simply that it *has* illocutionary force – in the revised framework all utterances do – but that it makes its force explicit: in 'I *promise* you', 'I *bet* you' or 'I *apologize*', the verb names the act it is used to perform.[2] It is also often possible to make the force of an utterance explicit by tacking on a preface containing a verb of illocution, as in '*I'm asking you*, Ms Smith, did you take that money?', '*We remind you that* smoking is not permitted in this area', or '*I order you to* put the gun down and place your hands on your head'. However, most speech acts do not have to be performed, and on many or most occasions are not performed, in this way. (Some actually cannot be: Jenny Thomas points out for instance that although 'insulting' is an act English speakers can perform in speaking, it cannot be done by saying 'I insult you'.[3]) Hence the question, in cases where illocutionary force is nowhere made explicit in the utterance itself, how do we work out what it is?

One source of information is the utterance itself. When Jenny Thomas refers to the 'meaning potential of an utterance' she is making the point that what people actually say does not have an unlimited range of possible interpretations. She gives the example of someone saying to an acquaintance 'how are things, Scott?', and comments that it is difficult to think of any circumstances in which Scott could reasonably interpret this utterance as a dinner invitation or a proposal of marriage (Thomas 1995: 23). But it does have the potential to be interpreted in more than one way (e.g. as an enquiry about the state of Scott's health, or a question about what he has been doing recently, or as a formulaic greeting that needs no answer beyond a brief acknowledgement). In considering these possibilities, people will make use of contextual information. For example, if 'how are things, Scott?' is produced by a doctor as the opening move in a medical consultation that is likely to strengthen Scott's commitment to the hypothesis that the utterance is an enquiry about his health. If it is produced in the course of a chance encounter in the street and the speaker is already walking away as he says it, Scott will probably surmise that it is a formulaic greeting.

In the account of speech acts developed by another philosopher, John Searle (1969), an attempt is made to account for people's ability to identify the illocutionary force of utterances by positing shared *rules* for the definition and felicitous performance of particular illocutionary acts (e.g. 'promising', 'asserting', 'apologizing'). To illustrate what Searle's rules look like let us take the case of 'promising'.

The rule-set for *promising* contains one specification of a 'propositional act' and three 'conditions'. The propositional act specification tells us what the basic content of a promise is: it is a 'predication' (roughly, statement) of something the speaker is going to do in future. Among other things the specification captures our

> **Rules for promising**
> **[S = speaker, H = hearer, A = act]**
> **Propositional act:**   S predicates some future act A of S.
> **Preparatory condition:** S believes that A is in H's best interest and that S
>   can do A
> **Sincerity condition:**   S intends to do A
> **Essential condition:**   S puts S under an obligation to H to do A.

knowledge that you cannot make promises about things that have already happened. However, it is possible to make statements about things you are going to do in future which are not promises, but predictions or warnings or threats or fantasies or lies. Therefore, the three conditions further specify the criteria on which a statement like 'I'll do X tomorrow' counts as a promise. The 'preparatory' condition says that X has to be something that is good for the hearer, rather than bad. (This is how we tell that 'pay up or I promise you'll get a good beating' is not actually a promise, but a threat – see note 2.) It also says that X has to be something the speaker believes s/he can accomplish. 'I'll take you to the moon on a unicorn' is on that ground not a felicitous promise. The next condition is 'sincerity' – something can only be a promise if the speaker really means to do what s/he promises. The 'essential condition' summarizes what the essence of 'promising' is – you put yourself under an obligation to do the act in question. Other speech acts in Searle's scheme also have rules comprising a specification of the propositional act and preparatory, sincerity and essential conditions. For *apologizing*, for instance, the propositional act is 'S expresses regret for a past A of S'. A preparatory condition is that the act was not in the interest of H, and the sincerity condition is that S should truly regret it.

Various criticisms could be, and have been, made of this framework. One is that Searle puts a great deal of emphasis on the speaker's intentions and state of mind. If, for example, a speaker says 'sorry' without meaning it, in Searle's terms s/he has not apologized, because the utterance does not meet the sincerity condition. But from a discourse analytic as opposed to philosophical standpoint it might be asked whether this is really sufficient reason to say that the apology does not 'come off' as an apology. It is relevant here to recall Jenny Thomas's point that 'meaning in interaction' cannot be equated solely with the intentions of individuals. Because we cannot read our interlocutors' minds, but can only attribute intentions, thoughts, feelings, and so on, to them on the basis of what they say and do, it is problematic to treat linguistic meaning as dependent on the accurate retrieval of a speaker's intentions by a hearer. In the case of apologies, it seems plausible to suggest that a significant proportion of utterances consisting of apologizing formulas like *sorry* are, precisely, formulaic, and that many speakers saying *sorry* on many occasions are not sincerely sorry at all. But if parties to interaction go on *as if* an apology has been performed – which they might do for all kinds of reasons[4] – then arguably it is irrelevant whether the apology was issued sincerely and whether the recipient privately believes it to be sincere.

Another issue that arises with Searle's approach to speech acts (and indeed with the philosophical approach in general, to the extent it involves introspective 'armchair' methods rather than empirical 'field' ones) is variability. *Whose* 'promising' or 'apologizing' behaviour are Searle's rules meant to apply to? Everyone's behaviour? The behaviour of people who speak a particular language, for instance English? Or do the rules only apply to some small subsection of the English-speaking community, perhaps the one to which Searle himself belongs? There has been a good deal of discussion regarding cross-cultural variation both in the range of speech acts that are recognized and the conditions that apply to their performance in different societies. The claim has also been made that even within one society there can be quite significant variation in people's definitions of common speech acts. Marga Kreckel (1981) undertook a study in which she set out to discover how speech acts were performed and understood in two British families. While there was consensus within each family, she found marked disagreement between the two. In one case, for instance, 'warning' was defined much as Searle defines it, as an undertaking by the speaker that some impending event or course of action is not in the hearer's interest. In the other case, however, family members understood a 'warning' as an undertaking that an impending event/course of action is not in the *speaker*'s interest! Kreckel suggests that the meanings of speech acts are negotiated among groups of people (e.g. families) in the course of regular interaction over time. (She does not mean they negotiate consciously and explicitly, but that a shared definition of what is meant by 'warning' or 'promising' emerges from repeated joint participation in the practical business of doing things with words.) In groups where people do not have a history of interacting regularly over time, by contrast, Kreckel believes there is no warrant for assuming that they all share the same rules for performing speech acts.

The discussion so far might suggest that speech act theory is of little relevance or use to those engaged in the actual analysis of spoken discourse data. However, without downplaying the problems critics have pointed to in the work of Searle in particular, there are a number of reasons why speech acts continue to be discussed by discourse analysts (and therefore continue to be part of the knowledge students of discourse analysis need to acquire).

FORM AND FUNCTION: A PROBLEM IN DISCOURSE ANALYSIS

One of the questions speech act theory addresses is how the (propositional) meaning of an utterance relates to its force: how the utterance of a statement like 'I'll do it tomorrow' comes to be taken as, say, a promise. This is one version of a more general question that discourse analysts are continually obliged to attend to, namely how linguistic *form* relates to communicative *function*.

Many studies of spoken language phenomena involve isolating one or more variables to examine in detail. In some cases the variable is identified using *formal* criteria – for example the analyst picks out every example in a data corpus of an expression like *well* or *y'know*, or every case of someone starting to speak before the previous speaker has finished, or every utterance that has the syntax of a question. What the analyst is usually looking for is regular patterns in the use of a given form – where in discourse does it tend to occur, and what is it used to do? An alternative approach is to begin with function, posing a question like 'how do people use spoken language to do X?' (e.g. accept a compliment, express disagreement). In this case the variable is a functional rather than formal category, and the problem facing the analyst is to identify all the data sequences that could be classified as compliment acceptances or disagreements – in other words, to find the linguistic forms in which the chosen function is realized. Although the two approaches begin from opposite 'ends', both require the analyst to make claims to the effect that 'form X in context Y has communicative function Z'.

This would not be a problem if the relationship of form to function were a simple matter of one-to-one correspondence – if the same form always communicated the same thing, and if a given function could only be realized in one linguistic form. But that is very far from being the case. For instance, the utterance of the stranger at the bus stop (p. 68), 'have you got a light?' has the linguistic form (syntax) of a question, specifically the kind of question that can be answered yes or no. Formally it resembles such questions as 'have you got a cold?', but any competent user of English will recognize that these two questions are doing different things. 'Have you got a cold?' can/should be answered with some variation on yes or no, but while 'no' is a possible answer to 'have you got a light?', 'yes' would be a peculiar one. On the other hand it is not peculiar to do what the second speaker actually did on this occasion: she provided no answer to the question, but simply handed the first speaker a lighter. All this becomes understandable if we consider that the function of the question is not to elicit information. Rather it is a request to the hearer to provide the speaker with a light. However, this particular function (requesting a light) does not have to be realized in the form of a question. One could do essentially the same thing by saying, for instance, 'give us a light', which is formally (syntactically) an imperative. Of course, there is something to say about what guides speakers in choosing different formal realizations of the same function – this is a subject I will return to later on – but for the purposes of this discussion the point is that the relation of form to function is not one-to-one but many-to-many. The same linguistic form (e.g. a sentence with interrogative syntax) can have different functions in discourse (e.g. question, request) and the same function (e.g. request) can be realized by different forms (e.g. interrogative, imperative).

To illustrate why the 'form and function problem' is indeed a *problem*, let us consider a couple of examples where the relation of form to function has been the subject of competing claims by analysts. My examples come from the field of language and gender studies, and I have chosen them because they are cases where it makes a considerable difference what you take the form/function relationship to be.

Robin Lakoff (1975) claimed that women made more use than men of tag questions (e.g. 'lovely day today, *isn't it?*'). Her argument was that tag questions are often used to solicit agreement or approval, so speakers who use them frequently appear insecure and lacking confidence in their own opinions. But later analysts disputed Lakoff's account of what tag questions do in discourse, suggesting that a

more important function was to 'facilitate' talk by offering someone else the opportunity to voice *their* opinion (Cameron et al. 1988; Holmes 1984). If this alternative
account is accepted, it follows that women who use a lot of tag questions are not
showing insecurity, but rather consideration for others. This claim has rather different
implications from the first one: for instance, it does not imply that women's use of
tag questions is necessarily a problem or a shortcoming.

Another example concerns the function of interruptions. Zimmerman and
West (1975) had famously found that in male–female dyads (pairs) it was overwhelmingly men who interrupted women, and they interpreted this as a marker of men's
dominance over women.[5] Deborah Tannen however argues that while interruption
can sometimes be a marker of dominance, it can also signal 'high involvement' – the
hearer expresses enthusiasm and support for the speaker by jumping in before
the end of the turn (Tannen 1994b). More generally, Tannen argues for what she calls
'the relativity of linguistic strategies', by which she means that the same form may
realize radically different or even opposite communicative functions (e.g. interrupting
someone can be a put-down or a sign of enthusiastic support).

Speech act theory is relevant to this discussion because questions about the
function of an utterance in discourse are quite often questions about what a speech
act theorist would call its [illocutionary] *force*. If, as Searle suggests, members of a
speech community share rules for defining and performing speech acts, then those
rules may help to explain how people in real situations do the necessary mapping
from form to function. Conversely, we might be able to explain certain kinds
of misunderstandings as the result of people *not* sharing the same rules for defining
and performing speech acts, and consequently arriving at different conclusions about
the relationship of form to function. In the study of cross-cultural communication
it has been pointed out that some common misunderstandings are of this type. A
well-known example is the tendency of Japanese learners of English to say 'sorry'
when English speakers would expect to hear 'thank you'. Though I am simplifying
for the sake of brevity (see further Coulmas 1981), the explanation is that in Japanese,
the speech acts of thanking and apologizing are not as distinct as they are for English
speakers. The act of thanking is an expression of indebtedness in both languages,
but in the Japanese case a debt not yet repaid calls for an apology from the debtor.
Apologizing is thus one way of expressing indebtedness. English speakers, however,
do not interpret apology formulas like 'sorry' as felicitous expressions of gratitude.

Even where there is no issue of cross-cultural difference, however, Tannen's
point about the 'relativity of linguistic strategies' raises the issue of *contextual*
differences, which pose a problem for rule-based approaches in the tradition of speech
act theory. As we will see in Chapter 7, for example, an utterance which has the syntax
of a question, and which in ordinary conversation would probably be taken as a
straightforward request for information, can have a very different force when it occurs
in a courtroom. People's knowledge of what courtroom interaction is typically
intended to achieve predisposes them to interpret many questions posed by lawyers
and magistrates as accusations or challenges rather than 'innocent' requests for
information. This kind of sociocultural knowledge is difficult to build into the kinds
of general rules which are formulated by speech act theorists in the tradition of Searle.

Some discourse analysts have tried to do it (an example is Labov and Fanshel's (1977) study of therapeutic discourse, where they adapt speech act theory to model the interpretation of utterances in a psychotherapeutic setting). Other analysts, however, are more attracted to the idea of general overarching pragmatic *principles*, which language-users apply together with other relevant knowledge to derive interpretations, not by rule but by *inference*. In the next section I examine this alternative approach in more detail.

ACTING ON PRINCIPLE

The originator of the idea of a 'pragmatic principle' is another ordinary language philosopher, H. Paul Grice. In what is probably his best known and most frequently cited essay on this subject, 'Logic and conversation' (1975), Grice proposed that when people interact with one another, a 'co-operative principle' is in force. The principle can be given the following general formulation:

> **Co-operative principle**
> Make your contribution such as is required, at the stage at which it occurs, by the accepted purpose or direction of the talk exchange in which you are engaged.
> (Grice 1975:45)

More specifically, Grice broke the co-operative principle down into four 'maxims', as follows:

> 1. **Quantity:** make your contribution as informative as is required (for the current purposes of the exchange). Do not make your contribution more informative than is required.
> 2. **Quality:** do not say what you believe to be false. Do not say that for which you lack adequate evidence.
> 3. **Relation:** be relevant.
> 4. **Manner:** avoid obscurity of expression. Avoid ambiguity. Be brief (avoid unnecessary prolixity). Be orderly.
> (adapted from Grice 1975: 45–6)

Even though they are expressed here as imperatives, the co-operative principle and its maxims are not rules which conversationalists are required by authority or social convention to obey. Rather they are principles which it is *rational* and *logical* for people to observe if their goal is to communicate meaning. When we converse, we find it logical to assume that others are using language for a purpose (namely to mean something), rather than simply uttering pointless remarks at random. Unless and until there is evidence to the contrary, we will try to interpret what others say on the assumption that they are behaving in accordance with our expectations of a rational communicator. When Grice uses the term *co-operative* about conversation, he means it in a special and limited sense – he is talking only about the kind and degree of co-operation that is necessary for people to make sense of one another's contributions. Even exchanges in which the parties are being highly unco-operative in the ordinary sense of that word – a furious argument, a tirade of vulgar abuse, a scenario in which one party refuses to do what the other wants – will be 'co-operative' in the sense that those involved are operating on similar assumptions about communication.

Of course, there are occasions on which people clearly do not observe all of Grice's four maxims – when what they say appears uninformative or over-informative, evasive or irrelevant or obscure or unnecessarily long-winded. Even then, however, we do not immediately conclude that they have abandoned the co-operative principle itself. Rather we consider the possibility that the speaker's 'deviant' behaviour is itself intended to be meaningful; that the speaker is trying to convey something to us by obviously flouting normal expectations regarding quantity, quality, relevance or manner – something s/he cannot or will not say directly, but expects us to *infer*. Grice calls the meaning which is inferred from the fact that a maxim is flouted *implicature*.

As an example, consider the following extract from a journalistic interview with the man who at the time was the leader of the (UK) National Union of Mineworkers, Arthur Scargill. The interview took place in the 1980s during a period of strike action by the miners; media coverage had focused on violent clashes between picketing miners and police.

> **Interviewer:**   Will you condemn the violence on the picket lines?
> **Arthur Scargill:** I condemn the violence of the police and the National Coal Board.

The journalist asks a question whose form ensures that the most informative, most relevant, least obscure reply would be some variation on 'yes' or 'no'. This presents Arthur Scargill with an unpalatable choice. If he answers yes, he will be heard as condemning the behaviour of his own union members, since they are implicated in 'the violence on the picket lines' – indeed, since they are the actual pickets, they are likely to be held primarily or exclusively responsible for it. If he answers no, however, he risks being heard as actually in favour of picket-line violence. He therefore decides *not* to supply a yes or no answer. Instead he condemns *some* violence – that of the police and of the National Coal Board, the employers with whom the miners are in dispute – but does not mention, either to condemn or to condone, violence on the part of the picketing miners themselves. This answer flouts the maxims of quantity (it is insufficiently informative as an answer to the question) and manner (it is ambiguous). The hearer (in this case, the media audience) is thus alerted to the possibility that Arthur Scargill intends to convey by implicature a meaning he does not actually utter 'on the record'.

What *is* the meaning Arthur Scargill conveys by providing an obviously under-informative and ambiguous reply to the journalist's question? The simplest inference for listeners to make is that Scargill does not condemn violent actions by striking miners on the picket line: this is the logical explanation of why he cannot simply answer 'yes'. Beyond this, however, the question arises of what else might be implied by his declining to condemn the pickets. One logically possible interpretation is that he denies that the pickets have engaged in violent actions – in which case there is nothing for him to pass judgement on. In fact this is unlikely, since television audiences at the time regularly saw films of violent incidents where miners were plainly not just passive victims. Perhaps, then, Scargill intended listeners to infer that miners did not deserve to be condemned for 'the violence on the picket lines' because even granting that they were involved in it, they were only responding to provocation by their opponents, the police and the employers. Another possible interpretation is that Scargill wanted his audience to infer that whereas he condemned the actions of the police and the National Coal Board, he actually *approved* of violent actions taken by members of his union on picket lines.

Clearly, Arthur Scargill did not actually say any of the three things I have suggested he might be taken by inference to have meant, and the form of his utterance by itself does not tell us which of the possible interpretations we should prefer. Utterances in which maxims are flouted cue us to look for relevant inferences, but the inferences we actually make are dependent on the assumptions and background knowledge we bring to bear on the interpretive task. Thus for instance I have already characterized the interpretation 'Arthur Scargill intends to deny that the pickets have acted violently' as 'unlikely'. In rejecting that interpretation I am making use of both factual knowledge (pickets' involvement in violence was a matter of public record when Scargill was interviewed) and logical assumptions (a rational person does not waste effort trying to communicate propositions he already knows his audience will not believe).

What about the other two possibilities? Here it may well be relevant to consider not only the knowledge available to listeners, but also the differing ideological and political beliefs they may have brought to the interpretation of Arthur Scargill's utterance. In mainstream political discourse, Scargill was frequently repre-sented as a political (left-wing) extremist intent on using an industrial dispute between mineworkers and their employers to pursue his covert goal of fomenting class warfare. Someone who accepted this as an accurate representation might find it reasonable to suppose that Scargill would approve of assaults on police officers by pickets, and might therefore understand his answer to the journalist's question as implying that he applauded the pickets' actions. By contrast, someone who believed in the legitimacy of the miners' cause, and/or was critical of the orthodox view of Scargill, might be less likely to draw that inference, and more likely to understand his utterance as a sort of plea in mitigation: some pickets might have resorted to violence, but they were less worthy of blame than those who provoked them.

This discussion is intended to illustrate one of the advantages that is claimed for the 'pragmatic principles' approach over approaches that attempt to specify rules for getting from the form to the force of utterances: the principles approach is more accommodating of variation in interpretation, or to put it another way, the existence of such variation is less of a problem in this approach. Gricean pragmatics treats utterances, not as *containing* the speaker's meaning but as providing *evidence* on the basis of which the hearer can work it out. Some of the evidence provided by Arthur Scargill is, of course, in the utterance itself. For instance, his utterance makes clear (and was presumably calculated to make clear) that he does not approve of violence per se. But he also provides evidence for meaning in what he does *not* say: his failure to mention the miners explicitly in connection with 'the violence on the picket lines' is what prompts the listener to search for implicatures. That search, however, does not have a single, predetermined meaning as its goal. Since all hearers do not come to the task of drawing inferences with identical assumptions and stocks of background knowledge, their interpretations of an utterance may differ. Nor can it be said that any of their interpretations is the final and definitive interpretation. Implicatures are 'defeasible': they are meanings which the speaker has only implied, not stated explicitly on the record, and consequently the speaker can later deny that what a hearer inferred is what s/he actually meant. Arthur Scargill, for example, could legitimately protest if someone suggested on the basis of the utterance analysed above that he had said it was acceptable for pickets to resort to violence under provocation, though what he did say could be taken to imply that.

It should be noted that not every failure to observe Grice's maxims necessarily gives rise to implicatures. Hearers will only look for implicatures if something prompts them to do so – it has to be obvious that the speaker is flouting a maxim. Clearly, it is possible for people to hold back information or utter untruths without making this obvious. A good liar systematically violates the maxim of quality, but s/he succeeds in deceiving others precisely because they do not realize that the liar is 'saying that which s/he believes to be false'. (Grice distinguished 'flouting' maxims from 'violating' them – flouting is meant to be noticed, violation is meant not to be.) It is also possible for people to utter what seem to be obscure or irrelevant remarks without *intending* to generate implicatures.

Why, it might be asked, do we need the complicated mechanism of implicature when it is perfectly possible just to say what we mean straight out? It is not difficult to appreciate the potential usefulness of a device which allows speakers to communicate propositions without fully committing themselves. A contentious statement made explicitly on the record (e.g. 'violence is acceptable in response to police provocation') is riskier than a veiled statement which leaves hearers to infer the contentious proposition. In the first case the speaker can be held accountable for saying something contentious; in the second case it is open to the speaker to deny that the contentious meaning was intended.

Above I have suggested that speakers who flout Grice's maxims may do so as a strategy for avoiding or reducing the risks associated with saying certain things directly. The idea that communication involves risk, and that communicators behave in certain ways because they wish to minimize risk, has been particularly influential in discussions of another set of pragmatic principles, those associated with *politeness*. One writer, Geoffrey Leech, has suggested that there is a 'politeness principle' which is even more compelling than Grice's co-operative principle: if speakers have to choose between being co-operative (informative, truthful, relevant and perspicuous) and being polite, they will normally choose to be polite (Leech 1983). Thus if I ask someone for an opinion on something I am wearing or something I am writing, and their opinion is unflattering, they may well choose to say something irrelevant, ambiguous or false rather than hurt my feelings by telling me directly what they think.

Not everyone agrees with Leech that there is an independent 'politeness principle', but many pragmaticists would agree that politeness affects the application of the co-operative principle and is therefore an important topic in pragmatics. Probably the best-known account of politeness as a pragmatic phenomenon is given by Penelope Brown and Stephen Levinson (1987), and it is useful to outline their model briefly here.

POLITENESS AND 'FACE'

Brown and Levinson begin from the assumption that all people have an attribute they call 'face'. The term *face* (borrowed by Brown and Levinson from the work of the sociologist Erving Goffman) is used in roughly the same sense as in the English expressions 'to save face' and 'to lose face'. Face is a kind of social standing or esteem which every individual claims for her or himself and wants others to respect. Brown and Levinson distinguish two kinds of face: 'positive face', the wish to be liked and approved of by others, and 'negative face', the wish to be allowed to go about your business without others imposing unduly upon you.

Many of the things people need or want to do in the course of interacting with one another are inherently 'face threatening acts' (FTAs): they have the potential to cause damage to the positive or negative face of the speaker, the hearer, or both. For instance, if you ask someone to do something for you, you are to some extent imposing on them, which is a threat to their negative face. If you criticize someone you are expressing disapproval, which threatens their positive face. If you thank someone or apologize to someone you are threatening your own face, since you are acknowledging that you have imposed on them. Brown and Levinson theorize politeness as a strategy for *mitigating* threats to face in verbal interaction. They offer a sort of 'decision tree' showing the options open to a speaker performing an FTA (1987: 69):

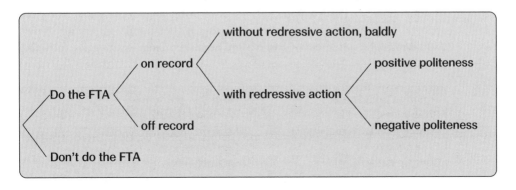

If a speaker perceives some action as face-threatening, the initial choice s/he must make is whether to perform it at all. If you notice that the important client you are meeting for the first time has his flies undone, you may well decide that the least embarrassing course of action is simply to pretend you haven't noticed. If the speaker decides to go ahead with a face threatening act, however, s/he must then choose whether to perform it 'on-record' or 'off-record', that is by implicature. For instance, a dinner guest might remark on the deliciousness of a meal as an 'off-record' strategy for getting the host to offer them more, rather than asking directly (which would be the 'on-record' strategy). The off-record strategy might be chosen in this case by a guest who is worried about appearing greedy, or who fears the host may take a request as a sign that s/he has been negligent in not making the offer unprompted.

If s/he decides to perform the FTA on record, the speaker's next choice is whether to perform it with or without mitigation. Brown and Levinson call the 'no mitigation' strategy 'bald on record': examples include asking someone to move by saying 'move!' or criticizing someone by saying, 'your work is rubbish'. In some circumstances it is rational to be bald – if the roof is about to fall on someone you shout 'move!' rather than casting around for some elaborate and indirect formula to mitigate face threat. A speaker may also, of course, have reasons for choosing to be deliberately impolite. However, in many instances speakers will choose a 'mitigated' way of performing a FTA, opting for a strategy that verbally displays to the hearer that the speaker is aware of the threat and wishes to minimize it – in other words, to be polite. For example, instead of using a bald imperative, a speaker might ask someone to move by saying 'I'm sorry, but I wonder if I could ask you to move over a bit?' This formulation makes clear that the speaker knows s/he is imposing on the other person (this is signalled by the prefatory 'I'm sorry') and it displays the speaker's desire to minimize the imposition through indirectness ('I wonder if I could ask you . . . ?') and hedging ('a bit'). It is a less efficient and straightforward way of expressing what the speaker means than the bald imperative 'move!': in Grice's terms, it is less in keeping with the maxim of manner ('avoid obscurity of expression . . . be brief'). But the clearer and briefer alternative is also highly threatening to the addressee's face: the desire to minimize face threat gives speakers a good reason *not* to choose the most direct and straightforward way of expressing what they mean.

'Politeness' in this model covers more than just fixed formulas like 'please', 'thank you', 'sorry', and so on; rather the term covers all the linguistic devices people may use to minimize threats to face. Just as face itself can be either positive or negative, so can politeness. 'Positive politeness' involves using language to signal liking and approval. Negative politeness involves using language to minimize imposition. Brown and Levinson list a number of positive and negative politeness strategies, including the following:

Positive politeness	**Negative politeness**
Show interest in H	Be conventionally indirect
Claim common ground with H	Minimize imposition on H
Seek agreement	Beg forgiveness
Give sympathy	Give deference

How do people decide whether and how to use the various strategies in real-life situations? Brown and Levinson suggest that they consider, in particular, three factors: how threatening the FTA they are contemplating is; how much social distance there is between the parties; and what the power relations between the parties are. The first factor, how threatening the act itself is, reflects the obvious point that some impositions are greater than others. A request to someone to pass the salt does not require a lot of elaborate minimization – 'would you pass the salt, please' will do. A request to someone to give you a large sum of money, by contrast, is fairly unlikely to be made in the words 'would you give me £100, please'. But the speaker's strategy in any case will also depend on the other two calculations, concerning social distance and power. The difference between distance and power is that distance is a symmetrical relationship whereas power is an asymmetrical, hierarchical one. The distance variable distinguishes, for instance, kin or friends from strangers (who may be of equal social status but are still socially distant from one another). We are inclined to perform FTAs differently with those we are socially close to and those we are more distant from. With family and friends we may use less elaborate politeness strategies, or we may use positive rather than negative politeness. We are also inclined to behave differently to our social equals and to people whose status is higher or lower than our own in a given situation (the 'power' variable).

Suppose I am trying to work in my office, but I am being disturbed by some people talking loudly in the corridor outside. I open the door intending to impose on these people by asking them to stop doing what they are doing, but what I actually say is likely to be affected by who they turn out to be. If they are a group of students (who in this context have lower status than I do) it is open to me to be minimally polite ('please could you stop talking, I'm trying to work') or even rude ('shut up, will you?'). If they are a group of colleagues (my equals, and people I know) I might do better to use the positive politeness strategy of 'claiming common ground' and then framing my request for them to stop disturbing me indirectly, as a question: 'hey, I've got a lecture to write. Is there somewhere else you could talk?' But if it turns out when I open the office door that the people disturbing me are the Director of the Institute where I work and some VIP guests he is showing round, I may well end up saying nothing, or perhaps even apologizing to *them*: 'oh, sorry, I heard voices and wondered who it was'. Maybe they will take the hint, but since my status is lower than theirs it would be impolitic for me to do much more than hint.

A POLITENESS PROBLEM: COMPLIMENTS

In this section we will consider a communicative act that poses an interesting challenge in terms of politeness: the act of complimenting someone. Complimenting might seem on the surface to be the *opposite* of a threat to the recipient's face, but in practice it may present the recipient with a potentially face-threatening interactional dilemma. Suppose, for instance, that A compliments B on her cooking by saying: 'this is delicious!' One 'polite' response B could make would be to *agree*: 'yes, isn't it!' However, while such agreement would show respect for A's face, B would run the risk of appearing immodest (which might threaten her own face, since it would imply she was a 'bad', conceited person). Alternatively, B could present herself more modestly by responding with a self-critical remark, such as 'I'm afraid it's a bit overcooked'. But then she would be disagreeing with A's complimentary assessment, which would risk threatening A's face. One way to resolve the dilemma would be simply to thank A for the compliment, or to say something like 'I'm so glad you like it!' There are other possibilities too, like drawing attention to the superior quality of the ingredients (as opposed to the skills of the cook) or recalling equally delicious meals prepared by some other person – perhaps even A herself – in the past. Compliments are interesting to look at because of the challenge they pose to their recipients. How people manage compliments in practice is the focus of the following activity.

ACTIVITY

Note: your data may be in any language or languages.

1 **Data collection**. For this activity it is impractical to tape record data: you need to keep a notebook and pen around, and aim to write down as accurately as possible any exchange containing a compliment that occurs in the interactions you witness over a period of several days. Minimally, you should try to record the compliment itself and what, if anything, the recipient said in response to it. You will also need to write down some contextual information (see 2 below). Obviously it is useful to record the data as soon as possible after you hear it, so that your recall of what was said will be reasonably accurate. It is better not to include compliments paid to you or compliments you pay to others, since doing this activity may make you unusually self-conscious about your own complimenting behaviour, but if you have difficulty in collecting examples involving third parties, you may use yourself as an informant. You may also use examples involving people not known to you, whom you overhear by chance, as well as examples involving family, friends and acquaintances. Your sample may not be very large (and for the purposes of this activity its size does not matter): it depends how common compliments are in the social groups and settings you have the opportunity to observe. If you find complimenting behaviour is rare or nonexistent in your everyday social encounters, that in itself is a significant observation! When you compare notes with other students, this may be an interesting issue to explore further (see 4 below).

2 **Contextual information**. As well as the compliment and the response (if any) you should record who addressed the compliment to whom and what their relationship was (or in the case of people you do not know, appeared to be), in what setting or situation the compliment occurred and (if the speech itself does not make it clear) what the compliment was directed to (e.g. grandmother to 6-year-old granddaughter in grandmother's kitchen; child presents grandmother with a drawing she has done).

3 **Analysis**. When you have collected a sample of compliments, consider the following questions.

- Was it easy or difficult to decide what utterances to record as compliments? If it was difficult, what made it difficult? Did you observe any 'problem cases' (e.g. did you hear compliments that seemed to you insincere or sarcastic – if so, how did recipients react?).
- Are there any patterns in who compliments whom (consider variables such as gender, age, social distance and power/status)?
- Are there any patterns in what compliments are about (e.g. appearance, dress, skill in particular activities like cooking, sport, drawing, academic work), and if so do these relate to the variables considered above?
- How do compliment recipients respond to compliments? What range of strategies do you find in your sample (e.g. say nothing, thank the complimenter, agree with the complimenter, disagree in order to be modest, praise something/someone else)? Does the choice of strategy seem to be influenced by Brown and Levinson's variables of distance, power, degree of face-threat? Does it seem to be influenced by other considerations (e.g. what the compliment is about, where the exchange occurs)?

4 **Discussion**. Compare notes with other students in a group. Did people find similar patterns in their data, or different ones? If there are differences, might they reflect differing conventions of politeness in the different social groups students belong to, or the varying social situations they collected data in?

5 **Optional extra**. On the basis of your data, can you formulate a set of rules and felicity conditions (on the model of Searle's rules for promising, see above, page 71) for the speech act of complimenting? What are the advantages and disadvantages of doing this?

ARE PRAGMATIC PRINCIPLES UNIVERSAL?

Both the co-operative principle and the principles underlying Brown and Levinson's model of politeness are often presented as applying very generally across cultures and languages. In Brown and Levinson's case the claim that their model has universal application is made explicitly: they recognize, and demonstrate with examples, that politeness itself takes varying forms in different cultures, but they suggest this can be explained with reference to considerations their model treats as variable in any case. For instance, variations in politeness behaviour may arise because different communities make differing judgements about the degree of threat associated with a certain act, or because their social relations are more or less hierarchical or asymmetrical, or because more or less emphasis is placed on social distance. But while the variables may be differently weighted in different cultures, Brown and Levinson assert that the same ones are operative in all; and people's face-wants themselves are fundamentally the same everywhere. Similarly, it has been argued that the co-operative principle captures something about the intrinsic nature of human communication and the reasoning faculty that underpins it. These are strong claims, and they have not gone unchallenged.

One well-known challenge to the universality of the co-operative principle was advanced by Elinor Ochs in a discussion of ways of speaking among the Malagasy (the people of the Malagasy Republic, which is an island in the Indian Ocean). According to her account, Malagasy 'regularly provide less information than is required by their conversational partner, even though they have access to the necessary information' (Ochs [Keenan] 1976: 70). Does this mean that the maxim of quantity does not apply to Malagasy speakers?

The linguistic anthropologist Don Kulick, whose work in the New Guinea village of Gapun we encountered in Chapter 5, notes a prevalent belief among Gapuners that people rarely if ever say what they mean: language, villagers assert, is used to *hide* meaning. Kulick recorded examples of the genre known as 'oratory': oratory takes place in the village men's house, and is remarkable for its obscurity and ambiguity. In one case, a man made an announcement about the fact that the local owners of an outboard motor had decided to begin charging others for its use. It might be thought that the primary purpose of such an announcement would be to inform people of certain facts that it was relevant for them to know, but what was actually said was so obscure and self-contradictory that it failed to convey any clear facts at all. When the speaker finished, it was impossible to be sure whether or not Gapun residents would be required to pay to use the motor, or if the charges only applied to people from neighbouring villages; if payment was required it was unclear whether this had to be in cash. On questioning people who had heard the announcement later, Kulick found that the villagers had no clearer sense than he did of what the situation would actually be if someone wanted to use the outboard motor. The main point that had been conveyed was one the speaker had not made explicitly at all: that the motor's owners were behaving in a selfish and unneighbourly manner.

Kulick explains the peculiarities of oratory in Gapun as a consequence of the fact that what is valued in this kind of speech is less informativeness or factuality than the creation and maintenance of consensus. Participants are concerned above all to avoid any hint of conflict, and to preserve at least the appearance of harmony and general agreement. It is therefore unthinkable for a conflict-generating topic like the possibility of having to pay cash to use a neighbour's outboard motor to be tackled in an unambiguous way. The speaker who made the announcement failed to observe the maxims of quantity (he conveyed virtually none of the information his listeners required), quality (he must have known that some of what he said was either false or, at the very least, misleading) and manner (the announcement was obscure, ambiguous and prolix). The question, though, is whether he *flouted* these maxims, inviting those present to draw their own inferences from the uninformative, contradictory and ambiguous nature of his discourse, or whether the maxims simply do not apply in this context.

Here we might recall that people in Gapun believe that speakers 'hide' their meaning in the words they utter. Hearers in this community expect to work hard at extracting meaning from the scanty and often misleading evidence provided by speakers. Evidently theirs is what some scholars (e.g. Ting-Toomey 1999) refer to as a 'high context' culture, meaning one in which communication relies heavily on the ability and willingness of hearers to retrieve relevant information from contextual knowledge, rather than having it spelled out for them by speakers. It could be questioned whether Grice's maxims offer the most persuasive account of communication in this kind of culture. The maxims are products of a 'low context' culture in which making meaning clear is implicitly considered to be the responsibility of the *speaker*. It is true that the Gricean approach gives hearers an active role in the production of meaning through inference, but the maxims themselves focus on speakers' behaviour rather than hearers', and suggest that in the 'default' case the speaker will leave the hearer with little interpretive work to do. Indirectness and inexplicitness, which place a greater burden on the hearer, are often treated by pragmaticists as deviations from the 'normal' case, and are sometimes described as 'risky' (because the intended meaning may not be retrieved) or 'costly' (because indirectness requires extra effort to process). But research on talk in places like Gapun, or the Malagasy Republic, or Japan (Clancy 1986), suggests that these perceptions are not shared by all communities in all circumstances. The ability to speak in what may strike an English-speaker as a bafflingly obscure manner may be accorded high value; the risk of confusion associated with indirectness may be less salient than the risk of disrupting collective consensus by making disagreement explicit.

The subject of cultural differences in pragmatic behaviour – and the misunderstandings they may cause when people from different cultures interact – is one we will return to in Chapter 8. Here, though, it should be pointed out that the existence of variation does not undermine the general argument that successful linguistic communication depends on participants' capacity for rational, purposeful and (in the Gricean sense) co-operative action. So far as I know there is no recorded instance of a community insisting that verbal interaction is a completely random and pointless activity. However, it cannot be taken for granted that members of every culture use the same assumptions in their reasoning, or that they co-operate in exactly the same ways for exactly the same purposes. Human communication practices, like human social practices more generally, are similar to one another in some ways, and different in others.

SUGGESTIONS FOR FURTHER READING ABOUT SPEECH ACTS, PRAGMATIC PRINCIPLES AND POLITENESS

A more detailed discussion of the ideas of Austin, Searle and Grice is provided in Jenny Thomas's *Meaning in Interaction* (1995). All three of these philosophers of language write relatively straightforward prose, albeit in the register of philosophy: interested readers may want to consult Austin (1962), Searle (1969) and Grice (1975). Stephen Levinson's *Pragmatics* (1983) also discusses these philosophical approaches at some length, and George Yule's *Pragmatics* (1996) provides a brief introduction. Geoffrey Leech's 'politeness principle' is set out in his book *Principles of Pragmatics* (1983), while Brown and Levinson's model of politeness is explained and exemplified in their own full-length study *Politeness* (1987). A useful shorter survey of the literature on politeness, which includes a critical assessment of Brown and Levinson's universalist claims, is Gabriele Kasper's essay 'Linguistic etiquette' in the *Handbook of Sociolinguistics* (Kasper 1997). Kasper is among those researchers who have studied pragmatics and politeness across cultures (see Blum-Kulka et al. 1989 and Kasper and

Blum-Kulka 1993). Another researcher in the field of intercultural communication, Michael Clyne, has attempted to reformulate Grice's co-operative principle in a way that is more sensitive to cultural differences (Clyne 1996). A full-length study of gender and politeness is Janet Holmes's *Women, Men and Politeness* (1995). Finally, a development of Gricean pragmatics which I have not considered in this chapter – mainly because it is most influential among researchers with a cognitivist orientation – is 'relevance theory'. One introduction to pragmatics written from this perspective is Diane Blakemore's *Understanding Utterances* (1992).

NOTES

1   *How To Do Things With Words* is based on a series of lectures Austin gave at Harvard in the 1950s: they were reconstructed from notes and published after his death.

2   Alert and critical readers may have noticed an objection to this general statement: performative verbs can sometimes be used to do an act other than the one they name, a good example being the use of *promise* to make what is clearly a *threat* (e.g. 'Pay up, or I promise you'll get a good beating'). This point will be discussed further below; and see also note 3.

3   A friend makes the point that one *can* insult someone by saying things like 'I spit on the grave of your mother'. This appears to be a performative (and it passes the 'hereby' test – one could say 'I hereby spit . . . '), but obviously it does not perform the act denoted by the verb, *spit*, which is not a verb of illocution. Rather it invokes the vulgar act of spitting in order to perform the illocutionary act of insulting. Another similar example, made popular by the *Monty Python* comedy team, is 'I fart in your general direction'.

4   For instance, if I keep a student waiting and then I apologize, s/he is likely to behave as though she accepted my regret as sincere, whether or not she really does (and whether or not it really is) because of the power differential between us. Or, to take a different kind of case which has been cropping up more and more frequently of late, if the Prime Minister of Australia apologizes publicly to the country's aboriginal peoples for abuses committed against them since the beginning of white settlement, it is extremely unlikely either that he sincerely regrets every act covered by the apology or that the aboriginal community believes he does. But what is most significant for political purposes is just that the apology has been issued: the act is by nature symbolic.

5   The finding that men interrupt women more than the reverse has not been replicated in all studies of gender and interruption, and the prevalence of the pattern reported by Zimmerman and West (1975) is a matter of dispute. For a critical review, see James and Clarke (1993).

7 Sequence and structure: Conversation Analysis

In this chapter I outline the approach to spoken discourse known as Conversation Analysis (commonly abbreviated to CA). I use the word 'outline' advisedly: CA has produced a voluminous literature, and there is far more to say about it than can be accommodated in a single chapter. Here I set out to explain what makes the CA approach distinctive, but I also focus particularly on those areas of its work which have been influential across the whole spectrum of approaches to spoken discourse.

In spite of its name, Conversation Analysis does not deal only with conversation: the approach has also been applied to talk in professional and workplace settings (Drew and Heritage 1992), to political speeches (Atkinson 1984) and to media genres such as radio phone-in programmes (Hutchby 1996). Many practitioners label their object of study not 'conversation' but 'talk-in-interaction'. This label is apt, since although CA can be used to analyse many different kinds of data, it was developed to analyse *talk* (rather than written text) and more specifically the kind of talk that is thoroughly *interactive* (as opposed to monologic sequences, such as narratives[1]). The fact that talking is prototypically a joint enterprise involving more than one person, and that people normally take turns at talk, is central to the CA approach, which is concerned above all to describe sequential patterns (regularities in what follows what) which are observable in the data being analysed. Claims about what is going on in any particular bit of talk are often supported by 'going to the next turn', that is, appealing to the evidence of what happens in the following bit of talk. Speech act theorists may define an utterance as, say, a 'question' in terms of whether it meets the felicity conditions for the relevant illocutionary act (see Chapter 6); practitioners of CA would be more interested in whether it is followed by an answer. It is in answering, CA practitioners point out, that the participants display their understanding of the previous contribution as a question, and their 'orientation' to the general principle that in properly ordered talk, questions will be followed by answers.

CA is a markedly 'data centred' form of discourse analysis: in 'pure' versions (it will become clearer later what I mean by 'pure' here), the analyst is not supposed to appeal to any evidence that comes from outside the talk itself. This makes doing CA a rather different proposition from doing, say, ethnography of speaking. As we saw in Chapter 5, the ethnographic approach relates verbal behaviour to the setting in which talk occurs, who the participants are, what languages or language varieties their repertoire includes, and what they believe about all kinds of matters, ranging from child development to the mysteries of salvation. Such 'external' considerations are taken to be potentially relevant in analysis whether or not anyone alludes to them directly in the piece of talk being analysed. In the extract from a Pentecostal meeting reproduced in Chapter 5, no one explicitly says that contributions are prompted by the Holy Spirit. The investigator Christine Callender discovered the significance of this belief by talking to community members outside the meeting, and she used that knowledge to illuminate certain features of the talk that occurred inside the meeting. CA, by contrast, does not require the analyst to gain detailed knowledge of participants' identities, their daily routines or their beliefs: instead their talk itself is treated as containing everything relevant for analysis.

Some CA practitioners (who adhere to what I am calling the 'pure' version of the approach) apply the principle that one should not look beyond the data very strictly. For them it is not just unnecessary but illegitimate for an analyst to make use of information that the participants themselves have not chosen to 'make relevant' in their ongoing interaction. This position reflects the origins of CA in a particular school of sociological thought, 'ethnomethodology'. Ethnomethodology developed in opposition to other sociological approaches (for instance structural-functionalism and marxism) which explain society – and the habitual behaviour of its members – in terms of abstractions such as 'the class system'. Ethnomethodologists reject this view: for them social order is created not by abstract structures, but by the concrete actions of people going about their everyday business. It follows that sociologists should concentrate on studying people's actions on their own terms, rather than trying to fit them into an abstract theoretical framework which may have no relevance for the actors themselves (in which case it can hardly constitute a satisfactory explanation of their actions).

Ethnomethodology raises complex theoretical and philosophical issues which I will not pursue here (but see the suggestions for further reading at the end of the chapter). In CA more specifically, the 'purist' stance which shows the influence of ethnomethodology has been the subject of heated debate, much of which revolves around questions of *power* in discourse. As Ian Hutchby notes, the position of some highly respected CA practitioners is that 'analysts should only have recourse to concepts such as power once they are forced to do so by virtue of some otherwise unexplainable interactional phenomenon' (Hutchby 1996: 482). Others, including people who use the techniques of CA as well as people who prefer other approaches, take a different view. For instance, some feminist practitioners of CA have argued that men tend to dominate conversations involving both sexes (Fishman 1983; Zimmerman and West 1975). From a feminist perspective this is a manifestation in discourse of the more general social fact of gender hierarchy: it is therefore relevant to refer to that social fact in an analysis of discourse data. To the CA 'purist', however, gender and gender hierarchy are only relevant to the analysis of a piece of data if the participants *make* it relevant in some way. If it is not explicitly an issue for the participants in their talk, the analyst has no warrant for making it an issue in the analysis of that talk.

In Chapter 11 I return to questions about power and inequality. In this chapter, though, I concentrate on the apparatus CA provides for describing spoken discourse empirically. Though CA's insistence on focusing on the data and nothing but the data is considered by some to have its drawbacks, it is also widely acknowledged to have certain advantages: if you cannot make reference to what is *not* in the data, you are impelled to pay very close attention to the fine details of what *is* there. CA is a 'microanalytic' approach, which takes apparently mundane and unremarkable spoken interactions and finds intricate patterning in the way they are organized. Just as putting a snowflake under a microscope reveals structure and complexity which are not visible to the naked eye, so putting talk under the CA microscope defamiliarizes what we normally take for granted, and reveals the unsuspected complexity of our everyday verbal behaviour.

INVESTIGATING THE OBVIOUS: THE ORGANIZATION OF TURN-TAKING

Several years before I encountered CA as a student, I came across a reference to it in the British satirical weekly magazine *Private Eye*, which has for many years run a feature called 'Pseud's Corner'. Items for inclusion in Pseud's Corner are sent in by readers, and are usually examples of artists or intellectuals stating the obvious in unnecessarily pretentious language. On this occasion, a reader had sent in an observation attributed to the pioneer of CA, Harvey Sacks, about turn-taking in conversation. The observation was that 'one speaker speaks at a time, and speaker change recurs'. What readers of *Private Eye* were being invited to ridicule was the presentation of such a banal observation as the fruit of some weighty intellectual endeavour. The implication was that the proverbial person in the street could have come up with this particular insight on the basis of no research whatever, except that ordinary people would have more sense than to find the issue worth thinking about. But in a sense that is exactly the reason why Sacks *did* find it worth thinking about. Things that appear obvious – so obvious, indeed, that in everyday life no one would ever remark on them – may turn out on closer inspection to be less obvious than they seem.

Here the observation is that conversation requires speakers to take turns, and this requirement is managed in a particular way. At any given moment, the turn that is in progress will typically 'belong' to a single speaker ('one speaker speaks at a time'). Participants in conversation will not usually all talk at once, and conversely there will not usually be stretches of time in which no one talks at all. That is not to say that simultaneous speech and silence never occur in conversations: they do. But when they occur they are often treated by participants as problems which need to be 'repaired' – in other words, as something other than the normal and desirable state of affairs. In the case of simultaneous speech, what typically happens is that one speaker wins the floor (the right to talk and be attended to by co-participants) while the other(s) fall silent. In the case of a silence that becomes long enough to feel awkward, what usually happens is that someone breaks into it and claims the floor.

In addition to noticing the 'one speaker at a time [no more and no fewer]' requirement, Sacks pointed out that 'speaker change recurs'. In other words, the floor is not given to any one speaker for the duration. Nor, in ordinary conversation, is it parcelled out in advance among the participants ('OK, you speak first, then I'll speak, then Joanne can have a turn'). Rather the floor is constantly negotiated and renegotiated as a conversation goes along. In fact this continual negotiation is a general feature of conversational organization. CA holds that talk is 'locally managed', meaning that its patterns and structures result from what people do as they go along rather than from their being compelled to follow a course of action that has been determined in advance.

The sceptical reader may still be asking, with the editors of *Private Eye*, 'OK, but so what?' There does not seem to be much of a puzzle about *why* the regularities noted by Sacks exist. If everyone spoke at once, or no one spoke at all, or the same person held the floor continuously throughout, what we would have would not be conversation, it would be chaos or silence or monologue. But the intriguing question is not '*why*?', it is '*how*?' How do conversationalists manage the organization of the floor in such a way as to produce the pattern that 'one speaker speaks at a time and speaker change recurs'? Certainly it might seem logical to suppose that conversation-alists would 'naturally' strive towards a pattern which enables conversation to proceed in an orderly, rather than chaotic, manner. But even if that is so (a qualification I make because later I will suggest that speakers or communities may vary in their ideas about what kinds of talk *are* orderly/chaotic), on its own it does not explain *how* they achieve the desired outcome. Nor can participants in conversation necessarily explain this themselves. Asking them questions like 'how do you know when it's your turn to speak?' is unlikely to elicit an illuminating response, because ordinary conversationalists take their ability to converse for granted – they do not have to think consciously about what they are doing when they interact. Making explicit what ordinary conversationalists take for granted is precisely what CA sets out to do.

So what, in fact, are conversationalists doing to produce the regularities noted by Harvey Sacks? Sacks, along with two colleagues, Emmanuel Schegloff and Gail Jefferson, proposed a model of conversationalists' behaviour which they presented under the heading of 'A simplest systematics for the organization of turn-taking for conversation' (Sacks et al. 1974). The model has two main elements. First, it says that speakers are aware that a turn consists of one or more (but not fewer) 'turn constructional units'. (Sacks et al. define these units as grammatical entities, like a complete clause or sentence; but it might also be suggested, for reasons explained in Chapter 2 above, that the units of spoken discourse are delineated primarily by prosody (intonation, stress, pausing) rather than grammar.[2]) People who are listening to someone else's speech can use their knowledge of the possible unit types to project the end-point of the turn currently in progress. Being able to do this is important, because the end of a turn constructional unit is potentially a 'turn transition relevance place', a point at which speaker change may occur (though as we will see, it does not have to). Projecting the end of a turn involves attending to a combination of things, including the content of what is said, the prosodic and grammatical structure of the speech, and aspects of nonverbal behaviour such as the direction of the speaker's gaze. For example, if someone utters the words, 'and that's what I did today', with falling intonation and a pause at the end, listeners are likely to take that as a possible turn transition relevance place. By contrast, if someone utters the words 'and she says to me?' (the ? denotes rising intonation), both the content and the prosody provide a clue that the clause boundary in this case does not mark the end of the turn: the speaker intends to continue with a report of what 'she' went on to say, and is entitled to continue holding the floor at least until that report has been completed.

The second element of the simplest systematics model is a mechanism for allocating turns to particular participants in a conversation. When a turn transition relevance place is reached, what ensues is not a random free-for-all, with everyone present having an equal chance of getting the floor next. Instead, Sacks et al. suggest, there is an ordered set of rules for the allocation of the next turn, which can be shown in summary like this:

1   Current speaker selects next speaker
    or if this mechanism does not operate, then . . .

2   Next speaker self-selects
    or if this mechanism does not operate, then . . .

3   Current speaker may (but does not have to) continue

The turn-allocation mechanism that takes precedence over the alternatives is for the current speaker to select the next speaker. If a speaker ends her turn by shifting her gaze to the person on her left and saying, 'and that's just like what happened to you last year, isn't it?' then the next turn is marked as belonging to whoever she has just addressed. If that person remains silent, it is an accountable silence – not just anybody's silence but specifically the silence of the person selected to speak next. There are many ways for a current speaker to select a next speaker, including asking them a question, naming them (as often happens in the classroom – 'Nahil, what do you think?' – and in broadcast talk – 'and now over to you, Bill') or aligning your body or gaze so you are seen to be addressing a specific co-conversationalist at the end of your own turn.

If the current speaker does not select a next speaker, the second option is for someone other than the current speaker to select themself, by starting to speak. When this option is activated, there is scope for simultaneous speech to occur because more than one speaker simultaneously self-selects; but as noted earlier, the normal pattern is for this situation to resolve itself, with only one of the self-selectors continuing to hold the floor. If, on the other hand, no one self-selects, it is open to the current speaker to continue. This is the third option offered by the simplest systematics model, and it ranks below the alternatives, i.e. it is only permitted if neither of the higher-ranked options has been chosen. At the next turn transition relevance place, the same options apply in the same order all over again.

The simplest systematics is, indeed, simple, and elegant in its simplicity, but how well does it account for what is actually observed in real conversations? Reading the account I have just given, you may well have thought of objections based on your own knowledge and experience of talk. For example, turn transitions are not always as smooth as my account might seem to suggest. I mentioned only one reason why we sometimes get stretches of talk in which two or more people speak simultaneously: the possibility of more than one speaker self-selecting at a turn transition relevance place where the current speaker has not selected a next speaker. But what about the fact that people often begin speaking before the previous speaker has finished rather than waiting for the end of the turn? Are they breaking the rules?

Some cases of simultaneous speech are classed as 'overlaps': they result from the new speaker's failure to project the end of the last speaker's turn with complete accuracy. The new speaker comes in at the point where s/he *thinks* the last speaker will finish, but either the timing is slightly 'off' or else the new speaker is mistaken in thinking the last speaker is close to completion of a turn. Overlaps of this kind are common, but they are typically short, and they start close to a potential turn transition relevance place. They are not instances of rule-breaking so much as unintended errors in the application of the mechanisms described by Sacks and colleagues. In other cases, however, a new speaker may start to speak at a point in the last speaker's utterance that cannot possibly be a turn transition relevance place. This is not overlap but interruption, and for some analysts (e.g. Zimmerman and West 1975) it is not just a violation of the turn-taking system but a hostile act designed to deny the current speaker their legitimate right to the floor.

For other analysts, however, the idea that simultaneous speech is either overlap (an honest 'mistake') or interruption (a hostile 'violation') is oversimplified, and does not account for some quite common instances of simultaneous speech. To illustrate the problem, let us revisit a piece of data I used in Chapter 3, involving two women friends (they are university students, and are talking about two other women students they both know).

Ali: and she didn't she didn't like Katie she didn't ge[t on with Katie at all   ]
Beth: [no she didn't get on with] Katie
[brackets mark sequences spoken simultaneously]

In this extract, Beth begins her turn at a point where Ali is right in the middle of an informational, a grammatical and (although to keep things simple I haven't shown it in this transcript), a prosodic unit. The word *get* in the phrase *didn't get on with* is unlikely to be taken to mark the end of any kind of unit, which makes it implausible to suggest that Beth is starting her turn on the assumption that Ali is about to finish hers. (A more likely point for that to happen would have been somewhere around the first utterance of *Katie*.) Is Beth, then, *interrupting* Ali? Two considerations make this unlikely, especially if interruption is understood as a hostile act. First, Beth does not deprive Ali of the floor: Ali does not fall silent (whereas in their study of gender and interruptions, Zimmerman and West (1975) found that the interventions they classed as interruptions often had the effect of making the interrupted party stop speaking). Ali continues speaking simultaneously with Beth until she finishes the unit she has started (that it is indeed complete at this point is signalled by a marked slowing down with emphatic stress on *at all*). Second, Beth's 'interruption' does not mark disagreement with what Ali has said, nor lack of interest in what she has said, nor any desire to change the direction of the conversation. On the contrary, it echoes both Ali's sentiments and Ali's actual words. At the point Beth starts speaking, just after Ali has begun producing the word *get*, she appears to have heard enough to guess accurately what Ali is in the middle of saying – 'she didn't get on with Katie' – and she interjects in order to say exactly the same thing. The function of Beth's contribution, then, is to *support* Ali in holding the floor rather than to take the floor away from her.

Jennifer Coates (1996) argues that simultaneous speech with this supportive function is particularly common in the talk of women friends; I have found examples of it in the talk of young men friends too (Cameron 1997). Carole Edelsky (1981) provides evidence that supportive simultaneous speech can also occur in institutional contexts. In analysis of talk at meetings, Edelsky distinguished two types of floor, which she labelled 'F1' and 'F2'. F1 conformed to the 'one speaker speaks at a time' model, whereas F2 involved more simultaneous speech (and according to Edelsky, enabled women to share the floor more equally with men than was the case with F1). It appears, then, that in both friends' talk and some kinds of institutional talk it is possible for the floor to be organized on a principle other than 'one speaker speaks at a time'. But the simplest systematics model assumes that 'one at a time' is both normal and fundamental: there is no obvious place in the model for simultaneous speech which is neither an error nor a violation, but merely a normal feature of certain kinds of talk.

The question this raises is whether Sacks and colleagues make assumptions about talk-in-general which are not, in fact, universally valid. In CA, analysts look not merely for regular sequential patterns in data, but for evidence that participants themselves are *orienting to* the existence of those patterns. Thus if the analyst's claim is that 'one speaker speaks at a time', one would expect participants in talk to display their orientation to that pattern by treating instances of simultaneous speech as problems requiring repair. This is what is happening when, say, a speaker who inadvertently overlaps another apologizes and stops speaking to let the other finish, or when three speakers who simultaneously self-select sort themselves out in such a way that only one continues. But in something like Carole Edelsky's 'F2' sequences, or in the conversation between Ali and Beth reproduced above, there is no display of orientation to the 'one speaker speaks at a time' pattern, and this is what motivates speculation that some other system of floor organization may be operative.

Some readers of my account of the simplest systematics – especially, perhaps, readers who do not live in an exclusively English-speaking society – may have wondered about the issue of *cultural* differences in relation to the organization of conversational floors. Ethnographers have reported on various societies which do not appear to fit the prototype assumed by Sacks et al., ranging from the Antiguan village in which Reisman (1974) observed 'contrapuntal conversation' (i.e. at least two speakers habitually speak at a time) to the Nordic and native American speech communities which tolerate extended silence in conversation (see Tannen and

Saville-Troike 1985). Anyone who has been exposed to a variety of cultural practices will be able to produce anecdotes about other differences. When I was teaching in Sweden, for example, an Argentinian student explained how hard it had been for her to learn Swedish turn-taking conventions. In Argentina, she said, the rule had been roughly 'grab the floor and then talk until someone interrupts you'; in Sweden the rule appeared to be something more like 'wait for the other to finish before you start speaking'. As a result, the Argentinian had often found herself in the midst of what struck her as an interminable monologue, desperately wishing for someone else to claim the floor from her. Meanwhile, as she later realized, her Swedish interlocutors were waiting for her to show some sign of finishing so they could take a turn. Both conventions basically conform to the 'one speaker at a time' model; the difference is subtler, to do with how and when the turn-allocating mechanism of self-selection may be used.

The existence of variations like these underlines the need for analysts of spoken discourse to be cautious about making quasi-universal claims. But that is not a criticism of the CA approach as such. Rather it restates what is actually a fundamental principle of CA – that analysts must be attentive, and analysis faithful, to the fine-grained detail of the particular data being analysed, and to the patterns that appear to be salient for participants themselves.

'ONE THING AFTER ANOTHER': ADJACENCY PAIRS

The turn-taking system provides a basic framework for the organization of talk-in-interaction, since it allows for the floor to be alternated systematically between speakers – in other words, for participants to *inter*act rather than simply acting individually in an uncoordinated manner. But if the orderly exchange of speaking turns is a necessary part of spoken interaction, it is not on its own sufficient to guarantee that there is genuine and meaningful interaction, as we can see from the following example (quoted by Labov 1972a: 299):

> Therapist: what's your name?
> Patient: well, let's say you might have thought you had something from before, but you haven't got it anymore
> Therapist: I'm going to call you Dean

In this exchange, the parties seem to have no problem coordinating the orderly exchange of turns. What makes the exchange odd is rather the apparent lack of co-ordination in the *content* of their turns. The therapist asks a question, but although the patient responds as expected in the sense that he unhesitatingly takes the floor, he fails to provide anything like a meaningful answer to the question he has been asked. A Gricean pragmaticist might say that the patient is flouting the maxim of relation. A practitioner of CA would not disagree with the assessment of the remark as irrelevant, but s/he would consider it important to clarify that the patient's response is irrelevant, specifically, *as a response to the immediately preceding contribution*. CA places great emphasis on the idea that conversation is 'one thing after another': it is an activity that unfolds in time, and what I say now must inevitably constrain what you can meaningfully say next. In the above example, the first turn is a question requesting information. The second speaker is thus constrained to provide the information requested – not in a minute or an hour or a year, but in the next turn.

Here it may be objected that questions are not always followed immediately by answers; sometimes, indeed, they may be followed by further questions (there is a parlour game based on this possibility, in which the players must speak entirely in questions – for instance 'how are you?', 'why do you ask?', 'what's the matter, are you paranoid?', 'what makes you think I'm paranoid?' etc.). But if one question is followed by another question, or indeed by an irrelevant remark like the patient's in the 'what's your name?' example, normally that only defers and does not cancel the expectation that the original question must be answered. The strength of that expectation is underlined, in fact, by what happens in cases where it is *not* met.

In a study called 'On questions following questions in service encounters', Merritt (1976) looked at exchanges like the following:

1   Customer: pint of Guinness please
2   Bartender: how old are you?
3   Customer: twenty two
4   Bartender: OK coming up
    [constructed example]

Merritt points out that the implication of responding to a request (turn 1) with a question (turn 2) rather than simply by supplying what has been requested is that the server's ability or willingness to provide the desired service depends on the answer to the question. In the above example, turn 2 conveys to the customer, not that the server is ignoring his request in favour of idle questions about his date of birth, but that the provision or non-provision of beer is *conditional* on the answer to the question 'how old are you?'. The question is taken as relevant by the customer, not only because of his background knowledge that alcohol can only be purchased by persons over a certain age, but also and importantly because of its position in the sequence of turns: it occurs immediately after a request for service, but before the server has fulfilled his obligation to provide that service. Hence what happens in turn 3 is that the customer fulfils his own obligation to provide an answer to the question posed in turn 2; the server then responds in turn 4 to the original request made in turn 1.

In the 'what's your name?' sequence, by contrast, when the therapist does not get a straight answer to his first question he uses his next turn to effectively answer it himself. That suggests he has some reason to believe the patient is not going to honour his obligation to provide an answer to the question. (In fact, he knows that the patient suffers from schizophrenia and for that reason often does not conform to 'normal' expectations in spoken interaction. He also knows the patient's name. Even so, he apparently is not content to let the question simply remain unanswered.)

The point that is illustrated by the examples given above is that spoken interaction is often structured around pairs of adjacent utterances (utterances which occur one after the other) in which the second utterance is not just related to the first but functionally dependent on it. If the first utterance is a question, the next utterance will usually be heard either as an answer to the question or, as in the Guinness example, as a move that has to be made in order to put the speaker in a position to answer the question subsequently. The sequence 'Question–Answer' is one example of what CA labels an 'adjacency pair', meaning a pair of utterances in which the second is functionally dependent on the first. Merritt's study of questions following questions shows that the two parts of an adjacency pair may become separated (and thus no longer adjacent). This separation is normally brief, however, and the second adjacency pair which is inserted between the two parts of the first one is understood to be necessary for the completion of the original transaction (as opposed to being some sort of digression from it).

Question–Answer is not the only type of adjacency pair identified by analysts. Another type is Greeting–Greeting. If someone produces an utterance that is hearable as a greeting, the person they are addressing is constrained to produce a greeting in return. They have a choice about what they say (or do: a nod, smile or raised eyebrow may be sufficient acknowledgement). But if the first part of the greeting–greeting sequence is not followed by a second part, this will be perceived as leaving an accountably empty slot – or in plainer English, as a snub. The fact that we perceive the non-return of greetings as rude, unfriendly or socially inept behaviour provides supporting evidence for the claim that a greeting is not a free-standing turn but part of a larger unit, an adjacency pair. If there is no second part we feel the return greeting is not merely absent but missing.

Some first turns present the producer of the second turn with a choice. For instance, invitations, offers, suggestions or proposals may be either accepted or declined. A turn which solicits the addressee's opinion on some proposition made by the speaker may be met with either agreement or disagreement. Analysts have noted an interesting pattern in the way the alternative possibilities are typically handled by conversationalists. Consider the following example, in which three friends are negotiating what they will eat for dinner.

Transcription conventions: ? = rising intonation; (.) = pause
1 Daphne: I was thinking we could have fish?
2 Julia: fine
3 Anita: well actually (.) I've stopped eating fish now because of you know
4   the damage it does to the ocean

In this sequence Daphne, who will be the cook on the occasion under discussion, makes the others a proposal regarding the menu: she suggests having fish. Julia accepts this proposal; Anita by contrast declines it. Whereas Julia's acceptance is brief and unelaborated, Anita's turn is considerably longer. It begins with *well*, a 'discourse marker' (Schiffrin 1987) which is commonly used to indicate that the speaker is about to say something which may conflict with the assumptions or wishes of a previous speaker. Anita also pauses briefly before she gets to the actual message, a polite rejection of Daphne's proposal that they should have fish for dinner, 'I've stopped eating fish now'. Finally, Anita provides an account of why she no longer eats fish: she has been persuaded to stop by ecological arguments about the damage intensive commercial fishing does to the ocean environment.

The difference between Julia's reply and Anita's illustrates the workings of what CA calls a 'preference system'. The 'preferred' response to a proposal is accep- tance, and it can be identified as the preferred option because it is typically performed without hesitation or elaboration. It is possible to accept proposals more elaborately, of course – Julia could have said something like 'ooh, fish! I *love* fish!' – but the point is, acceptance *can* be done without elaboration. Refusal by contrast is almost never done in the same way. Refusal is the 'dispreferred' response, and is identified as such because it is typically performed as Anita performs it here: she is hesitant about coming to the point and she elaborates her refusal by giving a reason for it. A similar pairing is agreement (preferred) and disagreement (dispreferred).

In discussions of the concept 'preference' in CA, analysts have often been at some pains to emphasize that the 'preferred'/ 'dispreferred' distinction is made purely on the basis of formal patterns: preferred responses are prompt and short while dispreferred ones are hesitant and elaborate. The word 'preference' is not intended, these analysts warn, to have its ordinary English meaning of something that is considered more desirable than something else. People's attitudes regarding what is or is not desirable are the province of psychology, and irrelevant to the concerns of CA. CA has simply noted the existence of a regular pattern in talk: acceptances and agreements are typically done in one way, while refusals and disagreements are done in a different way.

But one might ask whether this line of argument is either convincing or enlightening. There are, after all, some fairly obvious reasons why people might generally 'prefer', in the ordinary sense of the word, to accept invitations, offers and proposals rather than refusing them, or to agree with others' opinions rather than disagreeing. Readers who recall the discussion of politeness in Chapter 6 will probably have noticed that the 'preferred' option is also the less threatening to the addressee's face. In the 'fish' example, for instance, Julia can make her acceptance without miti- gation, because acceptance does not inconvenience Daphne or hurt her feelings. Anita on the other hand is doing something that both imposes on Daphne (she must think of something else to have for dinner) and hints at disagreement with or even disapproval of Daphne (Anita thinks commercial fishing and the consumption of its products are morally unjustified practices, whereas Daphne evidently does not share those views). It is not surprising that Anita chooses to mitigate the threat to Daphne's face by using politeness strategies such as hesitation. The particular patterns described by CA, then, could be seen as outcomes of the general politeness principles set out by researchers like Brown and Levinson (1987). People make choices about how to perform certain acts in the light of their assessment of how face-threatening those acts are. If this account is accepted, then the underlying difference between a 'preferred' and a 'dispreferred' move is that the latter is more face-threatening than the former and is therefore typically performed with more mitigation (for an extended argument to that effect, see Owen 1983).

At the beginning of this chapter I noted that Conversation Analysis has not confined itself to examining the kind of informal face-to-face talk that is most readily brought to mind by the term *conversation*. In the following sections I will consider some of the contributions CA has made to our knowledge and understanding of particular kinds of talk: talk on the telephone, and talk in institutional contexts.

WHY IS IT SO HARD TO GET OFF THE PHONE?

Telephone conversation has been studied quite intensively by CA practitioners. One argument for choosing this kind of data is that the phone restricts participants in talk to the oral–aural channel: there is no visual information available, and thus an analysis focusing on spoken language is not leaving out an important dimension of the participants' own experience. Not surprisingly, analyses of telephone conversation show that it is both similar to face-to-face talk in some ways and different in others. One example of simultaneous similarity/difference concerns the way calls often start:

> *Phone rings in Beth's location*
> 1   Beth: hello
> 2   Ann: hello
> 3   Beth: oh hello Ann what's up
> 4   Ann: nothing much just had something I wanted to ask you

The puzzle here is that on the surface it looks as if we have a sequence of three greeting turns ('hello', 'hello', 'oh hello Ann') when the normal organizational principles would lead us to expect only two, one from each of the participants. But what seems to be a deviation from the norm in face-to-face conversation actually conforms to the principle of the adjacency pair; it just adapts it to the particular circumstances of the phone call. Beth's first turn is not a greeting, but rather the second part of an adjacency pair whose first part is the ringing of the phone (strictly speaking I should have numbered this event as turn 1 in my transcript – it stands in for Ann's opening turn). Analysts of telephone talk refer to the first part as the 'summons' and the second part as the 'answer'. In support of the claim that the answer is not the first turn in an exchange of greetings, we might also note that people do not always use a greeting formula like 'hello' in this position. Many recite their telephone number, for instance; in some countries it is conventional just to say one's name.

There is, furthermore, a good reason for supposing that the person who answers the phone must be taking the second rather than the first turn in the opening sequences. The person who answers is by definition not the person who has initiated the conversation: the initiator is the person who decided to make a phone call in the first place. And since it is only the initiator who knows *why* s/he is calling (the responder may not even know *who* is calling), the initiator needs to be in the position of taking the first turn in subsequent adjacency pairs.[3] In the example above the initiator, Ann, produces the first greeting at turn 2 and the responder returns the greeting in turn 3, coupling this with an acknowledgement that she recognizes the caller and a formulaic enquiry ('what's up?') that could be either about the caller's general state or about her particular reason for calling. The caller then uses her next turn, turn 4, to introduce the actual business of the call: 'just had something I wanted to ask you'.

One question that is frequently asked by phone users is why it is difficult to *finish* a telephone conversation, and why getting off the phone with someone can become such a protracted business. In fact, CA practitioners have pointed out that conversations in general do not just 'end'; rather they have to be 'closed' (Schegloff and Sacks 1973). On the phone this requirement is particularly demanding linguistically: closure has to be done entirely through talk, since other options for disengagement, involving for instance body language or physical movement, are limited or unavailable.

So how do people in practice manage phone-call 'closings'? Here is an extract from a call made by Daphne, who is trying to get five people, including Paula, together for a meeting on a Saturday. At this point Daphne has elicited the information she needs, regarding which Saturdays in the next few weeks Paula has free.

Transcription conventions: (.) brief pause, ? rising intonation, : lengthened segment

1 Daphne: so that's any Saturday except the seventh (.) right I'll let you know when I've heard from the others
2 Paula: OK
3 Daphne: right then
4 Paula: I might be in London before that though shall I give you a ring?
5 Daphne: yeah do that
6 Paula: OK I will
7 Daphne: good
8 Paula: OK::
9 Daphne: take care then
10 Paula: you too
11 Daphne: bye
12 Paula: OK bye

The most obvious feature of this extract which might lead to the impression that the end of the call is 'dragging on' is the number of turns in which the participants merely utter formulaic remarks like 'good', 'right then', 'OK', rather than exchanging any actual information. Why does this happen? Essentially, because it is necessary for telephone interactants to make sure that there is joint agreement to end the exchange. Since it is possible on the phone to cut someone off at any time (by hanging up), and this is regarded as a highly aggravated act of impoliteness (akin to just walking off in the middle of a face-to-face encounter) phone users who do not wish to be impolite have to negotiate the breaking off of contact carefully. Before they can close, each participant has to signal she has no more to say by 'passing' on the opportunity to introduce new information (some CA practitioners refer to 'unmentioned mention-ables', things that could be mentioned but so far have not been). On the phone this 'passing' is signalled by taking a turn but putting no new content into it.

At turn 3 in the sequence above, Daphne 'passes'; she has an opportunity to go on to some matter other than the business the pair have just transacted, but what she says is merely 'right then'. This is potentially a 'pre-closing', an indication that she is ready to close and an invitation to Paula to pass on her own next turn. Paula, however, does not pass; she brings up the previously unmentioned topic of her intention to visit London. Daphne is thus obliged to respond to the new topic, and Paula completes the sequence by agreeing to ring when she makes the visit. At turn 7 Daphne again indicates readiness to close by saying 'good'. This time Paula also passes: she says 'OK', with marked lengthening on the last syllable which carries the implication of finality. With the pre-closing successfully accomplished by the two women each passing up the opportunity to introduce new matter, the actual closing can begin. It takes them ten turns to get from the end of their main business (at turn 2) to the end of the call, and it is not uncommon for this portion of a call to be far more extended than it is in this example. Since it is open to either party *not* to accept the other's invitation to pass, the endings of phone calls have a 'recursive' structure – the conversation in principle goes on until the parties manage to arrive at a mutual agreement to end it.

BEYOND THE 'BASICS': INSTITUTIONAL TALK

As I noted in Chapter 1, many discourse analysts are inclined to privilege what they call 'ordinary talk', meaning the kind that prototypically occurs in private or domestic settings between people whose relationship is close rather than distant. For various reasons, and in particular because children typically acquire their competence as conversationalists by talking to intimates (e.g. parents, siblings and other caregivers) in domestic settings, this kind of talk is regarded as 'basic'. Generally, CA practitioners follow this line of argument. In relation to 'institutional' talk – business meetings, service encounters, doctor–patient consultations, talk in courtrooms or in classrooms – analysis tends to be organized around the question, 'what special considerations apply that make talk in this institutional context different from ordinary talk?'

In their editorial introduction to a collection of articles on workplace interaction, Paul Drew and John Heritage summarize what they take to be the main differences between institutional and ordinary talk (Drew and Heritage 1992: 22):

1 Institutional interaction involves an orientation by at least one of the participants to some core goal, task or activity (or set of them) conventionally associated with

the institution in question. In short, institutional talk is normally informed by *goal orientations* of a relatively restricted conventional form.

2 Institutional interaction may often involve *special and particular constraints* on what one or both of the participants will treat as allowable contributions to the business at hand.

3 Institutional talk may be associated with *inferential frameworks* and procedures that are particular to specific institutional contexts.

To see what this means in practice, let us consider the case of interactions in a magistrate's court, which were studied by Sandra Harris (1984). The court Harris observed dealt mainly with people who had not paid previously imposed fines or maintenance orders. Defendants were questioned to determine why they had not paid and what resources they had to pay with. The purpose of this was to enable magistrates (in the English legal system, officials who preside over court proceedings which are too 'minor' to require a judge and jury) to determine how much the defendant should pay over what period. Thus the talk Harris observed in court had a very specific goal (cf. point 1 in Drew and Heritage's list), which was reflected in many features of the interaction: for example, that it took the form of a series of questions and answers on the topic of the defendant's intentions and financial resources, followed by the announcement of the magistrate's decision.

One 'special and particular constraint' which applied in the magistrates' court, and which often applies to some degree in institutional talk, though it rarely applies in ordinary conversation, was a constraint on the right to ask questions. Essentially, defendants were not permitted to ask questions, whereas they were obliged to respond to questions posed by the representatives of the institution. Harris observed occasional instances where defendants *did* ask questions, and were immediately censured for doing so (showing that their questions were not treated as 'allowable contributions to the business at hand'). She also observed that defendants were censured for answering questions in ways the magistrate deemed inappropriate. The following extract illustrates these observations (Harris 1984: 5):

Transcription conventions: italics = emphasis, (6) = pause duration in seconds, – = short pause, [= simultaneous speech

Magistrate: I'm putting it to you again – are you going to *make* an offer – uh – uh – to discharge this debt (6)
Defendant: Would you in my position
Magistrate: I – I'm not here to answer questions – you answer *my* question
Defendant: One rule for one and one for another – I presume (3)
Magistrate: Can I have an answer to my question – please (6)
 The question is – are you prepared to make an offer to the court – to discharge – this debt (2)
Defendant: What sort of minimal offer [would be required
Magistrate: [it's not a bargaining situation – it's a *straight* question Mr H. – can I have the answer

Here the defendant twice responds to the magistrate's questions with questions of his own. On the first occasion he is explicitly told that the magistrate is 'not here to answer questions' (which means it is inappropriate for defendants to ask any); on the second the magistrate cuts him off and complains that he is 'bargaining' rather than giving a straight answer. The magistrate asks the defendant three times in this short extract to answer the question he has been asked, demonstrating the validity of the defendant's presumption that there's 'one rule for one and one for another'.

The 'one rule for one and one for another' principle applies rather consistently in asymmetrical talk (that is, talk in which the participants do not have equal power, status, responsibility or control). Not only in courtrooms but also in other kinds of institutional encounters, such as medical consultations, interviews, radio phone-in programmes and school classrooms, there is an asymmetrical distribution of questions and answers. Typically it is the dominant party who has the right (and/or the obligation) to ask questions, while the subordinate party has a restricted right to ask questions. This is no coincidence, for the position of questioner gives its occupant considerable power to direct interaction. A question forms the first turn of an adjacency pair, and it does not merely require an answer, it also constrains what will count as a relevant or appropriate answer.

Magistrates in Harris's study often exploited this fact by putting questions in a particularly 'conducive' syntactic form, that is, a form which constrains the recipient to produce a particular answer. An example is the tag question 'that means you've got to pay thirteen pounds, doesn't it?' (Harris 1984: 17). The magistrate is not interested in the defendant's opinion on the matter; rather s/he is making an assertion ('you've got to pay thirteen pounds') and the purpose of encoding it as a question is to get the defendant to demonstrate understanding and agreement. The implication of a 'yes' answer is that the defendant recognizes the court's power to impose the payment and intends to comply with the order. A 'yes' thus serves the purposes of the institution, and the magistrate's discourse is designed to make the institution's preferred outcome the most likely outcome. Using questions obliges the defendant to respond rather than just remaining silent, but choosing conducive forms minimizes the defendant's opportunities to produce responses which are protracted, unexpected or challenging to the presuppositions of the court. Of course it remains *possible* for a defendant to say 'no' or embark on some other kind of response altogether – people are not sociolinguistic automata – but this will be treated as 'marked' and accountable behaviour. It transgresses both the norms of the context and the expectations embedded in the form of the question.

Drew and Heritage's third point about institutional talk is that it may be associated with particular *inferential frameworks*. In other words, people engaged in talk that has a certain institutional goal may use their understanding of what the institution wishes to achieve to make inferences about the meaning or function of an utterance that they might not make in other contexts. Sandra Harris noted that defendants in the magistrates' court regularly interpreted questions not as straight-forward requests for information but as *accusations*. Defendants anticipated that magistrates would treat their failure to pay off debts as a sign of unwillingness rather than inability to pay, and they often framed their responses to rebut the charge of deliberate non-compliance. For instance, one defendant, asked the question 'are you supporting anyone else?' answered 'not at all – no – I live on my own sir' (Harris 1984: 15–16). This answer, which is both emphatic and markedly deferential, suggests the defendant construed the question as implying that he had taken on a financial commitment to a new partner or family while neglecting to pay maintenance to his ex-wife and three children. In fact, it is unclear whether or not the magistrate who asked the question intended that inference. Magistrates need to know a defendant's circumstances before deciding how much their weekly payment should be, and 'are you supporting anyone else' could in principle be no more than an attempt to elicit relevant information. However, some questions posed by magistrates were clearly accusatory (for example, 'would you like to explain why . . . you've chosen to ignore the order of the court please' (p.19)). It is understandable that defendants extended the same inferential framework to questions whose status as accusations was less obvious: when talking to someone who has the power to send you to prison, it is advisable to err on the side of caution and adopt a defensive stance.

ACTIVITY: ANALYSING SCRIPTED TALK

To conclude this chapter, here is an activity that brings together some of the main themes discussed above, but in relation to a slightly unusual kind of data. In the discussion of turn-taking I introduced the axiom that talk-in-interaction is 'locally managed', organized by the participants themselves as they go along rather than following some preordained path. Recently, however, increasing numbers of companies providing service to customers, especially via the telephone, have been doing something that appears to be in conflict with this fundamental principle: writing standard scripts for routine transactions, which employees are required to perform. It is interesting to consider to what extent these scripts, which are usually designed by people with no expert training in the analysis of spoken discourse, embody the organizational principles which have been found by CA to apply in non-scripted, spontaneous interaction.

   Overleaf I reproduce (with slight modifications to disguise the identity of the organizations concerned) scripts which are given to employees in two call centres where people are employed to deal with customer enquiries by telephone. One centre provides directory assistance to phone users, and the other authorizes credit card transactions. Read the scripts and then consider the following questions:

ACTIVITY

1 In what ways does the script in example A reproduce features that are typical of unscripted spoken interaction, and in what ways (if any) does it seem to deviate from the normal organization of talk? If you notice 'deviant' features, what might account for them and what problems might you expect them to cause in practice?

2 How is example A affected by the fact that it is a script for a transaction conducted by telephone rather than face to face?

3 In example B, how would you describe the difference between the script for authorized applications and the script for unauthorized applications? Why are these scripts so different?

4 Do Drew and Heritage's observations on the characteristics of institutional talk (quoted above) seem relevant/illuminating in relation to these scripts? To what extent and in what ways do the scripted transactions exemplify 'asymmetrical' talk?

5 If you have experience of dealing with service workers who are following a script, or if you have ever done a job that required you to engage in scripted interaction yourself, how do you feel about the practice of scripting talk? Why?

Example A: Conducting a 'standard search' for a telephone number

Agent: XYZ Directories, which name please? 1
Caller: Jones
Agent: Jones, thank you.
 Which town please?
Caller: Cardiff 5
Agent: Cardiff, thank you.
 Which address please?
Caller: Number 28, Acacia Avenue
Agent: Number 28, Acacia Avenue, thank you.
 Just searching for you. (pause) 10
 Sorry to keep you waiting.
 Thank you. Your number is 0123 456789
Caller: Thank you.
Agent: You're welcome.
Caller: Goodbye. 15
Agent: Goodbye.

Example B: dealing with requests for credit authorization
When a transaction is authorized, say to the caller:
 This application has been accepted.
If a transaction is not authorized, say to the caller:
 Unfortunately this application has been declined but thank you for calling.

SUGGESTIONS FOR FURTHER READING ABOUT CA

An introduction to CA which is both detailed and accessible is Hutchby and Wooffitt's *Conversation Analysis: An Introduction* (1998). Max Atkinson's *Our Masters' Voices* (1984), a study of political speechmaking as a form of interaction (the audience doesn't get a speaking turn, but it does get the chance to clap and cheer) is a readable piece of empirical CA. Other 'classic' CA work is collected in edited volumes including Gumperz and Hymes (1972), Scheinkein (1978) and Turner (1974). On institutional talk, probably the best single source is Drew and Heritage's collection *Talk at Work* (1992). Some readers may be interested in the origins of CA and its theoretical roots in ethnomethodological sociology. One account is provided in John Heritage's *Garfinkel and Ethnomethodology* (1984). Harvey Sacks, who is generally regarded as the pioneer of the approach that became CA, died early in the field's history; he never wrote a textbook, but the lectures he gave on conversation have been a source of inspiration to many of the analysts who followed him. They circulated among insiders in unpublished form for many years, and were eventually edited for publication as *Lectures on Conversation* (Sacks 1995).

NOTES

1   CA does have something to say about narrative, and I pursue the subject further in Chapter 10 below.
2   For discussion of the relationship between grammatical and interactional structure, see Ochs et al. (1996); the specific issue of how conversationalists project turn transition relevance places is examined in detail in Ford and Thompson's contribution to that volume.
3   It should be noted here that technological change may raise new and interesting questions about telephone talk. For instance, Jane Davies (pers. comm.) comments that now many people have caller display on their phones (especially their mobile phones), which means they can identify certain callers as soon as the phone starts ringing, it is increasingly common for the responder's first turn to be a greeting like 'hi Jane!' rather than an answer to the initial summons. This might prompt the question whether callers who have been recognized and greeted in this manner then have to negotiate themselves back into first position to enable the call to proceed smoothly (caller display tells us who's calling, but not why); and if so, how they do it.

8 Small differences, big difference: interactional sociolinguistics

There is a popular self-help book whose title advises: 'Don't sweat the small stuff'. It is based on the idea that people often get themselves worked up unnecessarily over trivial issues; they would be happier and more productive if they learnt to tell the difference between things that really matter and things that don't. Then, they could resolve to save their mental and emotional energy for the important things, and stop wasting it on the 'small stuff'. In many areas of life, this may well be good advice. In relation to spoken language, however, 'small stuff' can make a big difference – communication may succeed or fail because of it. This chapter is about an approach to discourse analysis, interactional sociolinguistics, which has highlighted the importance of small and subtle variations in the way people use and interpret spoken discourse.

WHAT IS INTERACTIONAL SOCIOLINGUISTICS?

Interactional sociolinguistics has connections with other approaches to spoken interaction that we have already examined (especially the ethnography of speaking), but as its name suggests, it also has connections with sociolinguistics, the study of socially conditioned patterns of variation in language-use. Sociolinguists describe differences in the way people use language – their pronunciation, their grammar, the words they use for particular things, the way that bilingual speakers alternate between two or more languages – and seek to explain these differences by correlating them with nonlinguistic differences – for instance in speakers' class, race, ethnicity or gender, the formality of the situation, the subject people are talking about or the setting where they are talking. *Interactional* sociolinguists take a similar approach to phenomena which are important in organizing spoken interaction. It is not only in their grammar, vocabulary and pronunciation that language-users have, as sociolinguists put it, different ways of saying the same thing (e.g. referring to a carbonated soft drink as *pop* or *soda* or *juice*,[1] pronouncing or not pronouncing an /r/ sound in the word *farm*). Such aspects of interaction as turn-taking rules, conventions for indicating acknowledgement and agreement, the marking of utterances as particular kinds of speech acts or as containing important information are also 'variables' – that is, are used differently in different contexts or by different kinds of speakers. Interactional sociolinguistics is the study of this kind of variation.

As with many of the regularities studied by CA practitioners (see Chapter 7), the aspects of interaction that interest interactional sociolinguists are often ones that the participants in talk have little or no conscious awareness of. They could not explicitly explain how they recognize a certain intonation pattern as signalling important new information, or why one minimal response (a brief acknowledgement of another speaker such as *mhm, yeah, right*) sounds encouraging, while another sounds dismissive. They may also be unaware that these aspects of interactional behaviour are *variable*, with different meanings for different groups of language users.

The nature and significance of this kind of variation may be illustrated by an example which concerns nonverbal communicative behaviour (discussed by Callender 1997). Some British schoolchildren of African-Caribbean ethnicity have been observed to direct their gaze downwards when confronted by a teacher. This behaviour infuriates some white teachers, prompting them to issue commands like 'look at me when I'm talking to you!'. These teachers understand the children's gaze behaviour as evasive and disrespectful. For them, 'looking someone in the eye' is a mark of attentiveness and of honesty. However, in the children's own community a different assumption is operative: lowering one's gaze is a way of conveying respect.

This is an example of 'intercultural communication' – communication between people who are operating within two different cultural systems.[2] More exactly it is an example of intercultural *mis*communication. While misunderstanding is always a possibility in any kind of spoken interaction, it is a particular problem in intercultural encounters, because of systematic differences in the cultural assumptions and patterns of linguistic behaviour which are considered normal by those involved. Small differences in people's ways of doing things in conversation can lead to serious misunderstandings, and since the parties often do not understand what has gone wrong, the problem may not be identified as linguistic or communicative at all. Instead it may be taken as evidence that members of group X are just mean, or stupid, or crazy. In the example given above, for instance, the child who behaves in a way s/he considers respectful, and is then accused of disrespect by a teacher because of it, may well end up feeling both confused and resentful. Since the communicational difference that caused the problem is correlated with a highly salient social difference – in this case one of race/ethnicity – the experience, particularly if it is repeated over time, may contribute to reinforcing each party's stereotypical beliefs about the other. If the teacher thinks African-Caribbean students are badly behaved and disrespectful, s/he is likely to have that view confirmed by the child's behaviour. If the child thinks white teachers treat Black pupils unfairly because of racial prejudice, s/he will find supporting evidence for that proposition in the teacher's behaviour.

In communicative encounters between members of different groups, the smaller and subtler the differences are, the greater their potential to cause problems. If someone addresses me in a foreign language that I don't speak, I know immediately that I don't understand them, and it is obvious why. If someone speaks to me in an unfamiliar dialect of a language I do speak, and I have difficulty decoding their pronunciation, the source of my problem will be equally apparent to me: accent is something we pay attention to, and have a certain amount of explicit knowledge about. Something like the gaze behaviour variation described above is more subtle: teachers have no difficulty in pinpointing which aspect of the children's behaviour is at odds with their expectations, but they do not realize that the behaviour in question is not intended to mean what they think it means. Unlike the standard English speaker who is addressed in Japanese or broad Scots, the teacher may not be aware that s/he has not understood the student. The proposition that people speak different languages or pronounce words differently because they are from different places is common knowledge; the proposition that their gaze behaviour varies for similar reasons is not.

There are other cases of interactional variation in which the participants become aware that they are not understanding or being understood, but they cannot identify the variables which are causing the difficulty, because those variables are features of discourse which they do not attend to consciously. Readers who recall the discussion of spoken and written language in Part I, 'Preliminaries', will not be surprised to learn that the discourse features most likely to be obscure to ordinary language-users are ones which are not represented, or whose representation is impoverished, in writing. Prosodic and paralinguistic features, to take an obvious example, are not represented in written language with any precision, and unlike spelling, punctuation or grammar, they are not explicitly taught. Consequently, people tend to lack awareness about the important and systematic contribution they make to the meaning of spoken discourse.

CONTEXTUALIZATION CUES AND 'CROSSTALK'

Some significant research in interactional sociolinguistics has been conducted with a view to helping people who regularly engage in intercultural communication (such as teachers or workers in multi-ethnic schools or businesses) become aware of the differences that may cause problems, and take account of variation in their real-life encounters with speakers whose ways of interacting differ from their own. An example is the work of John Gumperz and his associates (Gumperz et al. 1979) on 'crosstalk' between members of Britain's white majority community and members of Asian minority communities. (The term *Asian* here denotes people who migrated from the Indian subcontinent, and their British-born descendants. This use of *Asian* is common in Britain, though there is some variation in the terms community members themselves prefer.) Communication problems involving Asian speakers are some-times attributed by white Britons to the fact that Asians are 'foreigners' and have difficulty with the English language as such. But while some Asians may indeed have a limited command of English, others, including many who were born in India or Pakistan, speak it fluently as a second language. However, what such people speak is not necessarily British English but an English variety developed in the Indian subcontinent itself. In Britain this becomes an 'ethnic' variety, a mark of membership in a particular minority ethnic community. Gumperz and his associates set out to investigate what systematic differences between this variety and the majority variety of English might be causing the perception of 'communication problems' between white and Asian speakers.

An example discussed by Gumperz (1982a) comes from a workplace in which white workers ate their lunches in a cafeteria staffed mainly by Asian workers. A customer who had chosen meat was addressed by a cafeteria worker who uttered the word *gravy*, pronouncing the word with falling intonation. The function of this utterance was to ask whether the customer wanted gravy, but it was not heard as an offer or a question. Rather it sounded like an assertion: 'this is gravy' or 'I'm giving you gravy' – which seemed rude and unnecessary, since customers could see for themselves what it was and decide for themselves whether they wanted any. Gumperz points out that British English speakers subconsciously expect offers of this kind to be pronounced with rising intonation (*gravy?*). When Asians did not produce the expected pattern, white workers inferred that they were deliberately being rude. But in Indian varieties of English, falling intonation on offers has the same meaning as rising intonation in British varieties – in other words, there is a systematic difference in the conventions used by the two groups for indicating the status of an utterance as an offer. Since neither group was explicitly aware of that difference, the result in this case was misunderstanding.

The use of rising or falling intonation to signal 'this is an offer' is an example of what Gumperz calls a 'contextualization cue'. When we speak, we have ways of conveying to the listener some quite complex information about how we intend them to treat the message: 'I am speaking to you confidentially as a trusted friend', or 'I am addressing you as a respected elder', or 'I intend this ironically, not seriously', or 'this is my main point, so listen carefully'. The means by which we communicate this kind of 'contextualizing' information include prosody (intonation, pitch and stress contrasts), paralinguistic cues (hesitation, pausing, contrasts of speed and volume, simultaneous speech), or switching to a different language, dialect, style or register for the part of the utterance we want to pick out as having a particular significance. If I am talking to someone and I do not understand their contextualization cues, I will miss part of the meaning they are trying to communicate. For instance, if I don't recognize that someone's tone of voice indicates irony, I may end up thinking they mean something different or even opposite from what they intended. If I do not pick up on the fact that speaking very softly and rapidly is meant to signal 'this is confidential and/or potentially damaging information' I may not infer that I should be careful about repeating it to others. If I cannot distinguish important from less important information using contextualization cues I will have trouble following the thread of the argument my interlocutor is making, and may wonder, 'what is the point here?'.

As a further illustration of the workings of contextualization cues, consider the following transcript of a role-play exercise devised for use in industrial language training (it is reproduced in Roberts et al. 1992: 151). The scenario involves a worker who wants to retrieve some timesheets from a colleague. In this transcript speaker A speaks Indian English and speaker B British English.

Trainees who heard a tape of this exchange – and also a tape in which the same scenario was role-played by two Anglo-British speakers – commented that the two speakers lacked rapport and that the Indian English speaker sometimes sounded 'irate' or 'slightly offensive'. Gumperz and colleagues note that 'an Asian person using

Transcription conventions: // major boundary; / minor boundary; under<u>lining</u> stress; ↑ rise in pitch; ? rising intonation.

A: excuse me David//   1
B: yeah
A: could I have those sheets <u>back</u> please//
B: those sheets?/ I put them on your desk <u>yesterday</u>//
A: haven't seen on my ↑ <u>desk</u>//   5
B: ah/ I'm <u>sure</u> I did/ I'm <u>sure</u> I did
A: no/ no/ I've not <u>seen</u> on my desk/ you're/ are you sure?
B: absolutely certain/ it said on the top/ <u>check</u>list for April// those are the ones aren't they//
A: no/ no/ not check<u>lists</u>/ I want the timesheets//   10
B: oh the timesheets// sorry/ yes/ I've got them here//

English makes much less use of tone and voice and stress than an English person. Asian English uses pitch level and rhythm . . . [it] has been much influenced by Indian languages in its use of prosody' (1979: 11). In this role-play, the negative impression commented on by trainees is produced to a large extent by the way speaker A uses *stress*, which is different from the British English way of using it.

At line 3, for instance, A says 'could I have those sheets <u>back</u> please', where the 'unmarked' British pattern would be 'could I have those <u>sheets</u> back please'. To the British ear, stressing <u>back</u> makes the request sound like an accusation – 'you took my sheets and you should give them *back*'. Then at line 10, when A has realized what the problem is – B is talking about checklists whereas A's request was for timesheets – A stresses *lists* in the word *checklists*, and puts no stress on the item which contains the really important information, *timesheets*. A British English speaker would probably use *contrastive* stress to clarify the point at issue here – something like 'no not the <u>check</u>lists, the <u>time</u>sheets'. The Indian English speaker's use of a different stress pattern makes the message confusing to the British hearer, who may wonder why *lists* is being emphasized. The impression of impoliteness conveyed by stressing *back* in 'could I have those sheets <u>back</u> please' is reinforced by the Indian English speaker's rise in pitch at 5 and his use of 'no, no' when B says 'I'm sure I did [put them on your desk]'. Rising pitch is associated by British English speakers with excitement or annoyance, while saying 'no' in this context may be heard as a suggestion that B is lying when he claims to have put the sheets on A's desk.

It is important to note here that miscommunication is not a one-way process. If discussions of crosstalk focus only on the ways in which minority speakers' behaviour deviates from majority expectations, there is a danger of simply reinforcing a perception of minority speakers as inadequate communicators. Gumperz and colleagues (1979) point out that Anglo-British interactional behaviour can baffle and irritate Asian English speakers just as much as the reverse. For instance, the way British English speakers use conventional indirectness as a marker of politeness (see Chapter 6) gives Asian English speakers the impression that white people do not say what they really mean. In the data extract above we saw an Asian speaker expressing disagreement by saying 'no, no' – a strategy that will strike many British speakers as overly blunt and thus impolite. Yet to the Asian speaker the preferred strategy of British speakers – expressing disagreeing by saying 'yes, but . . .', appears deliberately evasive. It would be hard to make a convincing argument that one group's conventions are inherently better than the other's; there is simply a difference in the degree of indirectness each considers 'normal'.

Miscommunication can result not only from variation in the use of contextualization cues, but also from conflicting assumptions about the norms and conventions of particular speech events. Roberts and colleagues (1992) cite cases where lack of familiarity with local assumptions has led Asian candidates at job interviews to make incorrect inferences about the interviewer's intentions in asking certain questions. The following is an example (Roberts et al. 1992: 131):

> A: What have you been doing since you were made redundant?
> B: Nothing

The question is actually a veiled invitation to the candidate to reassure the selectors that s/he has *not* simply been doing nothing since losing a previous job. But since this is not made explicit in the wording of the question, understanding it depends on sharing, or at least being aware of, certain culturally specific ideas about work and the lack of it. In the culture the interviewer belongs to, unemployment is often regarded less as a misfortune than as a moral failing – a sign that the unemployed person does not have the necessary 'work ethic'. Where a job applicant is not currently employed, s/he will often be expected to provide evidence that s/he is not merely idle and apathetic. But speaker B in the above exchange does not pick up on this hidden agenda; he takes it that the interviewer is concerned simply to elicit facts about his present situation, and answers accordingly (which is to say, truthfully).

'Crosstalk' between people of differing cultural backgrounds is not just a matter of surface linguistic features, then, but also (and often more importantly) of the assumptions language-users make about the kind of speech event they are participating in and what is appropriate or 'normal' in that context. Problematic exchanges like the ones just discussed provide a dramatic illustration of the point made by ethnographers of speaking and by pragmaticists – that in 'successful' communication, what is actually said is only the tip of the iceberg. Even the most seemingly straightforward interaction actually depends on a great deal of shared, tacit knowledge, both cultural and linguistic.

In this section I have explained the notion of 'contextualization' and given examples illustrating some of the problems that can arise when participants in talk do not recognize one another's intentions as evidenced by contextualization cues. I have not, however, said much about the *methods* used by analysts to investigate the workings of contextualization systematically. In the following sections I want to look more closely at two techniques that are commonly employed by interactional sociolinguists: distributional analysis and controlled elicitation of judgements on the meaning or function of particular ways of talking.

LOOKING AT DISTRIBUTION: THE CASE OF 'UPTALK'

In recent years, a particular intonation pattern in American English (it is also becoming increasingly noticeable in British English) has attracted copious and mostly negative comment. The pattern is known variously as 'uptalk', 'rising intonation', 'high rising terminals' and 'talking in questions'. What all these terms refer to is a pattern whereby declarative utterances (utterances that have the grammar of statements rather than questions or commands) are spoken with a marked rise in pitch at the end, as in 'I went to the mall today?'. This (invented) example reflects the social stereotype that has been constructed in discussions of the uptalk pattern. It is held to have originated among young women (typically in the 'Valley Girl' mould, which is to say affluent white girls who are or present themselves as shallow and unintelligent, and who do a lot of shopping). Since the function of rising intonation which is most familiar to most English-speakers is that of marking an utterance as a question or query, the use of rising intonation on statements about what the speaker believes, or has done (e.g. visited a mall), often puzzles and irritates people who do not use the pattern themselves. It is said to make the speaker sound as if s/he does not know what s/he is talking about, or as if s/he cannot express the most straightforward thought without looking to others for approval.

Negative attitudes to uptalk are not new. In 1975, the linguist Robin Lakoff drew attention to the pattern in her book *Language and Woman's Place*, which argued that women were socialized to talk in ways that lacked power, authority and confidence. Rising intonation on declarative sentences was one of the features Lakoff included in her description of 'women's language', a gendered speech-style which in her view both reflected and reproduced its users' subordinate social status. More than two decades later, the rising intonation pattern can be observed among younger speakers of both sexes (though it is still associated in popular thinking with women more than men). It continues, however, to attract negative evaluations, and has become the subject of frequent complaints from parents and teachers. In 1999, for example, the *Boston Globe* reported that several prestigious colleges and universities in the US were making a concerted effort to get rid of what the paper called 'mallspeak' among students, including their habit of using the rising intonation pattern. Professors interviewed by the *Globe* suggested that if students persisted in this way of talking as adults they would be disadvantaged in their professional lives.[3]

It is evident that older people find uptalk both irritating and difficult to see the point of – why would young people want to make every statement into a question? But this might be a case in which the function explicitly attributed to a discourse feature ('making statements into questions') is not its actual function for the speakers who use it. By studying the *distribution* of declarative utterances with rising intonation in people's naturally occurring talk, an interactional sociolinguist might be able to come up with a different account of what uptalk does or means – even though its users themselves may not be conscious of any regular pattern.

Just such an approach was taken by the linguist Cynthia McLemore in research she carried out for her PhD thesis (McLemore 1991). Since the most 'advanced' group of uptalk users appears to be young women, McLemore chose to collect data in a setting where young women form a distinct community and regularly interact on a variety of topics: a sorority.[4] She recorded a sample of interactions among sorority members and looked for distributional regularities in the incidence of uptalk. Her approach was based on two assumptions which are fundamental in any kind of sociolinguistic research. The first assumption is that there is likely to be *variation* in the use of a linguistically and socially meaningful feature. Speakers will not use rising intonation on every declarative utterance: it will be found on only some declarative utterances, while others will have the supposedly 'normal' falling intonation pattern. The second assumption is that the pattern of variation will not be random, it will be *structured*. When the analyst compares the utterances that manifest the uptalk pattern and those that do not, s/he will be able to make a generalization about the conditions under which the variant being studied (in this case rising intonation) tends to appear. It might hypothetically be correlated, for example, with the formality of the situation, the type of subject matter, the speaker's level of involvement in what s/he is saying or the speaker's status within the group.

In fact, the pattern McLemore uncovered had to do with the status of the *information* the speaker was relaying in her utterance. For McLemore's informants, falling or level intonation on a statement marked the proposition contained in that statement as something the speaker believes the hearer will be able to treat as 'given': it is a piece of shared, familiar knowledge. Rising intonation on the other hand marks a proposition as something the speaker considers important 'new' information for the hearer. For example, McLemore observed at sorority business meetings that announcements reminding participants about events or other obligations that had been discussed before were typically made with falling intonation. The implication was something like 'as you already know (or should know) . . . '. Announcements which introduced new plans, by contrast, were made with rising intonation.

Essentially, then, the alternation between rising and falling intonation on statements functioned for this community as a contextualization cue signalling the status of the information presented by speakers and the kind of attention hearers were expected to give it: 'take this information as given and/or routine' or alternatively 'take this information as new and important'. This is clearly not the function non-users of uptalk attribute to the pattern: it has nothing to do with trying to sound as if you aren't sure whether what you say is acceptable or valid.

It might be asked here, what enables someone like Cynthia McLemore to notice this kind of pattern when language-users themselves seem unable to get a fix on it, despite constant exposure to the behaviour being analysed? There are two main answers. First, if you want to uncover distributional patterns you need to look systematically at a relatively large sample of data (transcribing it and extracting every instance of the relevant variable – in this case rising versus falling intonation on statements). Second, the analyst has a better idea than the ordinary language-user of what kind of pattern s/he might be looking for. It is unlikely McLemore began her analysis with no hypotheses at all about the difference between rising and falling intonation patterns. Though she may not have recognized the relevant contrast (given versus new information) straight away, her knowledge about other kinds of variation in discourse, and about the sorts of functions intonation has in discourse, would have suggested a number (but not an infinite number) of possibilities which she could test against the data.

It is important to bear in mind, however, that the same formal feature may not serve the same purpose for every group of speakers or in every context: analysts must be attentive to what I referred to in Chapter 6 as the 'form and function problem'. I would be cautious, for instance, about assuming that McLemore's analysis of uptalk in a US sorority can just be applied without modification to the way the pattern is now used by (some) British speakers of English. We know that intonation is extremely variable across dialects of the same language; the US uptalk pattern also differentiates younger from older speakers. In the British case it is debated whether the increasing use of rising intonation on declaratives is an innovation modelled on recent/current usage in the US or whether the model is Australian English, where the feature was well established even earlier. It is also clear that some British varieties (e.g. the English spoken on Tyneside) have made use of rising, or at least non-falling, intonation on declaratives for decades – though not necessarily to serve the same purpose as more recent uses of uptalk elsewhere in Britain. In sum, the functions of any particular intonation pattern may be different in different communities.

The following activity is designed to give you practice in noticing distributional patterns and using them to work out the functions of common but 'taken-for-granted' features of spoken discourse. The activity focuses on a class of features called 'discourse markers' (Schiffrin 1987): 'little words' like *oh* and *well*, and phrases like *y'know* and *I mean*. Like uptalk, these features are often decried as marks of 'inarticulacy' and 'sloppiness' in speech. They are sometimes described as 'meaningless' and as 'fillers' (in other words, devices speakers use to 'fill out' their remarks when they do not really know what they want to say, or have nothing of substance to say). Once again, this view probably reflects the status of written language as most people's model and ideal for all language. Except in fictional dialogue, discourse markers rarely appear in writing. The fact that they are not necessary for written communication is taken to imply that they are not necessary for any kind of communication; rather they must be a regrettable consequence of people's inability to use spoken language with the same clarity, economy and precision they are able to achieve in writing. As analysts of spoken discourse, however, we have to reject the view implied by this kind of attitude, namely that speech is just an imperfect version of writing. Rather we should assume that even the smallest details of talk are functional and potentially meaningful: if something is 'there' in people's talk, then it must be there for some purpose. By looking at where a feature typically occurs, we can try to work out what purpose(s) it serves in their speech.

ACTIVITY⁵

For this activity you need about 15 minutes of recorded conversation: you may wish to use the tape you made for the transcription exercise in Chapter 3.

1   Listen to the tape, searching for instances ('tokens') of *oh, well, you know, I mean*. You are going to analyse **one** of these items. Make a checklist including all four before you start, and each time you hear a token of one of the items, place a mark beside it. The item with the most marks is the one you should choose for close analysis. Be careful, however, to distinguish discourse markers from cases where an item is being used in a different way (lexically). For example, *well* in 'she's not well' is not functioning as a discourse marker; nor is *you know* in 'you know what he's like'. It is characteristic of discourse markers that they are **detachable**: you could take them out of the utterance without changing its basic grammatical structure or its propositional meaning.

2   For each token of the discourse marker you have chosen, transcribe the segment of talk in which it occurs (this may mean more than just a single utterance or turn – how much of the surrounding talk you need to transcribe is a matter for your analytic judgement).

3   Now try to work out what the function of your chosen discourse marker is by examining what the examples that appear in your data have in common. The aim is to be **systematic** and to produce an account that will cover all your examples, or at least not be contradicted by any of them. It may be helpful to bear in mind that discourse markers are often used in connection with one or both of two conversational tasks. One is **managing information** (e.g. signalling that a proposition is 'given' or 'new' information, that it is important, surprising, etc.) and the other is **managing interpersonal relationships** (e.g. mitigating threats to face). More specifically, you should consider the following:

   • Placement and distribution: does the marker usually occur at the beginning/middle/end of a turn? Does it follow or precede a certain kind of speech act or grammatical construction (e.g. statement/declarative, question/interrogative)?
   • Context: does the marker tend to appear in a certain kind of context – e.g. when people are joking, or where there is an element of face threat? (Think about the elements of Hymes's SPEAKING grid (see Chapter 5), such as topic, purpose, key.)
   • Contrast: what is the difference between utterances in your data that do contain your marker and utterances that do not, though they are structurally/contextually similar? When would it be inappropriate/weird/impossible to insert the marker?

4   In the light of the analysis you have made, can you come up with a **generalization** about the function or meaning of your chosen discourse marker in conversation?

ELICITING SPEAKERS' JUDGEMENTS: INDIRECTNESS AND MINIMAL RESPONSES

Spoken interaction depends not only on what speakers do with language, but also on the ways in which hearers interpret their behaviour. In theory (and reality) these two aspects of communication are equally important, but an obvious problem for the analyst is that only one of them – the behaviour of the speaker – is amenable to direct observation. Evidence about the process whereby hearers attribute meaning to utterances, and indeed about the meaning they ultimately construct, is always indirect. In Chapter 7 we saw that the CA strategy for making claims about interpretation involves 'going to the next turn', the point in talk where the hearer *becomes* a speaker and produces a response to the previous speaker's utterance. That response provides evidence of how its producer took the previous turn. For instance, if A says 'hello' and B replies 'hello' then the evidence suggests that B heard A's turn as a greeting. If B replies not 'hello' but 'what is it?', however, that suggests B heard A's turn not as a greeting but as an attention-getting move.

There are cases, however, where looking at what happens next may not provide the evidence an analyst is looking for, because the hearer's interpretation of a particular utterance may only become apparent much later, or not at all. Some interactional sociolinguists try to address this by eliciting people's judgements about the meaning of (other people's) utterances. Researchers may play tapes and/or give transcripts to a sample of judges from the communities whose interpretive conventions they are investigating, and ask the judges to interpret a particular utterance, or choose between a small number of possible interpretations. They may also go on to ask the judges to explain or reconstruct the reasons why they chose the option they did.

The interactional sociolinguist Deborah Tannen used a test task to investigate cultural preferences for directness or indirectness among Greek, Greek-American and Anglo-American speakers (Tannen 1982). She constructed a scenario in which a married couple must decide whether or not to go to a party. The wife asks the husband whether he wants to go, and he responds 'OK'. The test question is what 'OK' means in this context. Has he taken his wife's question as a straightforward enquiry about his own preferences, in which case OK means 'yes, I'd like to go'? Or has he interpreted it more indirectly, as a strategy his wife uses to communicate to him that *she* would like to go, in which case 'OK' means 'I agree to your request that we should go to the party (though I don't necessarily have any active desire to go myself)'?

Tannen was interested in two possible axes of variation: ethnicity (Greek, American or Greek-American) and gender (women and men). She recruited informants from each ethnic group and presented them with the task in the form of a written questionnaire (Tannen 1982: 224). What she found was a correlation between 'Greekness' and preference for the indirect interpretation. Greeks were most likely to pick the indirect option, Anglo-Americans least likely to pick it, and Greek-Americans were intermediate between the other two groups. Tannen also found that the Anglo-Americans manifested a significant gender difference, with women being more likely than men to pick the indirect interpretation.

Deborah Tannen has investigated ethnic style in a number of contexts, but she is probably most famous today for her work on gender differences in language (Tannen 1990, 1994a). The work on ethnicity and the work on gender are connected, because Tannen's approach to gender differences treats them as being *like* ethnic or national differences. Tannen points out that as children and adolescents males and females spend most of their time interacting with peers of the same gender, learning either the rules that apply to girls' talk or those that apply to boys' talk, and on the whole remaining ignorant of the way talking is done in the other gender group. This means that when they come to interact with one another, women and men are engaging in what amounts to a form of cross-cultural communication. Like the Indian and non-Indian speakers studied by Gumperz, or the Greeks and the Americans in the indirectness study, they are likely to misunderstand one another in systematic and predictable ways.

There has been much debate on whether the comparison between gender groups and ethnic or national groups is valid or illuminating, and we will return to that question in Chapter 11. The issue which is relevant for the purposes of the present chapter is how an analyst can *identify* systematic differences in the discourse strategies used by members of two or more groups. Many of the claims that have been made in both expert and popular literature about male–female differences and male–female misunderstanding have not been subjected to the kinds of tests described above, and it is arguable that without such testing they remain matters of speculation.

One claim of this kind that has been repeated fairly frequently concerns a putative difference between women's and men's ways of using and interpreting minimal responses. In an early and influential paper proposing the gender difference/cultural difference analogy, Daniel Maltz and Ruth Borker (1982) suggested women use and interpret minimal responses like *yes* or *mm* to mean something like 'I'm listening, go on', whereas men use and interpret such minimal responses to mean 'I agree'. They suggested, further, that this difference in the function of minimal responses would explain why men have been found in a number of studies to use fewer minimal responses than women (one has occasion to signal agreement less often than one has occasion to signal that one is listening). It might also call in question the conclusion that has sometimes been drawn about men's less frequent production of minimal responses, namely that they are less supportive listeners than women. It would suggest that if women experience men's behaviour as unsupportive, that is because women mistakenly think that men are not listening or not interested, when really men are just not committing themselves to agreeing with everything other people say.

Maltz and Borker presented this as a suggestion rather than an empirical claim supported by evidence. A student of mine, Helen Reid-Thomas, decided to investigate it empirically using the method Deborah Tannen had used in her Greek/American study (Reid-Thomas 1993). However, whereas Tannen presented her judges with a written version of what the couple said, Reid-Thomas presented hers with extracts from tape-recordings of real conversations (accompanied by a transcript to ensure there were no problems in simply decoding the tape). She chose four extracts containing a minimal response whose form was semantically neutral – *mm* as opposed to, say, *yeah*, or *right*, which might bias the judges towards the 'agreement' interpretation – and asked an equal number of men and women (19 of each) to say whether the minimal response they heard would be best characterized as meaning 'I agree', 'I follow your argument', or 'I'm listening, go on'. A smaller group of ten judges were not given fixed options to choose between, but were simply asked to say in their own words what they thought *mm* in each extract meant. Below I reproduce two of the extracts, so that readers can make their own initial assessments of the function of *mm* in each. ((.) marks a short pause and ? marks rising intonation; both tokens of *mm* were realized with falling intonation.)

Extract [1]

K: In some ways the timing is quite opportune (.) you don't get this sort of offer all the time

F: I think (.) er (.) somehow I think (.) that it will probably generate (.) a (.) a little more (.) dynamism all round

K: mm

F: to have something like that

K: well obviously it's a thing for people to get their teeth into

In this extract from a conversation, do you think the listener's response 'mm' means
        I agree with you
Or   I follow your argument
Or   I'm listening to you: go on talking
        (put a tick against **one** *statement only)*

Extract [2]

M: How did you actually get (.) get a hold of the various people?

B: well (.) we were (.) you may remember we were organizing a conference

M: mm

B: and these were all people who offered papers for the conference

In this extract from a conversation, do you think the listener's response 'mm' means
        I agree with you
Or   I follow your argument
Or   I'm listening to you: go on talking
        (put a tick against **one** *statement only)*

The results of this test did not support the hypothesis that there is a systematic difference between women and men whereby women are more likely to hear *mm* as a sign of listening and men are more likely to hear it as a sign of agreement. Male and female judges showed a high degree of consensus in the choices they made for each extract; at the same time they made different choices about different extracts. For example, the *mm* in extract [1] above tended to be heard as meaning 'I agree with you' (55 per cent of judges chose this option, with a further 34 per cent opting for 'I follow your argument'), whereas the one in extract [2] was heard by 82 per cent as meaning 'I'm listening to you: go on talking'. Judges who were free to explain the meaning of *mm* in their own words came up with similar interpretations: 'yes, I agree' was a common response for extract [1], while extract [2] prompted responses including 'yes, I remember', 'carry on', 'go on', and 'I do remember that, and . . . ?'. If one looks closely at the extracts, these findings are not surprising. In the second extract, for instance, the *mm* would be hard to hear as 'agreement', since it does not follow any assertion to which the hearer could agree. It is also evident that the speaker has not finished, since the initial question ('how did you actually get a hold of the various people?') remains to be answered. Thus 'I'm listening, go on' is the most likely interpretation. In the first extract, by contrast, *mm* can more plausibly be heard as an agreement token, since it occurs at a point where the speaker has just expressed a personal opinion ('I think it will probably generate a little more dynamism all round').

It might be objected here that Reid-Thomas did not design a 'fair' test for gender differences, insofar as the extracts she chose did not lend themselves equally to the hypothetically 'masculine' and 'feminine' interpretations. But in a sense that is exactly the point of this study: the suggestion that men and women generally interpret *mm* differently is implausible precisely because any real instance of *mm* has to be interpreted in context, and the context will almost always favour one interpretation over the alternatives. Reid-Thomas's findings are consistent with the view that the judge's gender is a less significant determinant of the meaning s/he attributes to any particular occurrence of *mm* than information contained in the discourse to which *mm* is a response.

Another sociolinguist and discourse analyst who has written about minimal responses is Roger Shuy, whose comments on the subject are framed within a context where the 'small stuff' of ordinary interaction can take on unusually dramatic importance. Shuy is a 'forensic linguist' in the US, meaning he may be called upon to testify as an expert witness in cases where the charge against the accused person hinges on what that person said and what it meant. Shuy's book on this subject is titled *Language Crimes* (Shuy 1993). There are a number of crimes in which the offence is actually committed by speaking – examples include offering or accepting a bribe, or taking out a contract to do physical harm to someone. In such cases, the prosecution's evidence frequently consists of taped spoken interaction obtained by surreptitious recording. The interpretation of this evidence may however be challenged by lawyers for the defence. Often Roger Shuy's role is to suggest that the obvious common sense interpretation on which the prosecution is relying is not the only possible interpretation or even the most likely one.

In one case described by Shuy, a Japanese engineer allegedly tried to buy secrets from someone he believed to be an American company representative – who was actually an undercover agent of the FBI. Part of the conversation used in evidence went as follows (Shuy 1993: 8):

> Agent: you see, these plans are very hard to get
> Engineer: uh-huh
> Agent: I'd need to get them at night
> Engineer: uh-huh
> Agent: it's not done easily
> Engineer: uh-huh
> Agent: understand?
> Engineer: uh-huh

The prosecution argued that the engineer's use of *uh-huh* signalled his agreement to what the agent was proposing, which was an obviously illegal course of action (secretly obtaining confidential documents). Shuy points out that it may not be clear to a foreigner that obtaining plans with difficulty and at night implies anything illegal. But in any case, it is questionable whether any of the tokens of *uh-huh* in the extract above signal agreement, as opposed to polite acknowledgement of the agent's contribution. The last *uh-huh*, following the question 'understand?' could in theory mean 'yes, I understand', but it follows a whole series of *uh-huhs* which plainly do not have that function, which might lead us to suspect that the last one does not have it either. Elsewhere in the tapes, there is evidence that the Japanese speaker overgeneralizes the acknowledgement function of *uh-huh* in English, using it in positions where a native speaker would not: for instance, he produces *uh-huh* in answer to the enquiry 'how are you?'. Considered in context, then, the engineer's *uh-huh* appears to be a formulaic acknowledgement token ('I'm listening, go on') motivated by interpersonal considerations of politeness.

Roger Shuy reports on a number of instances where the application of knowledge drawn from interactional sociolinguistics has prevented, he believes, a miscarriage of justice. But he also mentions cases where judges have refused to allow him to testify, on the grounds that the jury does not need expert help to make sense of spoken discourse evidence. It is obvious to judges that juries need help interpreting the results of a post-mortem or a DNA test, since for most people pathology and genetics are unfamiliar and difficult subjects. Conversation, by contrast, is something with which everyone is familiar, and this leads to the supposition that there is nothing in taped talk that a jury would find difficult to interpret.

From the perspective of interactional sociolinguistics, or indeed of any kind of discourse analysis, this argument is partly right and partly wrong. The vast majority of people are, indeed, practised and skilled conversationalists; on the vast majority of occasions they are able to negotiate the intricacies of spoken discourse without difficulty. Typically, however, they have little conscious awareness of what the intricacies are that they are negotiating; nor do they always understand that the patterns which are natural for them may not be natural for everyone. Thus in a context like the courtroom, where someone's liberty is at stake, it is arguable that the expert does have a role to play, in suggesting to jurors that common-sense interpretations of spoken discourse evidence might be mistaken, and that they should consider alternative possibilities very carefully.

In this chapter we have focused on the kind of detail that will tend to strike most people, if they notice it at all, as fairly trivial. What meanings we should attribute to rising intonation on a statement, or falling intonation on the word *gravy*, or *OK* as a response to a suggestion, or discourse markers like *well* and *y'know*, or the minimal responses *mm* and *uh-huh* – these are not issues that ordinary language-users are apt to ponder very deeply. But as we have seen, this kind of 'small stuff' is both more important and more complicated than it might look, and it provides discourse analysts with a good deal to ponder.

SUGGESTIONS FOR FURTHER READING ABOUT INTERACTIONAL SOCIOLINGUISTICS

Deborah Schiffrin's textbook *Approaches to Discourse* (1994) contains a chapter on interactional sociolinguistics. Classic discussions of contextualization and cross-cultural (mis)communication can be found in John Gumperz's *Discourse Strategies* (1982a) and in a collection of papers he edited, *Language and Social Identity* (1982b). Other useful sources include Celia Roberts, Evelyn Davies and Tom Jupp's *Language and Discrimination* (1992) and Michael Clyne's *Intercultural Communication at Work* (1996). Deborah Tannen's scholarly work on gender differences is collected in *Gender and Discourse* (Tannen 1994a). On discourse markers, the standard text is Deborah Schiffrin's *Discourse Markers* (1987). Roger Shuy's *Language Crimes* (1993) is not exclusively a work of interactional sociolinguistics, but for those who enjoy both courtroom drama and delving into the minutiae of spoken interaction, it is a fascinating read.

NOTES

1   *Pop* and *soda* are found in different regions of North America; *juice* is common among speakers, especially younger ones, in Glasgow.
2   Another term that is sometimes used is 'cross-cultural' communication. One commentator, Aki Uchida (1998 [1992]), suggests that 'intercultural' is preferable in cases where the groups are located within the same society and are in regular contact with one another.
3   This report appeared in the *Boston Globe* (31 January 1999: A1) under the headline 'Talk is like, you know, cheapened: colleges introduce classes to clean up campus "mallspeak"'.
4   For readers unfamiliar with this type of institution, sororities are national organizations of female university students with 'chapters' (branches) located on US college campuses. The equivalent for men is called a 'fraternity'. Sorority members come together to pursue various social and charitable projects, and some of them may also live together in a house owned or leased by the sorority. They elect officers, recruit and select new members, and run their own affairs.

5   To encourage readers to approach this activity systematically and without preconceptions about what they are 'supposed to find', there are no 'answers' provided in this chapter. However, Chapter 10 includes some observations on the uses of *oh* and *well*, and frustrated readers who do not have a teacher to help them will find a full account of discourse markers' functions in English in Schiffrin (1987).

9 Hidden agendas?
Critical discourse analysis

The approaches examined in Chapters 7 and 8, CA and interactional sociolinguistics, were developed to analyse interactive talk. They are not generally applied, nor are they readily applicable, to the analysis of written texts. The approach examined in this chapter, by contrast, critical discourse analysis or CDA, can in principle be applied to both talk and text. Indeed, it is very much a 'textual' approach, which has most often been applied either to writing or to certain kinds of speech: analysts tend to work with 'institutional' rather than 'ordinary' talk, and many are particularly interested in the language of the media.

These preferences reflect CDA's concern with the 'hidden agenda' of discourse, its *ideological* dimension. This is an approach to discourse analysis in which the two senses of the term *discourse* discussed in Chapter 1 (the linguist's sense and the critical social theorist's sense) are equally relevant. The purpose of analysis is to show how discourse in its first sense (language in use) also functions as discourse in its second sense (a form of social practice that 'constructs the objects of which it purports to speak'). Institutions, including the media, are important sites for the operation of discourse in its second, ideologically significant sense, and that is why institutional and/or mediated discourse features so prominently in the work of CDA practitioners.

As I explained in Chapter 4, the 'critical' in 'critical discourse analysis' refers to a way of understanding the social world drawn from critical theory. Within that paradigm reality is understood as *constructed*, shaped by various social forces. These, however, are frequently 'naturalized' – in everyday discourse, as opposed to critical discussions of it, reality is presented not as the outcome of social practices that might be questioned or challenged, but as simply 'the way things are'. Naturalization obscures the fact that 'the way things are' is not inevitable or unchangeable. It both results from particular actions and serves particular interests. Many of the arrangements that currently regulate global trade, for example, are more congenial to rich people and rich countries than to poor people and poor countries, and they are particularly congenial to large multinational corporations. But that is not how the processes of economic 'globalization' are usually represented by mainstream commentators in politics, business and the media. Even when globalization is not presented as self-evidently a good thing, it is typically presented as an inevitable thing, with which governments, workers and consumers worldwide will have to learn to cope whether they like it or not.

Abstractions such as 'globalization' are to a significant degree grasped, made real and noticeable to us, by their representation in *language*.[1] Reality ('how things are in the world') is the most general 'object' of which discourse 'purports to speak', and the central claim of CDA is that the way certain realities get talked or written about – that is, the choices speakers and writers make in doing it – are not just random but ideologically patterned. These choices do much of the work of naturalizing particular social arrangements which serve particular interests, so that in time they may come to seem like the only possible or rational arrangements. However, the word *choice* here does not necessarily imply a deliberate decision, or a conspiracy, to represent the world in misleading or self-interested ways. From the standpoint of the language *system* a choice has been made (this word or this sentence rather than that word or that sentence), but from the standpoint of most language-users on most occasions, choice is not consciously an issue. Rather it appears obvious that this, and not that, is the most natural and neutral way to describe a given phenomenon.

DISCOURSE AND THE CONSTRUCTION OF REALITY

The Glasgow Media Group, who are sociologists rather than linguists but who approach some aspects of language in quite similar ways to CDA practitioners, provide a good illustration of naturalization through language in their early work on the media reporting of industrial disputes (Glasgow Media Group 1980; Eldridge 1995). In a sample of news reports dealing with disputes over pay and conditions in the workplace, they noticed a consistent pattern in the words that were used to describe actions taken by workers and labour unions on one hand and employers or managers on the other. The workers were described as 'demanding' more money or better conditions, and 'threatening' to walk out if their 'demands' were not met; the employers were described as 'offering' terms and as 'appealing' to workers to accept their 'offers'.

It would be possible to describe an industrial dispute by reversing this pattern, saying for instance: 'the workers *offered* to return to work in exchange for a 5 per cent pay rise, but employers *demanded* that they settle for 2 per cent'. I suspect, however, that most readers will find this way of putting the matter less 'natural' and less 'neutral' than the alternative. Attributing 'offers' to workers and 'demands' to employers will strike many people as overtly ideological, a clear sign that the speaker is on the side of the workers. Talking about workers' 'demands', however, will not necessarily be seen as an ideological gesture of support for the employers. It just seems like the obvious way to talk about an industrial dispute. (One piece of supporting evidence for this argument is that the Glasgow Media Group found the pattern in British television news reporting, which is subject to a strict requirement of political neutrality or balance: the BBC, for instance, evidently did not see its choice of words as 'biased'.) But as the Glasgow Media Group pointed out, words like 'demand' and 'threaten' carry overtones of aggression and menace, whereas words like 'offer' and 'appeal' suggest a more reasonable, conciliatory stance. The linguistic pattern found in news reporting thus naturalizes a view of industrial disputes as arising from the unreasonable and aggressive behaviour of workers. News reporters do not say explicitly that 'workers are responsible for industrial chaos', but their ways of describing reality implicitly carry that meaning.

In news reporting, only one discursive construction of reality is presented to the audience. In other kinds of discourse, by contrast, addressees are presented with *competing* constructions of reality. A case in point is judicial discourse. When a witness is examined in a courtroom, or a suspect is interrogated by police officers, the overt purpose of the interaction is to establish who did what to whom and with what intentions. This is accomplished largely through discourse: the alleged criminal act is not usually available for direct scrutiny, so judicial decisions regarding who did what and why have to be based on the accounts people give after the fact. But since judicial proceedings are adversarial, and there are conflicting interests at stake, the accounts given by different people will often represent the 'same' events in different ways. The question this raises for critical discourse analysts is whether and how a speaker's linguistic choices contribute to the judgement of their account as more or less credible than competing accounts.

The Canadian researcher Susan Ehrlich (1998) has examined this question in relation to a university disciplinary hearing and a subsequent court case dealing with a complaint of sexual assault. Two women undergraduates had brought charges against the same man, also a student, whom they previously knew as a casual acquaintance. In each case (the incidents took place two days apart), the complainant reported that she had invited the man back to her room, where he had then subjected her to unwanted sexual acts in spite of her clear unwillingness and repeated protests. As in many proceedings dealing with sexual assault and rape, particularly when the alleged attacker is known to the victim, the defence put forward by the accused ('Matt') was that the women consented to have sex. The proceedings thus turned on two competing constructions of reality: the complainants' account, in which they were forced to engage in sexual acts, and Matt's account, in which they engaged in those acts voluntarily.

Whereas the Glasgow Media Group's analysis of industrial dispute reporting focused on *lexical* (vocabulary) choices, Ehrlich's analysis of the judicial proceedings focuses on the *grammatical* resources used to construct a certain sequence of events as consensual sex rather than assault. Matt and his representatives frequently choose grammatical constructions whose effect is to downplay agency (the capacity to act freely and autonomously). They avoid describing actions for which Matt was allegedly responsible using grammatical constructions in which he is the agent of an action and the complainant's body or clothing is the object (e.g. 'I kissed her' or 'I took off her sweater'). Instead they frequently choose grammatical constructions which imply shared responsibility and thus mutual consent, such as 'we were fooling around' (a formula Matt repeats several times) and 'we started kissing'. Sometimes Matt or his lawyer uses 'agentless' constructions in which responsibility is explicitly attributed to no one. The lawyer asks, for instance: 'I take it that the sweater *was removed*?' Formulating this question in the passive leaves it unclear whether Matt removed the woman's sweater or whether she removed it herself. The complainants by contrast choose sentence structures that foreground Matt's agency: 'he took my shirt off and . . . he unclasped my bra . . . and he pulled my pants down'. Matt does not deny that the events referred to here actually occurred, nor that he participated in them, but by using reciprocal and agentless constructions to describe actions like kissing, touching and removing items of clothing, he challenges the portrayal of himself as the aggressor and the women as unwilling victims.

Ehrlich points out that Matt's way of representing events fits with the ideological belief that rape occurs because women 'lead men on' – appear willing to begin with, but then 'change their minds'. In many judicial systems it used to be part of the legal definition of rape that the woman must have shown 'utmost resistance' to a man's sexual advances, and that anything short of that might reasonably be construed as consent. This is no longer written into the law, but it persists as a common-sense assumption. Thus Matt explained to the tribunal that if a woman 'didn't say "no", didn't say "stop", didn't say, uh uh uh jump up and say "no I want you to leave", I am assuming, OK? . . . that that is consent' (Ehrlich 1998: 155).

The complainants operated on different assumptions. One of them explained why she tried to use persuasion to get Matt to stop rather than, say, pushing him away and screaming for help, by saying she was afraid he would get angry and hurt her if her resistance was any stronger. The women wanted the tribunal to understand that when you are faced with an assailant whose demeanour is threatening and who is physically stronger than you are, unequivocal refusals like 'no' and 'stop' may be assessed as too risky. From the complainants' perspective their patent lack of enthusiasm and their repeated attempts to persuade Matt to stop should have been enough to communicate to him that they did not want to have sex: 'consent' for them meant actively desiring sex rather than merely submitting to it. But while this way of understanding things would make sense within some interpretive frameworks (feminist ones, for instance), the women were not able to make their construction of reality credible and convincing in the judicial setting. The proceedings turned on questions about how Matt interpreted the women's behaviour and whether they had done enough – that is, resisted strongly enough – to make it clear they did not consent. The question of whether Matt's definition of consent was *itself* reasonable did not arise. Ehrlich sees this as one instance of a general phenomenon noted by the feminist linguist Sally McConnell-Ginet: 'men (and dominant groups generally) can be expected to have made disproportionately large contributions to the generally available background beliefs and values on which speakers and writers rely in their attempts to mean' (1988: 91). The outcome of the case, Ehrlich says, was to naturalize a definition of sexual consent that serves the interests of men rather than women.[2]

McConnell-Ginet's observation that what gets naturalized in discourse tends to be the common-sense beliefs of dominant groups is also relevant for the study of racism in discourse, as is Ehrlich's point that the beliefs in question may be *presupposed* in discourse rather than stated openly. The study of racist discourse in CDA is not usually the study of the propaganda produced by racist and fascist organizations, whose members do state their prejudices openly. This kind of discourse may, of course, be analysed critically, but as I have noted already, CDA has traditionally been most concerned with uncovering 'hidden agendas' in discourse – and in overtly racist discourse, the agenda is not hidden, but obvious. The crudest kinds of racist speech and writing are, in addition, a 'fringe' phenomenon, for in most western countries now there is a stigma attached to 'being racist'. Very few people are prepared to say that they speak 'as a racist' – even when they speak on behalf of groups that are racist by most people's definition. Recently even the Ku Klux Klan in the US has 'modernized' its image and based its public rhetoric on the notion that the organization is 'for' white people, rather than 'against' Black people. The neo-fascist political parties that have gained increasing public visibility and support in some European countries (like Austria, France and Italy) have recognized that their legitimacy as mainstream political organizations depends on avoiding the extreme language of their 1930s predecessors. In order to avoid being relegated to the fringe, proponents of racist arguments must take care to distance themselves from the stigma of 'being racist'. Critical discourse analysts have taken an interest in how this is done – that is, how racism is made 'respectable' in mainstream discourse.

The Dutch critical discourse analyst Teun van Dijk has examined the representation of race in mainstream sources including press reports, speeches made in European legislative assemblies, school textbooks, scientific and corporate discourse (van Dijk 1987, 1991, 1996). One issue that is significant is the *labelling* of the groups under discussion. It is characteristic of discourse on race that discussion is framed in a language of 'them' and 'us', with minority ethnic groups often marked as outsiders by using terms like *immigrants* and *foreigners*. In some cases these descriptions are factually accurate, but in many they are not, suggesting that facts are not the main consideration influencing the choice of label. The European-born children of immigrants, for example, are not themselves immigrants, since they did not migrate from anywhere. Referring to them as such conveys that unlike others who were born in a certain country, they do not really 'belong' there. At the same time, the term *immigrant* or *foreigner* avoids making direct reference to racial differences, and does not distinguish between members of minority communities who are structurally disadvantaged (e.g. Turkish 'guest workers' in Germany) and professional expatriates (who are typically white). This makes it possible for the politician who argues for more restrictive immigration laws, or for the denial of rights to 'foreigners', to deflect accusations of racism by saying that the issue has nothing to do with race as such.

The following extract from a report in the British popular newspaper the *Sun* illustrates a number of commonplace features of racist discourse (van Dijk 1996: 98).

BRITAIN INVADED BY AN ARMY OF ILLEGALS

Britain is being swamped by a tide of illegal immigrants so desperate for a job that they will work for a pittance in our restaurants, cafés and nightclubs.

Immigration officers are being overwhelmed with work. Last year, 2191 'illegals' were nabbed and sent back home. But there were tens of thousands more, slaving behind bars, cleaning hotel rooms and working in kitchens . . .

Illegals sneak in by:

- DECEIVING immigration officers when they are quizzed at airports.
- DISAPPEARING after their entry visas run out.
- FORGING work permits and other documents.
- RUNNING AWAY from immigrant detention centres.

Source: *Sun*, 2 February 1989

This report uses two metaphors which van Dijk found to be common in discourse on the subject of immigration: immigrants are figured as an invading army or a 'tide' threatening to 'swamp' the native population. The advent of migrants is thus likened to a military incursion or a natural disaster, which also suggests that fear and resistance are reasonable responses. Two other common features reproduced by the *Sun* are high but vague numbers (undetected illegal immigrants are said to number 'tens of thousands') and the attribution of dishonest or criminal behaviour to the group under discussion (cf. the verbs *sneak, deceive, disappear, forge, run away*).

As van Dijk notes, there are some surface indications of sympathy for the plight of the illegal immigrants, who are described as 'desperate', 'working for a pittance' and 'slaving'. However, he goes on to make the important point that what is actually communicated by a text may not be only/exactly what is explicitly said in that text. As we saw in Chapter 6, communication involves inference, and meaning is produced by placing new information in the context of existing background knowledge and established frameworks (some cognitive scientists call these 'scripts' or 'schemas') for interpretation. Here the relevant framework is one in which immigrants/foreigners pose a threat to the economic wellbeing of native workers because they are sufficiently 'desperate' to work 'for a pittance'. In other words, 'they take our jobs'. This idea is sufficiently familiar from a whole history of racist discourse that the report does not have to spell its relevance out: it can be 'cued' by a couple of significant lexical choices like *pittance* and *slaving*.

Van Dijk points out that press reports on the subject of illegal immigration very rarely make any reference to the employers who knowingly take on immigrants to work illegally, using their economic desperation and precarious legal position to exploit them by paying 'a pittance'. Logically, the actions of these employers are as much a part of the 'problem' – and just as much against the law – as the actions of the immigrants themselves. But in press reports the immigrants are consistently foregrounded while the employers are backgrounded. The *Sun* article quoted above, for instance, goes on to report that in one raid, immigration officials 'ended up taking away 13 Nigerians, all employed illegally'. The grammar of this sentence deletes the agent of the verb *employ*, focusing on the Nigerians rather than the (presumably British) businesspeople who illegally employed them.

Both this analysis of racist discourse and Susan Ehrlich's discussion of sexual assault proceedings illustrate that in analysing the ideological significance of a text, attention needs to be given not only to its surface linguistic features but also to what is *not* said, but is indirectly hinted at or presupposed as obvious. On 'sensitive' subjects like immigration or sexual violence, speakers may actively avoid stating contentious propositions 'on the record', relying on the ability of a competent addressee to infer those propositions. For instance, in the report quoted above the *Sun* makes no direct statement to the effect that immigrants are in unfair competition with native workers for a limited supply of jobs; that meaning emerges from an *interaction* between what is in the text and what is available to the reader from other sources. Among the relevant sources are other texts: rather than treating each new text as a separate and self-contained instance of communication, readers routinely make connections between the discourse they are dealing with now and the discourse they have encountered previously. Over time, as we will see, relationships among texts and discourses have become an increasing focus of interest in CDA.

In all the work we have looked at in this section, an important part of the analysis is to demonstrate the existence of consistent *patterns* in a text or set of related texts. Analysis, in other words, has to be systematic, and not just a matter of picking out isolated examples for comment. It is not any one instance, but the repetition of the same pattern in many instances and on many occasions, that does the work of naturalizing a particular view of reality. Of course, this argument does still raise questions about how the significance of a given pattern should be interpreted, and whose interpretation should be privileged. I will return to that issue at the end of the chapter.

DISCOURSE AND SOCIAL CHANGE

During the 1980s and 1990s, a number of critical discourse analysts, notably the British linguist Norman Fairclough, turned their attention to a rather different kind of project from the ones we have looked at so far. Their examination of 'language and power' or 'language and ideology' broadened out into an investigation of the role of discourse, and the manifestation *in* discourse, of ongoing and significant social changes which were increasingly being discussed by 'critical' theorists across disciplines.

The 1980s and 1990s have been analysed as a time when the social and political order that had been established after the Second World War was radically and irrevocably changed. The fall of communism and the ending of the Cold War between two global superpowers (the US and the USSR) coincided with, and enabled the spread of, a new political consensus based on liberal democracy and free market capitalism. Capitalism itself took new forms as the movement of capital across national borders was deregulated by governments which subscribed to a free market ideology. Together with the 'information revolution' made possible by new computer technology, the removal of restrictions on free movement of capital led to the development of a global market system beyond the control of any one nation state. In many western countries, the free market also became a model for non-capitalist institutions such as hospitals, schools and universities. In Britain, for example, the National Health Service (NHS) began to be managed as if it were a business – not to make a profit, but because of an assumption that all organizations work better when run on market principles. Users of public services were increasingly treated as if they were 'customers' (even when, as in the case of Britain's NHS, most people had nowhere else to take their 'custom').

What has any of this to do with discourse analysis? One answer is that social changes of this kind and magnitude are bound to manifest themselves in all areas of social life, including the way people communicate; thus studying the discourse in which people communicate during a period of major social change is one way of studying change itself. Another answer is that if an institution wants to change the relations it has traditionally had with people – for instance, to recast hospital patients or university students as 'customers' – then one of the things it has to do is instruct them in their new roles and relationships by changing the way it addresses them. Not only does this put them in the position of 'customers' in particular exchanges, arguably it has the more general effect of encouraging them to think about hospitals or universities in a 'consumerist' frame, while discouraging the use of an older, 'public service' frame. From this point of view, the emergence of new kinds of discourse is not only a *consequence* of social change, but also an *instrument* of social change.

Norman Fairclough has argued (see especially Fairclough 1992) that a number of general tendencies representing social change can be discerned in contemporary institutional discourse. One of these, which goes along with the adoption of the capitalist free market as a model for all kinds of transactions, is a tendency for discourse genres which were once primarily 'informational' to become more 'promotional' – they are no longer designed simply to 'tell', but also to *sell*. One salient way in which the shift is expressed is through the incorporation into non-commercial genres of features from the genre of commercial advertising. An example Fairclough has examined by comparing earlier and later texts is the British university prospectus. Recent prospectuses have much in common with advertising brochures in their appearance and the language they use: the reader deciding where to study is now positioned as a 'customer', for whose business the university must compete by drawing attention to its 'selling points'. Earlier prospectuses read very differently. They inform readers about the courses on offer, the admissions requirements, and so on, but pay less attention to framing this information in ways designed to appeal to the reader as a consumer.

Another notable development is the incorporation of 'therapeutic' discourse (the kind of talk found in therapy or counselling contexts) into genres which have no therapeutic function, such as job selection and appraisal interviews. Interviewees may be invited to talk about their personal attributes and feelings, strengths and weaknesses, and so on, as if the goal of the encounter were self-understanding and self-development, and as if interviewees were like clients interacting with helping professionals rather than subordinates being judged by their superiors.

This kind of borrowing from one genre of discourse to another is sometimes discussed in CDA using the notion of *intertextuality*, which is itself a term borrowed from the study of literature and other forms of artistic production. Most works of art are not 'original' in the sense of being totally unlike and unrelated to any other works of art; rather they are full of allusions to and echoes of the works that preceded them. These allusions create 'intertextual' (between texts) relationships: in alluding to other texts, an author can transfer something of those texts' qualities and their cultural significance into his or her own text.[3] Similarly, the informational document which alludes to advertising in its use of language (and other features, such as layout and graphic illustration) creates a sort of intertext or generic hybrid. It is neither purely an advertisement nor purely a digest of information, but has some of the qualities – and some of the meaning – of both.

A very general development to which Fairclough has called attention is a shift away from formal and impersonal modes of address, which affects both writing and speech. In fact, Fairclough suggests that there is a general tendency for institutional discourse, both written and spoken, to make intertextual reference to the kind of discourse that is least 'institutional': ordinary casual conversation.

Consider, for example, a telephone conversation in which I recently participated (I did not tape-record it, but wrote it down immediately afterwards. Underlining indicates emphatic stress):

Caller: hi this is Roberta from [name of a local newspaper] how're <u>you</u> doin today
DC: fine thanks but the person you want isn't here

The purpose of this call was to sell the person whose house I was staying in a subscription to the local newspaper. It was, in other words, a business (sales) call, and has some of the features one would expect in a business call (for instance, the caller states her affiliation to the newspaper in her first turn). The exchange also, however, has some features that are more typical of a personal call made by one friend or acquaintance to another. The caller uses only her first name, and she chooses a greeting formula typical of casual conversation (*hi*). Moreover, instead of introducing her business at the earliest opportunity, she finishes her first turn by uttering a formulaic enquiry ('how're <u>you</u> doin today'). In the part of the US where the exchange took place, 'how are you doing?' is as likely to be a greeting as a 'genuine' enquiry, but either way it is the first part of an adjacency pair, which requires the addressee to take the floor and produce an appropriate response. So Roberta's uttering this formula both involves me in the exchange and defers the point at which she will have a chance to move into the actual business of the call. Just as in a conversation between friends, we are apparently in no hurry to get to the point here. In fact, Roberta and I are total strangers, but her way of addressing me implies that she knows and cares about me. Had it not been for the mention of the newspaper she works for I might even have thought that I actually did know her, and racked my brains trying to remember who she was.

Of course, the mention of the newspaper gave the game away: as my contribution to the exchange shows, I knew that this was a sales call by the end of the opening turn. I was not confused by Roberta's incorporation of conversational features like first naming and informal pronunciation (*how're, doin*), or by her failure to state her business upfront, because these have become ubiquitous strategies in sales and service encounters. They exemplify an aspect of the more general 'conversationalization' of discourse which Norman Fairclough has dubbed 'synthetic personalization'. As Fairclough explains it:

> One finds techniques for efficiently and nonchalantly 'handling' people wherever one looks in the public institutions of the modern world. Equally, one finds what I shall refer to as *synthetic personalisation*, a compensatory tendency to give the impression of treating each of the people 'handled' *en masse* as an individual. Examples would be air travel (*have a nice day!*), restaurants (*Welcome to Wimpy!*) and the simulated conversation (e.g. chat shows) and *bonhomie* which litter the media. (1989: 62)

Institutional encounters tend to differ from ordinary conversation between acquainted persons (see Chapter 7), because the participants' talk is designed to accomplish institutional goals rather than to carry on a personal relationship between individuals. However, Roberta in the example above simulates personal conversation in her call to me, a stranger, because she believes, or has been instructed by her employer, that constructing personal rapport with a prospective customer is an effective way of accomplishing her institutional goal, which is to sell. I am more likely to buy, the theory goes, if I feel I am being treated *as* an individual, *by* an individual. If the seller can draw me into quasi-personal conversation using formulas like 'how're you doin today' which oblige me to respond similarly, I will find it more difficult to rebuff her at a later stage.

What are the linguistic markers of synthetic personalization in discourse? One is the frequent use of names, especially first names, and another the use of pronouns *I* and *you*. There is a preference for informal styles and registers, which connote a higher degree of intimacy or solidarity than more formal ones. These strategies could be analysed as examples of positive politeness – that is, the kind of politeness that says 'I like you' rather than the kind that says 'I don't mean to impose on you' (see Chapter 6), and positive politeness in general is extensively used in synthetically personalized talk. Roberta, for instance, does not make use of a negative politeness strategy which is sometimes used in sales talk, where the salesperson apologizes for taking up the customer's time or asks if s/he may have a moment of their time. Rather she says 'how are you doing today', a move that invites me to take up *her* time by replying.

In research on the regulation of spoken discourse in service workplaces (described in Cameron 2000a, 2000b), I found a variety of positive politeness strategies being incorporated into scripts, routines and rules for speaking to customers, with the aim of personalizing interaction. For instance, workers may be advised to create rapport by showing empathy (that is, the ability to feel *with* as well as *for* another) using minimal responses and 'mirroring' statements. One insurance company tells employees who deal with claims relating to traffic accidents that they should respond to the customer's account of what happened by saying things like 'that must have been very distressing for you'. In other contexts, it is suggested that employees should tell the customer who has a problem or a complaint: 'I know exactly what you mean' or 'the same thing happened to me', responses which use the positive politeness strategy of 'claiming common ground'. Empathy can also be displayed in the nuances of intonation and voice quality. One text on the subject of 'customer care' advises: 'If a customer comes across as cold and diffident, convince yourself that beneath the surface is a warm, caring, loving human being. Try to reach that suppressed warmth by injecting emotional warmth into your own words.'

It is not entirely clear what ideological meaning should be ascribed to the tendency for institutional talk to borrow features of 'ordinary' conversation. It could be argued that this is a manifestation in discourse of the commitment that now exists in contemporary western societies to conducting social relations on a basis of equality and solidarity rather than status and social distance. On this view, institutions are adjusting to, or playing their part in, a general shift away from the formal and hierarchical relations of the past, which are no longer felt to be appropriate, or tolerable, in a modern democracy. It could also be argued, however, that conversationalizing institutional encounters tends to *mystify* the real nature of those encounters: it reinforces the widespread belief that society is becoming more egalitarian, and so obscures the continued existence of hierarchy and inequality. The boss who addresses employees in a friendly, informal conversational style is still, in fact, their boss. The interview between a job candidate and a prospective employer, or a client and a social worker, or a student and a teacher, may resemble a casual chat, but it is not a casual chat: one party is being judged, the other is doing the judging, and their encounter will have material consequences for the less powerful participant.

One side-effect of conversationalization is to foreground the issue of *sincerity* in institutional and public discourse. When institutional encounters become personalized, and when institutional representatives are routinely encouraged to project positive *feelings* towards the strangers they deal with, the question arises of whether the feelings they express are 'sincere'. Someone who greets you with a courteous 'good morning' does not lay claim to much in the way of sincerely felt emotion, but a greeting like Roberta's 'how're you doin today?' may prompt the customer to formulate the unspoken question, 'what's it to you?'. Many customers on the receiving end of synthetically personalized talk complain about its patent insincerity, while for the producers of this kind of talk, the work involved in creating an impression of sincere concern for the customer can be a source of stress (see Cameron 2000a).

Sales and service talk are not the only kinds of institutional discourse in which sincerity is an issue. The critical media discourse analyst Martin Montgomery (1999) remarks on the increasing emphasis on sincerity in more formal kinds of public discourse too. The case he discusses in detail is the reception of various public tributes to Princess Diana following her death in a car accident in 1997. Many commentators praised the sincerity of a tribute paid on television by the British Prime Minister Tony Blair, while a television tribute paid by the Queen was felt to lack a certain authenticity and emotional depth by comparison.[4] One commentator noted that although the Queen was 'clearly moved' she was also 'very composed'. A member of the public asked to comment by a reporter assessed the speech as 'very good', but then said: 'I hope it's true that she feels it you know and these are her own words and nobody else's' (Montgomery 1999: 15–16). It appears then that the Queen's tribute was received as a performance, which left some room for doubt as to whether she was expressing her true feelings in her own words. Tony Blair's tribute evoked no such doubts; but this cannot be because Blair was not 'performing', for it is very unlikely that a prime minister addressing the nation on such an occasion would not have thought in advance about what he was going to say. As Montgomery notes, however, the use of sincerity as a criterion for judging public speech demands a kind of performance that *conceals* its own status as a performance. Rather like the Pentecostalists whose discourse we examined in Chapter 5, who claimed that their interventions were inspired by the workings of the Holy Spirit, 'sincere' speakers are understood to be moved by their feelings at a particular moment. If they are obviously performing – which implies planning or calculation – their sincerity may be called into question.

The value placed on sincerity in public speaking, Montgomery argues, is largely a product of the rise of television, an 'intimate' medium which gives viewer access to the emotions of those who address them (for instance, by showing facial expressions in close-up). If Tony Blair's tribute was judged 'more sincere' than the Queen's, that may be because Blair, whose public persona was formed in the age of television, is more skilled in meeting the demand for an intimate, personalized and apparently spontaneous form of address on camera. By contrast, the Queen acquired her public speaking skills before television became such a dominant medium. She belongs to a tradition in which formal public speech was judged mainly on the criteria of appropriateness or 'decorum'. A 'decorous' public speaker utters those sentiments which it is conventional to express in a given situation, but does not set out to create intimacy with the audience or engage in displays of spontaneous feeling. In this tradition of public speaking, it is more important to observe social convention than to express individual emotion. In her tribute to Diana, the Queen did mention feelings of shock and grief, but her speech was delivered in a decorous ('composed') manner which did not convey the same strength of feeling as Blair's performance.

ACTIVITY: 'SPEAKING SINCERELY' ABOUT THE DEATH OF PRINCESS DIANA

This activity focuses on the spoken discourse characteristics that distinguished Blair's tribute to Princess Diana as an exemplar of sincerity in public discourse. In line with the general preoccupations of critical discourse analysis, it also asks what kind of ideological work is being done by the choices Blair makes in his speech. The transcript is reproduced from Martin Montgomery's article (1999: 6) and the comments that follow it are also based largely on Montgomery's analysis.

ACTIVITY

Read the transcript below and consider the following questions. You should complete this activity before you read the discussion that follows it.

1 How and to what extent does Tony Blair's speech exemplify 'conversationalization', importing characteristics of casual, unplanned conversation into a more formal/institutional speech event?

2 What features of the speech are suggestive of a more 'rhetorical', highly planned and/or formal kind of discourse?

3 How is emotion displayed in the speech?

4 In the light of your answers to the questions above, what do you think people were responding to in the speech when they characterized Tony Blair as 'sincere'?

5 Tony Blair is not just reacting to Diana's death as a private individual but also addressing the nation as a political leader. How is that signalled in the way he constructs his tribute, and what is the ideological effect?

Transcript

Transcription conventions: (2.5) pause measured in seconds (.) hearable pause less than 0.2 seconds, / tone unit boundary, ___ tonic syllable (syllable carrying a tone, i.e. pitch movement),' prominent (stressed) but non-tonic syllable

BBC: Prime minister can we please have your reaction to the news

BLAIR: (2.5) I feel like / everyone 'else in this 'country to<u>day</u> / (0.3) / <u>utterly</u> / (0.7)
/ <u>dev</u>astated / (3.3) / our 'thoughts and <u>prayers</u> are / <u>with</u> / (.) Princess
Di'ana's <u>family</u> / (1.0) in par<u>tic</u>ular / her <u>two</u> / (1.5) <u>sons</u> / the two <u>boys</u> /
(2.5) /our 'hearts go <u>out</u> to them / (3.5) / we 'are to<u>day</u> / (2.2) a <u>nation</u>/ (0.8) /
in <u>Brit</u>ain / in a 'state of <u>shock</u> / (1.5) / in <u>mourn</u>ing/ (0.5) /<u>in</u> / (1.2) grief
(1.3) / that is so <u>deep</u>ly painful for us / (4.0) / <u>she</u> / (1.2) / was a <u>won</u>derful /
(1.3) / and a 'warm human <u>be</u>ing / (3.5)

[several lines omitted]

/ you <u>know</u> uh / (0.3) / how <u>diff</u>icult things/ <u>were</u> for her / (.) from 'time to
<u>time</u> / (1.1) / I'm 'sure we can only <u>guess</u> at / <u>but</u> (2.7) / the <u>people</u> / (.)
/ <u>every</u>where / (.) /not just / <u>here</u> in Britain/ <u>every</u>where / (1.3) / they 'kept
<u>faith</u> with Princess Diana / (1.0) / they <u>liked</u> her / they <u>loved</u> her / (2.4) / they
re<u>gard</u>ed her / (0.6) /as 'one of the <u>people</u> / (3.0) / she <u>was</u> / the 'people's
<u>prin</u>cess / (4.0) / and that's how she <u>will</u> / (1.5) / <u>stay</u> / 'how she will re<u>main</u> /
(2.3) /in our <u>hearts</u> / (.) / and in our <u>mem</u>ories / (1.0) / for <u>ev</u>er / (3.0)

Martin Montgomery suggests that the most obviously 'conversational' feature of the speech transcribed above is its lack of fluency. It is a markedly hesitant performance, containing many long pauses; furthermore, the pauses occur, as they would in casual unplanned speech, not only at major boundaries but also between smaller units of discourse. Blair's delivery thus lacks the degree of fluency we generally associate with planned performance, and this contributes to the impression that he is in the grip of strong emotions. That impression is reinforced by Blair's explicit references to emotional states, which are described in such 'extreme' terms as 'utterly devastated', 'in a state of shock', 'so deeply painful'.

The Queen's tribute – made in a live television broadcast, but on the eve of the funeral rather than immediately after the announcement of the news – gives a very different impression from Tony Blair's, as the following extract illustrates (Montgomery 1999: 14, transcription conventions as above):

QUEEN: / I <u>hope</u> that / tomorrow / we can <u>all</u> / wherever we <u>are</u> / (1.0) / join in
expressing our <u>grief</u> / (.) at Diana's <u>loss</u> / (1.0) / and <u>grat</u>itude / (.) for her all
too short <u>life</u> / (2.2) / it is a <u>chance</u> / (0.5) / to <u>show</u> / to the whole <u>world</u> /
(0.5) / the <u>Brit</u>ish / <u>na</u>tion / u<u>nit</u>ed / in <u>grief</u> / (.) and re<u>spect</u> / (2.5)

This passage consists of two complete sentences, which are also grammatically complex, containing multiple clauses: the Queen's syntax thus suggests a higher degree of planning than Blair's. Her delivery is also much less hesitant: the only pauses longer than one second mark the two sentence boundaries (and although I have reproduced only a short extract from the whole text, Montgomery finds the same pattern throughout). The longest pauses in Blair's tribute (especially the first part of it) are also used to mark major grammatical boundaries, but the fact that he also inserts relatively long pauses in other positions makes his delivery sound more spontaneous and less calculated. Many of his pauses sound like pure hesitation phenomena, whereas most of the Queen's have rhetorical functions to do with rhythm and emphasis.

Montgomery remarks on the way Blair repeatedly uses parallelism ('they liked her/they loved her'; 'in a state of shock/ in mourning/ in grief'; 'how she will stay/ how she will remain') where the terms shift from weaker to stronger (e.g. *like* to *love*) and/or from less to more formal (e.g. *stay* to *remain*). He also uses a number of conventional formulas, like 'our hearts go out to them' and 'a wonderful and a warm human being' (which is a parallelism as well as a cliché). These are rhetorical techniques, common in many genres of verbal art, which might well suggest advance planning. At the same time, ordinary unplanned discourse tends to be repetitive and formulaic: even if Blair is using parallelism for rhetorical effect, it does not detract from the overall impression of spontaneity. The Queen's use of parallelism (for instance 'grief (.) at Diana's loss and gratitude (.) for her all too short life') is, once again, more markedly rhetorical – Montgomery calls it 'measured', and links it with the tradition of public speaking which emphasizes decorum rather than overt emotional display. The paired terms are explicitly co-ordinated with *and*, and in the case just quoted even the pattern of pausing and stress is exactly the same in both phrases.

Both the absence of marked hesitation and the 'measured' use of rhetorical devices probably contributed to the assessment of the Queen as 'very composed'. No doubt it is reasonable for a tribute delivered several days after the event to be more 'composed' than one delivered only a short time after hearing the news. Nevertheless, it seems that some hearers found the Queen's performance *too* composed, and equated her measured rhetoric with a lack of deep and sincere feeling.

The political/ideological aspect of Blair's discourse that Montgomery singles out for comment is the way the Prime Minister constructs himself as voicing a collective response to the event on behalf of the whole British nation. He immediately aligns his personal reaction with the reaction of the country at large: 'I feel like everyone else in this country today'. His characterization of his own response to Diana's death – 'utterly devastated' – thus has the covert function of telling his audience how they are or ought to be feeling. From then on the pronouns that predominate in the speech are first person plural ones, *we* and *our*. This tends to imply that the attitudes expressed by Blair are common to the nation as a whole: for instance, that his invocation of religious belief ('our thoughts *and prayers*') and his assessment of the late princess as 'a wonderful and a warm human being' will naturally be shared by his compatriots.

Towards the end of the extract Blair shifts to the pronoun *they*, denoting people 'not just here in Britain' but 'everywhere', who 'liked [Princess Diana], they loved her, they regarded her as one of the people'. The word *people* is ideologically interesting here: Blair has not previously used it in connection with the nation, and when it occurs in the phrases 'one of the people' and 'the people's princess' it clearly does not mean just 'British people', but something more like 'ordinary people everywhere'. It is significant that Blair puts emphasis on the 'ordinariness' of Diana. A princess is by definition not ordinary, not just 'one of the people': the relationship of 'the people' to royalty is symbolically one of feudal subjection, not democratic equality. But by juxtaposing contradictory ideas in the phrase 'the people's princess', Blair implies that Diana, by contrast with other real or hypothetical princesses, managed to be both ordinary and exceptional, simultaneously 'one of them' and 'one of us'. Here it is worth recalling that Diana's death occurred at a moment when other members of the British royal family were attracting criticism for being arrogant, remote and out of touch with their ordinary subjects. By emphasizing that Diana was different, and that she was loved by people everywhere because of it, Tony Blair could be seen as discreetly taking a position in the ongoing debate about the monarchy.

PROBLEMS OF INTERPRETATION

It will be seen from the examples discussed in this chapter that CDA has developed over time, in terms both of its theoretical framework and of the kinds of phenomena it is interested in, but it remains essentially a form of textual analysis. Typically it involves (a) finding a regular pattern in a particular text or set of texts (involving lexis, grammar, modes of address, intertextual relations with other texts and genres, etc.), and then (b) proposing an interpretation of the pattern, an account of its meaning and ideological significance. Arguments about whether the proposed pattern is actually there or not are in most cases fairly straightforward (though analysts are sometimes accused of looking at too few examples and giving too little weight to counterexamples), but the *interpretations* proposed by CDA have led to controversy. What is the evidence, critics ask, that these are the 'correct' interpretations and not just meanings which the analyst is 'imposing' on the data because of her or his own ideological commitments (e.g. to socialism, feminism, anti-racism, and so on)?[5]

Practitioners of CA, for example, argue that an interpretation is not 'correct' if it cannot be shown to be the interpretation of the participants themselves. What an utterance means is what participants take it to mean, and what they take it to mean is evidenced in their response to it. But this assumes that the data consists of interaction among participants, in which they will have the opportunity (or indeed, the obligation) to demonstrate their understanding of a previous speaker's turn in their own next turn. When the text being analysed is something composed for presentation to a mass media audience, by contrast, the analyst will not be able to make reference to any evidence in that text of how the audience understands it. The question arises, then, of how to 'validate' a particular analysis. Do all readers of the *Sun*, for example, pick up on the presuppositions about immigrants which are identified in van Dijk's analysis of BRITAIN INVADED BY ARMY OF ILLEGALS? Did everyone who heard Tony Blair's tribute to Princess Diana feel equally implicated by his representation of Britain as a nation wracked by shock, grief and pain?

A student in one of my classes once remarked that the *Sun*'s description of immigrants using 'criminalizing' verbs such as *sneak, deceive, disappear, forge, run away* reminded him of the prisoners in the film *The Great Escape*, who are not presented as despicable criminals but as resourceful heroes. If we did not know certain 'extra-textual' facts about the editorial politics of the *Sun* – for example that it has a history of opposing non-white immigration to Britain – could we not read the report as expressing admiration for illegal immigrants who outwit the authorities? This student's challenge exemplifies a not-uncommon kind of scepticism towards CDA. Even if a critic does not suspect analysts of having their own 'hidden [political] agendas', s/he may argue that since texts can support an infinite variety of readings, and we do not have independent access to the intentions of the text producers, it is impossible to 'prove' using discourse analytic techniques that a text exemplifies a particular ideological stance.

A number of things could be said in response to this challenge. First of all, the 'infinite variety' argument should not be taken too far, for clearly it is not true that texts support *any* reading the analyst might care to produce. As Jenny Thomas points out (1995; and see Chapter 6 above), meaning-making involves *interaction* between the reader and the text: the text puts limits on what the reader can do with it. Just as 'how are things, Scott?' could not reasonably be taken by Scott as a proposal of marriage, so BRITAIN INVADED offers nothing to the analyst who wants to claim that the *Sun* reproduces sexism, or homophobia, or an obsession with football. To anyone familiar with the *Sun* these are all quite plausible claims, but they find no support in this particular piece of discourse.

Second, it is important, as I have said already, to pay close and systematic attention to the *whole* text, bearing in mind that it may contain internal contradictions. The BRITAIN INVADED text may appear simple, but on inspection it offers more than one frame for interpretation. As we noted above, some lexical choices (*desperate, pittance, slaving*) suggest a frame in which the immigrants are victims of exploitation; this is in tension with the frame in which they themselves are exploiting the host society (signalled by metaphors of invasion and swamping). There is also a slight undercurrent of 'jokiness' (cf. colloquial expressions like *nabbed* and *sneak in*), which appears at odds with the serious point about the 'problem' of illegal immigration. A convincing analysis of this text would have to acknowledge there is linguistic evidence for several contrasting stances: the issue would then be how to decide what effects the juxtaposition has and which, if any, is the dominant interpretive frame.

On that issue, we would surely acknowledge some arguments as better than others (i.e. it is not 'just a matter of opinion'). For example, someone who argued that the dominant frame was an 'anti-immigrant' one might point to the significance, in this genre (that is, popular tabloid news reporting) of the headline, as that part of an article which most clearly sets its agenda (in this case, not an agenda sympathetic to the immigrants). This would be a discourse analytic argument, relating the text to general properties of its discourse genre (the importance of headlines in framing news reports is widely accepted by analysts of media discourse). Another kind of potentially relevant argument might be based on statistical evidence about what frame dominates the reporting of race and immigration issues in popular news texts generally. This kind of evidence derives not from close linguistic analysis of a small corpus of texts but from 'content analysis' of a large corpus. Content analysts have claimed (and van Dijk reports a similar pattern in his own fairly large corpus of racist discourse) that news reports dealing with minority ethnic groups are overwhelmingly framed in terms of *problems*, particularly crime and violence (rather than, say, the enterprise and cultural contributions of migrant groups). This observation could be adduced to support the argument that BRITAIN INVADED is most likely to be placed in the 'immigrants are a problem' frame, that being the frame most familiar to *Sun* readers from previous experience.

Even then, though, it has to be conceded that there is always potential for variation in the reception of a text by its actual readers. To describe the ideological frame(s) a text offers is not to say (and certainly not to 'prove') that all or most recipients actually interpret it in a particular way. As my sceptical student's 'Great Escape' challenge shows, it is not impossible that someone could read BRITAIN INVADED and think 'good for the illegal immigrants!'. (Or, 'I blame the employers', or 'what a skilful piece of racist journalism', or any number of other things.) What the analyst has to explain is why a number of different meanings (but not, as noted earlier, just any meaning whatsoever) can be made from the same text. Explaining this could involve teasing out internal contradictions in the text, but it could also involve making use of insights from pragmatics which take us beyond the text. Pragmaticists argue that variations in interpretation are an inevitable consequence of the fact that communication involves inference, and inference requires the mobilization of background knowledge, which may differ significantly from person to person – or vary systematically among groups of people. The text itself remains the same, but if different recipients bring different assumptions and beliefs to the process of making meaning from it, the result will be differing interpretations.

This point is illustrated in Ulrike Meinhof and Kay Richardson's study of a television documentary series titled 'Breadline Britain', whose subject was poverty in Britain in the 1990s (Meinhof and Richardson 1994). Meinhof's textual analysis of 'Breadline Britain' is supplemented by Richardson's account of an audience study in which she investigated how particular viewers of the programme interpreted and judged its representation of poverty. Richardson set up focus groups in which people watched and then discussed selected parts of the series. The groups were made up of members of several pre-existing organizations, including a branch of the Townswomen's Guild (a social organization for middle-class women), a Citizen's Advice Bureau (a voluntary organization providing free advice on various social and legal problems) and a 'grass-roots' support group for single parents. Richardson found that these different groups produced differing interpretations. The Townswomen were more inclined to think that the programme presented poverty too uncritically, that the people shown were not 'really' poor or that their poverty was the consequence of their own inadequacy, than either the Citizen's Advice Bureau volunteers, who had encountered many poor people in their advice sessions, or the single parents, many of whom had experienced poverty themselves. Meaning, then, was not only in the text itself, but was affected by what viewers brought to bear on it from their own knowledge and experience.

Of course, Richardson does not claim to have uncovered the entire range of possible interpretations of the text. Her study tells us only about the interpretations produced by the particular groups in her sample (and it may also be relevant that those groups were interacting in a particular context, that of a research encounter – I discuss this issue further in Chapter 10). Nevertheless, the focus group study enables Richardson to say something about the meaning and ideological significance of 'Breadline Britain' for a selection of real viewers in a concrete situation. The members of Richardson's groups may not represent 'everyone', but they do represent *someone*, whereas the idealized reader of many purely textual analyses is open to the criticism that s/he represents no one, and has simply been invented for the analyst's convenience.

CDA has tended to prompt particularly sharp criticism because of its openly 'committed' agenda, which challenges the orthodox academic belief in objective and neutral description. But you do not have to be opposed to committed scholarship per se to find some of the criticisms levelled against CDA worth taking seriously. In this discussion I have attempted to argue that reading off the ideological significance of discourse on the basis of textual analysis alone is a problematic proceeding. I have suggested that the analysis is enriched, and the risk of making overly subjective or sweeping claims reduced, by going beyond the single text to examine other related texts and to explore the actual interpretations their recipients make of them. This latter point reflects a principle that informs the discussion throughout this book, since it is central to the study of language in use: *all* discourse, and all communication, is fundamentally interactive. In the next chapter, we will consider the implications of that for social researchers who work with spoken discourse.

SUGGESTIONS FOR FURTHER READING ABOUT CRITICAL DISCOURSE ANALYSIS

There is no single 'orthodox' version of CDA, and to get a sense of the range of work done under this heading, readers should look at the work of more than one scholar or 'tendency'. Carmen Caldas-Coulthard and Malcolm Coulthard's collection *Texts and Practices* (1996) contains work by a number of analysts, including some of the best-known names but also representing some diversity of national and cultural contexts. One approach that has become influential, particularly in the UK, can be tracked through the various works of Norman Fairclough (1989, 1992, 1995a, 1995b), while another very influential figure is Teun van Dijk (1987, 1991, 1993). Though CDA has adherents in many parts of the world, it is better known and more widely practised in Australia, continental Europe and the UK than it is in the US. One US-based discourse analyst whose work is broadly in the 'critical' tradition is James Paul Gee, whose approach is outlined in his book *An Introduction to Discourse Analysis* (1999).

Finally, a general issue which readers may have found themselves pondering at various points in this chapter is the relationship between language, thought and reality. The postulate of 'linguistic relativity' (what we take to be real is 'relative' to the language we use to represent it) is obviously relevant to the project of CDA. As Michael Stubbs (1997) observes, CDA reworks the classical relativist idea that different languages may lead their speakers to embrace radically different worldviews, suggesting that different patterns of usage in a single language may have a similar effect. For readers who want to pursue this much-disputed issue at a more theoretical level, thoughtful recent treatments of linguistic relativity include Lucy (1992) and Gumperz and Levinson (1996).

NOTES

1   There are, of course, other media of representation, and 'naturalization' can occur through visual images, or through a combination of language and images. The idea of 'famine' as a kind of natural disaster, caused by food shortage rather than the global economic systems that distribute resources unequally, has probably been constructed as much by images of starving children in television reports on famines as by any amount of talk or written text.

2   The disciplinary panel found that Matt's behaviour had fallen short of the standards expected in the university community, but rejected the proposal that he should be expelled (instead they barred him from university dormitories). In court Matt was found guilty on one count of sexual assault but acquitted on the other.

3   As an example, consider the Quentin Tarantino movie *Pulp Fiction*. 'Pulp fiction' was the disparaging name given to the sort of 'trashy' novels (e.g. about crime) which were printed on very cheap paper (hence 'pulp') and were popular in the first half of the twentieth century. The movie is not a novel, nor does it belong to the period of pulp fiction, nor is it trash (it is artfully made and became a critical success), but titling it *Pulp Fiction* points the viewer who 'gets' the reference to the possibility that Tarantino is reworking, in a different time and medium, the conventions of the pulp fiction narrative. Thus the cultural meaning of 'pulp fiction' becomes part of the meaning of *Pulp Fiction*. (And possibly vice versa, for people who encounter the earlier genre after they have seen the Tarantino movie.)

4   A third tribute, the eulogy delivered at Diana's funeral by her brother Earl Spencer, attracted some controversy. While its sincerity was widely remarked on (indeed certain passages were applauded by the congregation – a very unusual occurrence at a funeral in Westminster Abbey), some commentators found it inappropriate to the occasion, because it did not just praise the dead princess but also criticized various parties (including journalists, paparazzi and the royal family) for the way they had treated her in life.

5   One critic who has pursued this issue vigorously is Henry Widdowson (see in particular Widdowson 1995). The journal in which Widdowson's critique of CDA appeared subsequently published a response from Norman Fairclough and a further rejoinder by Widdowson. This exchange can be found in vols 4 and 5 of *Language and Literature*. For a more sympathetic critical discussion of CDA see Stubbs (1997).

III Applications

10 Working with spoken discourse in social research

I began this book by quoting the observation that 'life is in many ways a series of conversations', going on to point out that for many social researchers, studying people's talk is not an end in itself, but a means for studying other aspects of their lives. The interpretation of spoken discourse data as a source of evidence about people's lives is the central concern of this chapter. An argument that runs through the discussion is that research subjects' talk is not just 'data', it is also *discourse*, and there is something to be gained by approaching it *as* discourse, using the insights and techniques of discourse analysis.

The talk social researchers work with may, of course, be 'naturally occurring' in the sense explained in Chapter 1, but in this chapter I will concentrate on the kinds of talk that are elicited specifically for research purposes, such as interview talk and group discussion. I will also make some observations on spoken narrative, since research subjects often produce stories in the course of a research encounter,[1] and in some kinds of social research, such as oral history, eliciting extended narratives may be an explicit aim in interviewing. In the discussion that follows we consider how the evidence research subjects provide when they interact with a researcher may be enabled, constrained, and in general shaped by the fact that what is going on is a particular kind of talk.

'Approaching data as discourse' does not necessarily require the researcher to undertake a lot of highly technical linguistic analysis: I am not suggesting that everyone who works with talk, whatever their academic discipline, needs to be an expert on the minutiae of spoken language. Outside linguistics, those minutiae are only relevant insofar as they affect the interpretation of data in ways that matter for a particular piece of research. Since the research aims of a sociologist, say, are likely to be different from those of a linguist, their analytic procedures may also legitimately differ. Nevertheless, there is one significant point analysts of any kind of talk need to bear in mind: that *talk is always designed by those who produce it for the context in which it occurs*. In the words of Ian Hutchby and Robin Wooffitt, 'it is not the case that respondents are simply imparting information to a passive recipient' (1998: 201). Rather they are actively constructing the accounts they give for a certain kind of recipient in a particular situation. Let us pursue this point first of all by looking at some of the characteristics of the research encounter.

THE RESEARCH ENCOUNTER AS A SPEECH EVENT

However 'conversational' the tone of an interview or a focus group discussion, it is not just any encounter between just any two or more people, nor is it the case that just anything can be discussed in just any way. Rather it is a certain kind of speech event, an encounter that takes place for a particular purpose among persons who are playing particular roles, and which is conducted according to certain more or less well-defined conventions. Its characteristics will accordingly be shaped by what participants take its purpose to be, how they interpret their roles and how they understand the norms for producing and interpreting talk.

The sociolinguist Nessa Wolfson (1976) tells a cautionary tale about her attempts to conduct 'unstructured interviews' in a community in Philadelphia. What Wolfson was interested in was the use of the 'historic present' (retelling past events in the present tense, as in 'so last week she comes into my office and she tells me there's been an accident'). In the hope of eliciting stories in which this variable might occur, and knowing that the historic present tends to occur particularly where people are very involved in telling a story, she tried to encourage her informants to talk at length about subjects that interested them. Unfortunately for her, though, this way of proceeding struck many of those she spoke to as a deviation from the form of a 'proper' interview. Interviews, as far as they were concerned, were not 'unstructured', but structured around a series of questions asked by the interviewer, to which respondents were supposed to provide relevant answers. Some of them clearly thought that Wolfson was just incompetent: they suggested she come back when she had decided what she really wanted to know.

The anthropologist Charles Briggs (1986) provides a different kind of example in which the interviewer's understanding of what is happening differs from the understandings of interviewees. For Briggs's subjects, members of a Spanish-speaking Mexicano community in New Mexico, the 'research interview' was not a culturally recognized speech event at all, and they clearly did not define the nature and purpose of the transaction in the same way Briggs himself did. 'Even though fieldworkers may define the situation as a focus on the explicit transmission of data', Briggs remarks, 'respondents may see the process as entertainment, pedagogy, obtaining cash income, protecting his or her neighbors from outside scrutiny, and so forth' (1986: 49). In his own case, some of the informants he was closest to were senior to him in age; following community norms regarding the behaviour of older people towards younger and less experienced ones, they treated his questions as opportunities to instruct him in the ways of the community. Since the ways of the community were what he was interested in, the resulting interactions were not irrelevant, but they were often frustrating nevertheless. Because the informants adopted a parental/pedagogic role and cast the ethnographer in the role of child/pupil, they considered it their prerogative, not his, to decide how much and what kind of information was relevant at any given point. As Briggs points out, an illuminating analysis of the resulting data would need to take account of the fact that informants saw what they were doing not as 'answering an expert's questions' (the typical western definition of a research interview) but as 'educating a young and ignorant newcomer'.

Briggs is also critical of the way social scientists often treat interview data at the analysis stage, noting that 'the usual practice . . . consists of extracting statements that pertain to a given theme. . . . These responses are then juxtaposed, yielding a composite picture of things that seem to go together in the eyes of the researcher on the basis of referential, decontextualized content' (1986: 102). What Briggs is talking about here is the tendency to treat informants' talk as primarily a 'container' for information, paying attention to *what* is said in a stretch of transcript but not how it is said or how it fits into the overall flow of the event. As he points out, many social scientists code their data (nowadays often with the aid of computer software) in order to be able to retrieve chunks of talk from different interviews or different parts of the same interview, take them out of their original locations in the interaction and put them together in a new location. Typically, this kind of analysis groups sequences of talk on the basis that they are *referentially* linked, that is, the speakers who produced them were apparently talking *about* 'the same thing'.

The crucial difference between this way of proceeding and almost any kind of discourse analysis is that discourse analysts do not treat language, especially spoken interactive discourse, as exclusively or even mainly referential. The reason it is important to consider communicative acts in their original context is, precisely, that they will always and inevitably be performing functions other than just referring to states of affairs in the world. Of course speakers do refer to states of affairs in the world when they talk, but at the same time they are deeply concerned with such non-referential tasks as the management of relationships with others involved in the interaction and the construction of identities for themselves. As we saw in Chapter 6, the desire to maintain one's own and others' 'face' – an interpersonal consideration – often overrides referential considerations like being informative, truthful and relevant. This principle operates in research encounters just as it does in other kinds of interaction. By extracting research subjects' talk from the interactional context in which it was produced (separating an answer from the question that elicited it, or a story from the talk that led up to it), analysts risk losing sight of the interpersonal factors that motivated the informant to produce just that response at just that moment.

GIVING AN ACCOUNT OF YOURSELF

One motivation that is often relevant in research encounters is the desire of informants to present themselves as certain kinds of people. The questions they are asked in many kinds of social research implicitly or explicitly require them to 'give an account of themselves' – to display to a researcher their experiences, their opinions, their attitudes and their feelings. Inviting people to do this is at least potentially a face-threatening act (see Chapter 6). It is both an imposition (a threat to negative face), and an act which risks exposing the informant to negative judgement (a threat to positive face). Methodology texts place emphasis on what researchers can do to manage the risks involved in asking people 'personal' questions; but analysts must also pay attention to the way *informants* try to manage the risk in designing the answers they give to those questions. As I pointed out in Chapter 1, no one ever answers a question without thinking about the other's motive for asking it and their likely reception of various possible responses. I illustrated the point by noting that answers to questions from health professionals about how much the respondent drinks are almost invariably oriented to the probability that the questioner disapproves of 'excessive' drinking. (Conversely, there are contexts in which people will orient to the opposite possibility, and exaggerate the amount they drink.) The answers people produce to questions about their experiences, habits, affiliations, opinions and preferences are not just designed to convey relevant factual information, then, but also very often to address what the respondent rightly or wrongly believes to be the intentions and preconceptions *behind* the question.

The social psychologist Susan Condor (2000) carried out interviews with English people from a variety of backgrounds, in which she tried to elicit their views about 'this country' (a phrase she employed deliberately because she was interested in whether they would spontaneously name the country 'Britain' or 'England'). A striking feature of the interview data she collected was the apparent reluctance of many informants to engage with her questions in a straightforward manner. Here is one of the extracts Condor reproduces (2000: 185):

Transcription conventions: I interviewer; R respondent. (2) pause in seconds (.) hearable pause less than a second; [simultaneous speech; : lengthened segment; [heh heh] chuckling within talk; underline stress; ? rising intonation; ° quote intonation; = latching (no gap or overlap between adjacent turns)

```
I:   so what d'you think about this country?                                    1
     (2)
R:   what do you mean?
     (1)
I:   well um just say something about (.) what you think this is like (1) as a country
     (1)
R:   what I think?
I:   yes (2) just tell me something in your own words (1) what you think          5
     (2)
R:   you mean anything that typically (.) typically [British
I:                                                   [yea
R:   the food [heh heh heh]
I:   yea
R:   and there's (1) we::ll (.) there's this stereotype of (1) of how it's (.) like (.)    10
     like we've got a long history and (.) and tradition and all that (.) people still
     'drink tea in the afternoons' and 'policemen ride bicycles' and we're all (.)
     old fashioned (.) and then there's things like of course we always lose at sport
     and (.) I suppose that one's true (.) [heh heh]
```

That the question is received as problematic is signalled by the long pauses before the respondent's first two replies and the fact that her first three turns focus on clarifying the task itself ('what do you mean?', 'what I think?', 'you mean anything . . . typically British?'). Then, when the respondent begins to answer the question, she begins with a reply which is marked as non-serious by chuckling. She goes on to produce a collection of what she explicitly describes as 'stereotypes' about British people having 'a long history and tradition and all that', drinking tea, putting police officers on bicycles and losing at sport. The tea-drinking and bicycling observations are ironized by the use of an intonation that signals one is quoting some other source, and the respondent's final comment 'I suppose that one's true', delivered with a chuckle, marks every generalization except the one about losing at sport as *un*true. Condor observes that the respondent adopts the role of a 'relayer' (the term is the sociologist Erving Goffman's), someone who does not speak for herself but just relays the views of others – in this case those unspecified others who subscribe to various stereotypical beliefs about the English. So although she produces a number of observations about 'this country', the respondent uses various strategies to distance herself from them.

This kind of distancing occurred frequently in Condor's corpus of interviews. Informants commonly received the initial question with long pauses, requests for clarification or replies like 'I don't know'; many adopted the 'relayer' role, producing stereotypes from which they distanced themselves by laughing or using quoting intonation. In other cases stereotypical attitudes were attributed explicitly to some other person, to whom the speakers just as explicitly contrasted themselves. One respondent said, for instance, 'my dad is very British . . . he hates foreigners he'll only eat British food and things like this (.) but uh (.) I'll try anything . . . ' (Condor 2000: 191). People who wished to express positive views about 'this country' sometimes prefaced them with quasi-apologies like the following (Condor 2000: 189):

> R: well (.) I don't know if I'm allowed to say this (.) [but
> I: [it's OK you can say anything
>   you want (.) I don't mind=
> R: =OK then (.) speaking in general terms now of course (.) I know that's a
>   stereotype but I do think it's true on the whole y'know the j the justice system
>   and all that [heh heh] and I like that our police don't have guns (1) not like
>   in America where they shoot people at the drop of a hat [heh heh heh]

This speaker is at pains to mark the opinion he is about to express as something one might not be 'allowed to say', and as a generalization or stereotype which might not be universally valid. Evidently he anticipates that his praising British justice or comparing British police officers favourably with their US counterparts might be negatively evaluated by the interviewer.

Condor suggests that the responses given by English people to her questions about 'this country' are designed in the knowledge that expressing pro-English sentiments is commonly equated with xenophobic ('foreigner-hating') or racist attitudes.

Whether or not they make that equation themselves, interviewees have to reckon with the possibility that positive comments about England and Englishness may be taken by others (including the researcher) as evidence of xenophobia/racism. Since few people wish to present themselves publicly as racists, questions about 'this country' present respondents with an interactional dilemma. If they make no reference to what is clearly common knowledge about how England and the English are perceived, they may come off as ignorant or disingenuous; but if they seem to endorse the stereotypes uncritically they will come off as prejudiced. The solution is to display awareness of stereotypical representations of Englishness by alluding to them, but in such a way as to make clear that the speaker her/himself is not that kind of English person.

Condor's research may not provide an 'objective' picture of what her informants 'really think' about 'this country', but the interesting point revealed by her analysis is that so many English people both recognize and resist the discourse in which 'proud to be English' implies 'racist and xenophobic'. That discourse is powerful enough to shape the answers they give the researcher (or withhold from her), but they are able to use various interactional resources to avoid being personally identified with it. This study provides one example of discourse analysis producing insights that other research methods might not. For instance, if Condor had presented people with a list of written statements about 'this country', asking them to indicate their agreement/disagreement, the interactional dilemma the issue presented would not have been 'visible' in her data.

Another example comes from a study for which the researcher, Sue Widdicombe, carried out interviews with members of youth subcultures – punks, goths, skinheads – in Britain, focusing on why young people join groups of this kind (the study is described in Widdicombe and Wooffitt 1995). Approaching subculture members who were highly visible as such because of the way they looked, the interviewer asked them first to describe their style or appearance – a question designed to elicit a subcultural self-identification such as 'I'm a punk'. But while some respondents did produce that kind of answer, others behaved more like Susan Condor's informants. Consider for instance the following extract (it is reproduced in Hutchby and Wooffitt 1998: 180):

> I: how would you descri:be (.) yourself and your appearance and so on
> (.)
> R: describe my appearance
> I: yeah
> (1)
> R: su- su- slightly longer than average hair

As in Condor's data, there is noticeable hesitation throughout this sequence, and the respondent begins not by answering the question but by confirming that the interviewer has asked for a description of his appearance. When the interviewer confirms that this is indeed the case, there is another pause and the respondent then provides a description which suggests his appearance is in no way remarkable: 'slightly longer than average hair'. In another interview involving two young people, the question 'can you tell me something about your style and the way you look' is followed by a lengthy pause. When the interviewer follows up with 'how would you describe yourselves', there is a further silence which eventually ends when one respondent says: 'I dunno I hate those sorts of questions'.

Some analytic approaches would take the replies just quoted at face value: for instance, the first respondent's answer might be analysed as suggesting genuine confusion about what the interviewer wanted, and the second respondent's answer might be coded as a 'don't know'. But Wooffitt and Widdicombe treat these replies as calculated, designed to do a particular kind of interactional work. They argue that in resisting or challenging the demand for answers identifying them as 'a punk' or 'a goth', young people were marking their objection to what they took to be a common view of subculture members as exotics or 'weirdos'. The strategies they used were designed to make the point that underneath the make-up and the mohicans[2] they were really 'just like anyone else'. By representing the interviewer's concern with their appearance as extraordinary, subculture members presented themselves as the opposite, ordinary. Like Susan Condor's informants, these young people were concerned to manage the way the interviewer *categorized* them. Informants in both studies knew that they were potentially categorizable in ways that carry a stigma (as 'a typical English racist' or 'one of those mindless punks'), and they designed their responses to questions which they took to be based on that presupposition to pre-empt or problematize the categorization.

TELLING STORIES

Another study in which Robin Wooffitt was the researcher involved interviewing people about their experiences of the paranormal – encounters with poltergeists, visitations by the spirits of dead relatives, and so on (Wooffitt 1992). On this topic, the most obvious self-presentational problem informants have to manage is credibility: as they well know, many or most people do not believe in the existence of supernatural entities and are inclined to judge others who do as dupes, cranks or lunatics. Wooffitt found that people's stories about paranormal events were often structured in a particular way. The narration of the actual event – such as a poltergeist suddenly manifesting itself – would be preceded by a series of utterances describing particularly mundane details, such as 'I was sat on a chair' or 'I was going through the doorway'. He suggests that this is a deliberate design feature of stories about the paranormal, and its purpose is to deflect sceptical challenges to the effect that the speaker had the experience because s/he was in a highly emotional state, or that s/he cannot distinguish between reality and fantasy. By situating the central, startling event in a flow of very routine events, the narrator claims credibility as a normal, even dull person whose account of a non-normal occurrence should therefore be taken seriously (see Hutchby and Wooffitt 1998: 186–201).

Juxtaposing startling events with banal ones also increases the dramatic effect. Consider this example (Hutchby and Wooffitt 1998: 195):

> *Transcription conventions:* (1) pause in seconds, (.) hearable pause less than 0.2 seconds, :: lengthened segment, (( )) nonverbal behaviour, __ emphatic stress, hh audible outbreath
>
> ah came home from work at lunchtime (1)
> an I walked into the sitting room door (.)
> in through the sitting room door (1.5)
> an:: right in front of me (.)
> was a sort of alcove (.)
> and a chimney breast (.)
> like this (0.7) ((pointing to wall))
> and a photograph of our wedding (1)
> came off the top shelf (0.2)
> <u>floated</u> down to the ground
> hh completely came apart
> but didn't break

One striking feature of this sequence (although I concede I am working from the published transcript only, and not the tape) is the number and length of pauses it contains. Right up until the moment when the paranormal event is reported ('<u>floated</u> down to the ground' – before that we are not sure anything remarkable has happened, since the photograph could simply have fallen), the narrator pauses – sometimes for a second or more, which is a long time in talk – at every clause boundary (and some phrase boundaries too). This might suggest that the narrator is artfully building up suspense, particularly given that when the moment of revelation does arrive, the three last clauses are delivered without further pausing. The piling on of mundane details (coming home for lunch, walking through a door, seeing an alcove and a chimney breast in front of you) is an effective strategy for creating anticipation in the listener. On the basis that such commonplace experiences are not worth recounting for their own sake, listeners infer that the narrator is working up to some experience that *is* worth recounting, and wait for all to be revealed. Researchers who elicit narrative material from informants should bear in mind that oral narrative is an 'artful' speech genre, and choices about how to tell a story may be made for aesthetic as well as other reasons.

Probably the best-known and most influential discourse analytic account of spoken narrative structure is that given by Labov and Waletzsky (1967; see also Labov 1972b), and their approach may have some uses for social researchers dealing with data in the form of narrative. The prototypical spoken narrative, these analysts claim, falls into a series of sections which can be identified by their linguistic characteristics as well as their place and function in the story:

1 **Abstract:** a clause summarizing the point of the story/how it is supposed to be taken

2 **Orientation:** a series of clauses filling in background information, for instance the characters, location and time of the story. Often (though not always) these clauses have verbs which denote states rather than actions, like 'there's a woman lives up the road' or 'it was September 1976'

3 **Complicating action:** a series of clauses each of which describes an event. The clause order is understood to represent the order of events in reality, so this section moves the story forward in time from the beginning to the end. Complicating action clauses have action verbs, typically in the past tense.

4 **Coda:** a section that shifts to present time-reference to restate the meaning or moral of the story. In addition, Labov and Waletzsky note the important point that throughout the narrative it is possible to find

5 **Evaluations:** talk in which the action has temporarily been suspended and the narrator comments on the action from outside the story world. This may be signalled by a shift of tense, away from the narrative time-frame.

Another of Wooffitt's paranormal stories illustrates this structure (Hutchby and Wooffitt 1998: 195–6). I have modified the transcript to eliminate non-structural details (for instance, re-spellings representing pronunciation) while bringing out the structure more clearly (for instance by laying the text out clause by clause, since the clause is Labov and Waletzsky's unit of analysis). Solid lines indicate the section boundaries (though the narrative, at least as represented in the published source, has no coda), and italics are used for evaluations.

---

1 It's quite funny actually

_____ *abstract*

2 cuz there's somebody up the road
3 I was talking to and uh (0.2)
4 she reckoned that uh he
5 he bought the house bought er bought it off his sister (0.5)

_____ *orientation*

6 and his sister was uh getting ready one night to go out
7 *she hadn't been drinking*
8 and the hairspray *apparently* lifted itself up
9 and went to the other side of the dressing table

_____ *complicating action*

For researchers dealing with narrative material, one of Labov and Waletzsky's most useful insights is that some parts of a story (its abstract, coda and any interpolated evaluation sequences) do not advance the action, but are designed to convey how the narrator from her/his present perspective views the events being related. As such, they merit particular attention, for they contain important clues about how the narrator wants the story to be understood, and by implication, perhaps, *why* it is being told.

In the story above, for instance, the narrator in clause 7 shifts *back* from the point where the action begins – with the sister getting ready to go out – to tell us that prior to the action, the sister 'hadn't been drinking'. The narrator suspends the action to make clear that whatever happens next should not be written off as merely a drunken hallucination. Again, in clause 8, the narrator interpolates an evaluation (this time into an action clause) by saying that 'the hairspray *apparently* lifted itself up' (my italics), whereas the same event could have been reported by saying just 'the hairspray lifted itself up'. *Apparently* is a comment on the action rather than part of it, and reminds the listener that the narrator did not personally witness the event in question. (People often append *apparently* to a piece of information they obtained at second hand, such as 'they're getting married, apparently', or 'apparently she was furious'.) In *apparently* we have an indication that the narrator may not wish to be understood as absolutely committed to this version of events. In 'she hadn't been drinking' on the other hand the implication is that the narrator is not committed to the opposite view either – the story is not wholly fantastic or deluded. Together, then, the two evaluations offer valuable information about the narrator's stance (neither unduly credulous nor unduly sceptical) in relation to the events the story concerns.

FOCUSING ON FORM

The interpolation of evaluations in narrative sequences functions like the contextualization cues discussed in Chapter 8 – by displaying the narrator's stance towards the events s/he is relating, it cues the recipient to make particular inferences which are relevant in interpreting the meaning of the story and/or the narrator's motive for telling it. To get at this kind of information, it may be necessary to pay attention to the form as well as the content of talk (for example, to look closely at shifts of tense and time reference). Indeed, this is an important consideration in all discourse analysis, not just narrative analysis: important contextualizing information may be carried by small details that are easily overlooked because they have little or no *referential* content.

The nurse-researcher Christine Webb interviewed women about their experiences of hysterectomy. One of the extracts she quotes from the transcript of an interview begins like this (Webb 1984: 252):

INTERVIEWER: Did he explain the operation to you?
SUBJECT: To tell the truth, this man was very arrogant and offhand.
                        [response continues]

It is worth posing two questions about the form of the subject's utterance – questions it might not ordinarily occur to a medical researcher to ask. First, why does the subject not answer the question directly? She is asked whether 'he' – the doctor – explained the procedure she was about to undergo, but the reply she provides is not an affirmative or negative answer to that question, it is a (very negative) general assessment of the doctor's personality and behaviour. The rest of her quite lengthy reply does not resolve the issue of whether he made any effort to explain the operation, though it is not difficult to infer that he did not in her view provide a satisfactory explanation. A researcher might not consider the 'mismatch' between question and answer significant – indeed, if s/he extracted the answer from the flow of interaction in the manner criticized by Briggs (see above, pages 146–7), the issue of its relationship to the preceding question might disappear from view altogether. But is there something to be said about that issue?

Second, what does it mean that the subject prefaces her assessment of the doctor with the formulaic expression 'to tell the truth'? A researcher might feel that this is just one of those clichéd 'filler' phrases which people insert into their discourse for no special reason: the 'meat' of the reply, the part you would want to code, is in the proposition 'this man was very arrogant and offhand'. But as I noted in Chapter 8, the discourse analyst's assumption is that this kind of small and apparently insignificant feature is found in spoken interaction for a reason. What kind of work might it be doing here?

The subject's response turns out to be the preface to a narrative about her encounter with the doctor, in which she represents herself as 'petrified' and him as totally insensitive. In Labov and Waletzky's terms it is an *abstract*, and as such it conveys to the interviewer what the subject thinks the central issue is: not simply whether the doctor explained the operation but more generally his arrogant and offhand attitude. The doctor's (unstated but inferrable) failure to provide a satisfactory explanation is one symptom of a 'deeper' problem, and the subject designs her reply to foreground that problem – a strategy which implicitly challenges the interviewer's somewhat narrower view of what is relevant.

What about the formula 'to tell the truth'? The default assumption, as we saw in the discussion of the 'co-operative principle' in Chapter 6, is that speakers' contributions represent the truth as they see it. Since a declaration that one is not telling lies is more information than a co-operative conversationalist requires – the point is normally taken as read – the subject's prefatory comment could be interpreted as implicating that maybe she is *not* going to tell the truth in what follows. However, the content of her following remark, a disparaging assessment of the doctor's behaviour and personality, suggests a rather different interpretation of 'to tell the truth', as a sort of justification-cum-apology for having to represent another person in such unflattering terms. The subject here is 'giving an account of herself' as a person who understands the rules of politeness; she wants the interviewer to understand that the doctor's arrogance was so extreme as to override the normal order in which politeness takes priority over truthfulness. The work the formulaic preface does here is to indicate that the subject views the act she is about to perform – criticizing the doctor – as a distasteful but necessary task.

Formulaic prefaces very often have the function of indicating a stance towards the information that follows and the recipient of that information. In the extract above, for instance, 'to tell the truth' conveys something like 'I am about to tell you something courtesy might normally require me to suppress'. In context, as I have argued, this is a way of emphasizing just how offhand and arrogant the informant took the doctor to be. Other common formulas work in comparable ways. The discourse marker *well,* for instance, which is commonly found prefacing answers to interview questions, is often used to indicate that the respondent does not entirely agree with the presuppositions of the question, or that s/he suspects the answer s/he is about to provide is not exactly what the questioner expects or wants. *Oh* as a preface can indicate that the previous contribution has been received as new or surprising information. Sometimes it prefaces a disagreement or a rejection of an account offered by the previous speaker, as in a (constructed) sequence like: 'so did you feel you were being exploited?', 'oh, no, they never exploited us'. Here, *oh* conveys something like 'not only am I going to reject your account, I'm surprised you should have been thinking along those lines'. If the response were 'well, no, they never exploited us', the implication might be rather different: an acknowledgement that the speaker does not entirely accept the proffered account, but can see how someone else might have come up with it.

The hedges in the last few sentences (*can, might*) are because the precise meaning of any particular preface will be dependent on the specific context in which it occurs; but the important point is that it does mean something, rather than being mere 'filler'. Looking carefully at these small aspects of discourse may provide support for an interpretation the analyst is considering, or otherwise tell the analyst something potentially useful about what is going on in a piece of talk.

DISCOURSES IN DISCOURSE: ANALYSING 'CONTRADICTIONS'

It is not uncommon for informants in the course of an interview or a group discussion to give more than one account of the same thing, and sometimes these accounts may appear to contradict one another. Even in a single continuous sequence of talk, the speaker may begin by advancing one view and end up at what seems to be the opposite view. If one takes the position, traditional in many kinds of research, that interviewing and other qualitative methods are techniques for getting at individual subjects' 'true' experiences, attitudes and beliefs, then this is a puzzle or a problem. Which of the accounts is the 'true' one, if any? What is causing an informant to 'misrepresent' matters in some or all of what s/he says? Is s/he confused or uncertain about the issue under discussion?

Discourse analysis offers an alternative way of thinking about 'contradictions'. In Chapter 1 I quoted Jay Lemke's remark that:

> We speak with the voices of our communities, and to the extent that we have individual voices, we fashion them out of the social voices already available to us, appropriating the words of others to speak a word of our own. (1995: 24–5)

I noted that discourse analysis could be considered a method for studying the 'social voices' (or, to use the term preferred by followers of Michel Foucault, whose meaning in this context is not dissimilar (see Chapter 1), the *discourses*) that are available to a community. It need not surprise us, nor trouble us, if one individual draws on more than one of the 'social voices'/ 'discourses' available to them in the course of a research encounter. Indeed, we have already examined some cases in which individuals were seen to do this. The English people, punks and believers in paranormal phenomena discussed above all faced interactional dilemmas which essentially arose from the existence of competing discourses (for instance one discourse in which ghosts exist and another in which they do not). To manage these dilemmas they had to draw, at least indirectly, on more than one of the available discourses. By speaking in more than one voice, social actors are providing evidence about their multiple ways of understanding the world. Arguably, 'normal' understandings *are* multiple and shifting rather than unitary and fixed. Traditional research methods have attracted criticism for treating evidence of multiplicity, such as contradictory accounts, as 'flaws' in the data to be eliminated by developing 'better' research instruments or interview techniques. Contradictions in informants' spoken discourse, these critics argue, are often particularly interesting and valuable data.

Elizabeth Frazer (1992) carried out research with groups of high school age young women to investigate how their experiences and perceptions were shaped by the interactions of gender, class and race. One of the groups consisted of young women who attended a private boarding school. They were all white and most were from the upper classes of British society (Frazer had approached the school precisely because she wanted this highly privileged social stratum to be represented in her sample). In one discussion, when Frazer had posed a question about what kinds of girls would not 'fit in' at the school, she noticed that group members had produced a particularly contradictory kind of discourse. Some participants repeatedly offered conflicting views within the space of a few minutes; the discussion became strikingly incoherent, and some participants became extremely distressed.

The group suggested a number of reasons why a girl might not fit in to their community – for instance, if she wore white socks and had a name like 'Sharon'. These are characteristics stereotypically associated with British working-class culture, and in picking them out as things that would prevent someone being accepted, the group was describing a form of class prejudice. The contradictions appeared when they turned to the subject of who held this prejudice and why. Frazer suggests that they were drawing on more than one way of understanding and speaking about class differences and class relationships; but the conditions of the research encounter (which required speakers to explain and justify their positions) brought underlying tensions and contradictions to the surface.

Frazer identifies two main discourses in the girls' talk about class. On one hand, they used an 'individualist' discourse in which class prejudice was attributed to the stupidity and ignorance of certain individuals – by implication, not including the members of this particular group (Frazer 1992: 103–4):

> EF: why Sharon?
> Arabella: oh it's just a name that some people
> Kate: it's a name that a lot of people look down on
> Sara: yes but I don't agree with that, I think it's just people's individual opinions
>   here, I think that half this form wouldn't take a second's notice, it's just the
>   half with all their stupid prejudices . . .

In this sequence, the participants refer to the category of prejudiced individuals using the phrases 'some people', 'a lot of people', 'the half with all their stupid prejudices'. They disagree about what proportion of their peers subscribe to prejudice, but no one suggests that everyone is implicated in it, or that it is essentially a collective view determined by one's own class position rather than 'just people's individual opinions'. At other times, however, the young women used a discourse in which they implicitly recognized that class prejudice had a systemic nature and that they themselves were not unaffected by it.

> Kate: but most of the people down in the working cl . . . well
> Sara: yes, just when we walk in, just because we're [name of school] girls if we
>   walk into [nearest town] when we're wearing uniform
> Annabel: yes they're shouting
> Sara: tripping us up
> Kate: we've got these people with milk bottles threatening to smash them in our
>   faces

In this sequence, there is a very literal polarization of 'them' and 'us'. 'They' shout, trip 'us' up, threaten to smash milk bottles in 'our' faces, just because 'we' are recognizable as pupils at a certain school (which is also to say, as members of a certain class). The pronouns *we/us/our* and *they* clearly index contrasting class affiliations – they do not refer to random collections of individuals expressing their own idiosyncratic opinions. This way of talking contradicts the earlier claim that class is something this group of young women 'wouldn't take a second's notice [of]'. Yet the same informants, Kate and Sara, are major contributors to both the sequences reproduced above.

The two discourses identified by Frazer embody ways of thinking about class which are fundamentally incompatible (one says that only stupid and ignorant people would take any notice of class, the other suggests that class differences are unavoidably salient and produce real hostility). In Frazer's analysis, both the incoherence of the discussion and the distress it caused arose from the participants' inability to reconcile their two ways of talking.

Frazer points out that there are discourses which no one in the conversation seemed to have access to – those that place class, race and gender in some kind of political framework, socialism and feminism for example. Thus participants could not interpret their experiences of class-based hostility in terms of wider social structures that might have made the issue both more understandable and less 'personal' to them. Other, less privileged groups Frazer worked with had other ways of talking available to them. For instance, one group drawn from a local (non-private) school ended their involvement with Frazer by producing, at their own suggestion, a version of a teenage girls' photo-story magazine. This text combined two discourses they had drawn on in their talk during the research: a discourse which appropriated the 'voice' of the magazines themselves, which they took pleasure in reading regularly, but also a 'feminist' discourse in which they pointed out the unrealistic, 'soppy' and sexist nature of the same magazines, showing that they did not in fact read them uncritically. One of Frazer's conclusions was that the discourses circulating in society as a whole are unevenly distributed across different social groups: what Lemke calls 'the voices of our communities' may be multiple and internally contradictory voices, but they are still *particular* voices, distinctive combinations of possible ways of speaking.

In the next chapter, we will return to the issue of 'multiplicity' in discourse in a somewhat different guise, as we consider the construction – or in interactive discourse, the *co*-construction – of *identities* by participants in talk. We will also consider in more detail an issue that has been mentioned only in passing in this chapter: the fact that many kinds of talk are 'asymmetrical' and may involve differences of power between participants. Identity, difference and power relations are topics investigated by many social researchers, and in many cases, perhaps most, they also affect the actual research encounter. In Chapter 11, then, we consider how identity, difference and power can be located in spoken interaction using the techniques of discourse analysis.

SUGGESTIONS FOR FURTHER READING ABOUT WORKING WITH SPOKEN DISCOURSE IN SOCIAL RESEARCH

Any textbook on qualitative research methods is in some sense also a book about working with spoken discourse in social research. One such text that focuses on the analytic phase (as opposed to the design and data collection phases) is David Silverman's *Interpreting Qualitative Data* (1993). For feminist researchers, a comprehensive resource that includes relevant material is Shulamit Reinharz's *Feminist Methods in Social Research* (1992). Other texts consider the pros and cons of using discourse analysis as a method in a particular academic discipline, or on a particular kind of research data. Arguments for discourse analysis as a legitimate and useful method in social psychology are set out in Jonathan Potter and Margaret Wetherell's *Discourse and Psychology* (1987). Sue Wilkinson and Celia Kitzinger's *Feminism and Discourse* (1995), also written by and for social psychologists, takes up the question whether discourse analysis is, as some have argued, a particularly appropriate method in feminist research. Shirley Brice Heath (2000) summarizes the contribution discourse studies, as well as other kinds of linguistics, have made to educational research. Rosaline Barbour and Jenny Kitzinger (1999) have edited a book about the possibilities and problems associated with using focus groups in social research, which contains an interesting discussion of focus group talk by Greg Myers and Phil Macnaghten. Anthropologist Charles Briggs's book *Learning How to Ask* (1986) deals with problems of interviewing across cultures, while Hutchby and Wooffitt's *Conversation Analysis* (1998) contains a useful chapter on the applications of CA to interview talk.

NOTES

1   Throughout this chapter I refer to any interaction that takes place for purposes of research as a 'research encounter', using more specific terms like 'interview' to denote particular kinds of research encounter.
2   A 'mohican' is the British name for a hairstyle worn by some punks. The sides of the head are cropped or shaved and the hair in the centre is made to stick up in a series of spikes. The hair may also be dramatically coloured. In the US this style is known as a 'mohawk'.

11 Identity, difference and power: locating social relations in talk

If 'life is in many ways a series of conversations', it is by no means an irrelevant or insignificant fact that those conversations take place among persons who occupy certain places in the world and have certain kinds of social relationships with one another. They are not all the same, nor are they all necessarily equal in any given social situation. Language using is among the social practices through which people assert their identities – who they are or take themselves to be – and distinguish themselves from others who are 'different'.[1] It is also among the social practices through which people enact relations of domination and subordination. Discourse (language in use), then, is a resource for understanding how identity and difference, or/and dominance, are constructed (or in various other theoretical terminologies, 'done', 'accomplished', 'performed') in verbal interaction – in the routine transactions of an institution, say, or the mundane exchanges of everyday life.

A number of the chapters in the 'Approaches' section made reference to discourse analytic work in which identity, difference and power were at issue. In the chapter about CA (Chapter 7), for example, we considered Sandra Harris's research on talk in magistrates' courts (Harris 1984). In this case the powerless position of defendants relative to magistrates is not just reflected, but to a considerable extent established and maintained, by an unequal distribution of interactional rights and responsibilities: one key inequality is that defendants are obliged to answer questions but prohibited from asking them. In the following chapter about interactional sociolinguistics (Chapter 8), I gave a number of examples illustrating 'intercultural' communication between people of different races, ethnicities, nationalities or genders. Issues of identity and difference are foregrounded in such encounters; power is also relevant, since although the misunderstandings studied by interactional sociolinguists may reinforce prejudices and stereotypes on both sides, relations between the 'sides' themselves – majority and minority ethnic groups, or women and men – are not necessarily symmetrical and equal. An effect of intercultural misunderstanding, therefore, is to reproduce not merely certain individuals' prejudiced attitudes, but the larger societal structures of racism or sexism. CDA, an approach which is very overtly concerned with issues of power (see Chapter 9), might say that racist and sexist discourses are both reproduced and naturalized in the interpretation of, say, Black people's communicative styles as 'disrespectful' and women's styles as 'lacking authority'.

Yet the discussion in Chapters 7–9 also made clear that identity, difference and power are contentious issues within discourse analysis. There are CA practitioners who, because of their commitment to ethnomethodological perspectives on the social world, are unwilling to look to general structural phenomena like 'male dominance' or 'racism' for interpretations of data. There are interactional sociolinguists, an example being Deborah Tannen in her work on gender differences, who believe variation is simply a matter of culture and has no necessary connection with social inequality. (The social problem as Tannen sees it lies not in the fact of difference itself, but in the fact that many people are unaware or intolerant of difference.) There are discourse analysts like Henry Widdowson (1995) who charge practitioners of CDA with imposing interpretations on data to fit their own ideological presuppositions. In this chapter I look more closely at the questions raised by these debates – *how* can one locate the workings of power or identity in discourse data? – and examine some of the research in which discourse analysts have tried to answer those questions.

ASYMMETRICAL ENCOUNTERS: LOCATING POWER

Discourse analysts using a range of approaches have often addressed the issue of power by focusing on kinds of interaction in which participants are positioned 'asymmetrically'. One party, that is, has responsibility for the conduct of talk, while the others have less control over it.[2] This is the case in many kinds of institutional talk, including for instance courtroom discourse, classroom discourse and interaction between doctors and patients. In some cases, research is undertaken, or commissioned, because the degree of asymmetry between participants in a particular kind of institutional talk is seen as a problem for the institution itself. Do the patterns of talk observed in courtrooms, classrooms and clinics serve those institutions' goals of delivering justice, enhancing learning and successfully treating illness? If they do not, is that an argument for changing the norms of institutional interaction (for instance by training teachers or doctors to use different discourse strategies)?

Sandra Harris's work on magistrates' courts, cited in Chapter 7, illustrates one common feature of asymmetrical talk: an unequal distribution of *speaking rights and obligations*. Courtroom defendants may not speak unless they are spoken to, but when they are spoken to they *must* speak, and what they say must conform, moreover, to the dominant party's definition of an acceptable contribution. Another setting where power is enacted using similar means is the classroom, where it is typically the prerogative of teachers to ask questions and also to evaluate the answers they elicit. Pupils may be encouraged to ask their teachers certain kinds of questions, but they are certainly not encouraged to pass judgement on the answers they receive ('very good, miss'): that would be impertinence. It is also teachers rather than pupils who decide what is talked about and who allocate turns to other speakers.

It would be inaccurate to suppose that asymmetry only affects institutional talk, however. In a classic study of heterosexual couples' domestic talk, Pamela Fishman described a very unequal distribution between women and men, not of rights so much as *responsibilities* (Fishman 1983). Women asked more questions and made more conversational moves whose function was to initiate talk on a certain topic, but it was men who essentially determined what was talked about by either accepting or rejecting the topics women proffered. Fishman analysed this asymmetry as the result of a gendered division of labour, similar to the division of domestic labour (housework) in most households, whereby women took responsibility for the 'menial' work of interaction. If they wanted the benefits of conversation with their partners, women had to be prepared to do the work of finding something the man was willing to talk about, and then asking questions to keep talk going. According to this analysis, women in heterosexual couples have responsibility for the conduct of talk, but it is men who ultimately control its direction.

If you are interested in questions of power in discourse, it is always worth asking, in relation to your data, the question 'who is allowed, or obliged, to say what, and when?'. But speaking rights and obligations are not the only aspect of interaction where power and inequality may be located. Ian Hutchby, a practitioner of CA, has studied the organization of talk between hosts and callers on radio phone-in programmes. In a discussion of his data, Hutchby (1996) argues that the power of the host in this context is not just a matter of his speaking rights and obligations (though these are one relevant consideration). Rather it is dependent on the host's ability to exploit the existence of certain *sequential* regularities in phone-in talk.

The phone-in programmes Hutchby studied featured argumentative talk on topical or controversial subjects. Hutchby observes that in argumentative exchanges involving two participants, there are advantages in taking the *second* turn rather than the first. The first speaker is obliged to state an opinion on the topic under discussion; the second speaker, however, does not have to advance an opinion of their own, but can choose to develop the argument by taking issue with what the first speaker said. Speaking first puts you in a defending position subsequently, while speaking second puts you in an attacking position. Second speakers can win the argument by undermining their opponent's case; they are not obliged to produce a convincing alternative.

Phone-in hosts exploit this second turn advantage. They do take the first turn in the opening of each interaction, but they use it only to identify the caller and invite them to state their view. In Hutchby's data sample, the host's next turn was typically used to comment on the caller's contribution, and a move hosts often made was to challenge the relevance of what the caller had just said. In this example (Hutchby 1996: 489) a caller is complaining about the number of appeals she receives from charitable organizations:

Transcription conventions: lengthened segment, (0.2) pause in seconds, ? rising intonation, . falling intonation, hh audible outbreath, CAPS loud, [simultaneous speech.

Caller: I: have got three appeals letters here this week (0.4) all a:skin for donations. (0.2) .hh two: from tho:se that I: always contribute to anywa:y

Host: yes?

Caller: .hh but I expect to get a lot mo:re

Host: so?

The host uses his first turn to encourage the caller to continue, but his second turn, 'so?', is an argumentative move – one that returns the floor to the caller and challenges her to explain or justify the relevance of what she is saying. The host implicitly evaluates the caller's contribution as less than clear and convincing, and also controls the progress of the interaction, without having to produce any substantive comment on the subject under discussion, the tactics of charities soliciting money from the public.

There were, however, cases where callers succeeded in getting the second turn advantage for themselves. In this extract (Hutchby 1996: 492), the caller is complaining about the use of taxpayers' money to pay for luxurious accommodation for a member of the Royal Family making a visit to another country:

Caller: WE'RE paying that money for her to stay there and I think it's obscene.
Host: Well we're not actually paying th[e the money
Caller: [well who:s paying for it.
Host: Well thee:: e:rm I imagine the the: r the money the Royal Family has h is
         paying for it

By choosing to make a substantive point of his own ('we're not actually paying the money'), the host 'gives away' his advantage, enabling the caller to do to him what he has previously done to her – that is, challenge his point and return the floor to him using a question ('well who's paying for it'). That this move puts the host on the defensive is evident from his use of hesitation and hedging ('well', 'I imagine') in his next turn. Later, the caller issues a further challenge that picks up on the vague and hesitant quality of this reply, to the effect that the host is not sure that the Royal Family rather than the taxpayer is footing the bill: 'you're only imagining that she's paying for herself you don't know either do you' (Hutchby 1996: 494). On the basis of examples like this, Hutchby argues that if the host loses the advantage of his sequential position in the exchange, he will find it difficult to exercise the power and control which are supposedly his by institutional right. This analysis fits neatly with the more general argument to which many CA practitioners are committed, that things like 'power' and 'control' must be constructed locally by the participants in an interaction.

In some cases, power may be exercised not in following the rules of institutional talk, but rather in *breaking* those rules. Sylvia Shaw (2000) has drawn attention to this point in a study of the speech behaviour of men and women Members of Parliament (MPs) in debates in the British House of Commons. The House of Commons has a set of highly codified and rather arcane rules regulating who may speak when, how, and about what. For example, it is a fundamental rule that contributions to a debate can only be made by an MP who is standing up; calling out comments from one's seat is prohibited. The person who has responsibility for enforcing this and other rules is called the Speaker (note the initial capital letter: the distinction between the Speaker and the speaker will be important in the following discussion). The Speaker has the right (and obligation) to call MPs to speak, and to censure them if they break the rules. The other participants, MPs themselves, are supposed to be positioned as interactional equals. One notable asymmetry does exist: the MP who is currently speaking is in a position of power relative to others who wish to claim the floor. MPs claim the floor from a current speaker by requesting them to 'give way'. When this happens, though, it is the prerogative of the MP who is already speaking either to grant the 'give way' request or refuse it: s/he has no obligation to cede the floor.[3] Nor, if s/he does give way, has s/he ceded the floor altogether. 'Give way' interventions are not speeches in their own right, but interventions in someone else's speech. At the end of the intervention the original speaker still has the floor and is entitled to resume speaking.

Officially, the House of Commons debate is very much an 'F1' in Carole Edelsky's terms (Edelsky 1981; and see Chapter 7), where 'one speaker speaks at a time' and there are strict rules governing the allocation of speaking turns. Unofficially, however – as anyone will recognize who has watched this institution's proceedings on television – MPs are constantly breaking the rules by making comments from a sitting position while the official floor is held by someone else. Some of these comments are akin to minimal responses in conversation: they are formulaic collective utterances such as 'hear hear!' (which signals agreement or approval) or 'shame!' (which signals disagreement or disapproval). Other comments, however, are substantive interventions by individuals in the official speaker's speech. In theory such interventions are censured by the Speaker as soon as s/he becomes aware of them; and they are not recorded systematically in the official proceedings of the House (a document called 'Hansard'). However, the fact that they are recognized as 'illegal' does not necessarily mean they are inconsequential. Those present during the debate get information through both the official and the unofficial channel. Contributions made 'unofficially' may impact on the proceedings by influencing the reception of the official contributions they are addressed to, or by putting the official speaker off their stride, or on occasion by introducing through the unofficial channel a point that is subsequently taken up in the official one.

In a close study of floor organization in five debates, Shaw found that male MPs were far more likely than women to make 'illegal' interventions in other people's speeches. This was not simply one manifestation of a general reluctance on women's part to intervene at all. It was specifically the 'illegal' interventions that women appeared to avoid. Shaw also found that in practice, these interventions were rarely censured by the Speaker. Rule-breakers, in consequence, were able to claim a larger share of the 'real' floor (as opposed to the 'official' one) than people who stuck closely to the rules. Men, more than women, seemed both to recognize and to exploit the fact that certain kinds of rule-breaking are treated as normal and acceptable.

In the following extract from Shaw's data, the subject under discussion is whether a proposed legal amendment lowering the age of consent for homosexual sex (making it equal to the age of consent for heterosexuals) has the 'hidden agenda' of ceding the UK Parliament's control over such matters to the institutions of the European Union. The amendment was supported by the governing Labour party, which was generally pro-European as well as somewhat sympathetic to gay rights, while the opposition Conservative party was dominated by a strongly anti-European faction and was also against the lowering of the age of consent for homosexuals.[4]

Transcription conventions: CMP = currently speaking MP, IMP = intervening MP, f = female, m = male, L = Labour, C = Conservative, LD = liberal democrat [political party affiliation], (Give way) = turn is part of a legal intervention, (.) = short (less than 1 second) pause, __ = stress , CAPS = nonverbal behaviour

CMPf (C):   it is very significant that this has not taken place (.) there is an element
            in my view of deceit in the way in which this legislation has been
            protect er presented in this house
IMPm(L):   would the right honourable lady give way
CMPf (C):   I will
IMPm(L):   (Give way) has the honourable lady been asleep for the last two years?
            the European Court of Human Rights have ordered us to change our
            laws we have to we have to change the law
IMPm(C):   rubbish
IMPm(L):   (Give way contd.) the honourable gentleman from his lazing position
            says rubbish (.) unfortunately life is life (.) and life says we've got to
            change the law and we're doing it (.) it's not there is no hidden agenda
            there
IMPm(C):   of course there is
IMPm(L):   (Give way contd.) oh rubbish Winterton (.) you really are a silly man
MPs: LAUGHTER
CMPf(C):   gentlemen (.)
IMPm(C):   no more silly than you
CMPf (C):   I'm really I'm as aware as he is that there's been a debate on the issue
            from that perspective and that the honourable gentleman opposite has
            made his (.) contribution to some extent but that does not alter the fact
            that we are still here debating (.) what is going in this case to be
            domestic legislation

Here the first 'official' speaker is a woman belonging to the Conservative opposition party. When she finishes her point she is asked to give way by a male MP representing the government party, and agrees to do so. The man begins speaking and is assailed by a cry of 'rubbish' from another opposition MP, a move to whose 'illegal' status he draws attention ('the honourable member from his lazing position says rubbish' – that is, the speaker is sitting down and thus breaking the rule which states that official contributions must be made from a standing position). When the illegal intervener persists, however, contradicting the assertion that 'there is no hidden agenda there', the legal speaker chooses to deal with this by addressing the culprit directly, saying 'oh rubbish Winterton you really are a silly man'. Although this remark comes from the 'legal' holder of the floor, its *form* breaches another House of Commons rule, which decrees that all references to others must be made in the third person ('the honourable member . . . says rubbish' rather than 'you say rubbish'). The MP thus criticized responds in kind: 'no more silly than you'. At this point the talk has become an exchange between two men who are both in breach of the rules, and the attention of MPs in general is focused on this exchange, as is suggested by their laughter in response to the 'silly man' comment. The original, female speaker has been marginalized, and is forced to appeal to the two other speakers ('gentlemen') in a bid to recapture the floor. At no point in this sequence does the Speaker intervene to point out breaches of official procedure.

Shaw found other examples in which illegal contributions by or exchanges between men had the effect of sidelining women who were in the middle of making a speech. She also noted that illegal contributions were not always ignored (as they effectively are in the example just cited), but often elicited a direct response from the 'legal' floorholder. Another extract from the age of consent debate illustrates this (and also shows that some women do break the rules). Here the illegal intervention, phrased as a question ('how do they know?'), comes from an opponent of the proposal under discussion, whereas the current speaker supports it; the question is therefore heard as a challenge, to which the speaker promptly responds.

CMPm(LD):	the council of the BMA which is not a radical organization was unanimous in its recommendation of a of a unified age of consent at 16 for the very reason that it would er er reduce the spread of HIV among young people
IMPf (C):	how do they know?
CMPm(LD):	well they do know from other places that where you criminalize an activity and drive it underground you are not able to get the information you are entitled to

It seems, then, that MPs can influence a debate (as opposed to merely disrupting it) by breaking the rules. Again this suggests that rule-breaking can be a source of power, giving the rule-breaker access to influence through two channels, the official and the unofficial, rather than just one. And since women in the House of Commons exploit that potential less than men do, Shaw concludes that they are, in that context, disempowered by comparison with men.

DOMINANCE AND/OR DIFFERENCE

Sylvia Shaw's findings raise a question that has been much disputed in the study of language and gender. The question is whether systematic differences in the interactional behaviour of women and men should be explained as an effect of hierarchical gender relations (that is, male *dominance*), or whether they are better seen as the outcome of quasi-cultural *differences*, which may happen to disadvantage one group in a particular situation, but are not 'caused' by gender inequality as such. The pattern analysed by Shaw is not a case in which men are knowingly and wilfully setting out to dominate women; it is produced, rather, by women's not taking advantage of a possibility (gaining extra turns and exerting influence by breaking the official rules) which men more routinely exploit. The question might arise, then, of how we explain the women's behaviour. Do they feel *unable* to intervene in the same ways as men (for instance because women as a subordinate group lack confidence, or because they believe they would not 'get away with it'), or do they simply not wish to intervene in these ways (for instance because women are less concerned with status and point-scoring)?

Sylvia Shaw's evidence points to both accounts as potentially relevant. In her sample women who broke the rules often did not get away with it: the Speaker intervened to point out their breaches of procedure. However, gender is not the only variable that might be influencing this pattern: others are status (whether an MP holds a ministerial post or not) and seniority (how long someone has been an MP). Women until the 1997 British General Election were a very small minority in the House of Commons, and therefore most women MPs have neither high status nor seniority. It may not be just their gender, then, that makes it harder for them to be successful rule-breakers.

On the other hand, when Shaw interviewed women MPs, some did explicitly tell her that they consciously avoided behaving in certain ways which they knew were acceptable in practice even though they were illegal in theory. Some, for instance, did not join in the collective cheering and jeering that is such a noticeable feature of exchanges in the House of Commons, and expressed disapproval of other women who did. The behaviours they avoided were ones they associated strongly with a particular kind of masculinity, which was objectionable as well as alien to them.

The extracts reproduced above demonstrate that the House of Commons is a highly adversarial forum, in which people not only compete for the floor, but also contradict and insult one another with comments like 'rubbish' and 'has the honourable lady been asleep for the last two years?'. It is a widely held view that this style of debate is a consequence of the institution's 'maleness'. When the 1997 election brought a record number of women MPs into Parliament, many media commentators looked forward to a change in the culture of the House of Commons, suggesting that the women would 'civilize' debate and make the place less of a 'bear garden'. Shaw's evidence suggests that this has not happened (or at least, not yet). It does not however rule out the possibility that at least some women behave as they do because they *reject* the adversarial culture of the institution, rather than because they are unable to participate in it on equal terms with men.

The view that adversarial debate is more congenial to men than to women fits with a generalization proposed by a number of analysts, namely that women tend to prefer a co-operative, consensus-building style of discourse, whereas men tend to be more comfortable with competition and conflict. For instance, Janet Holmes (1995), a researcher who has taken a particular interest in the effects of gender on interaction in public contexts, argues that women speakers are generally more concerned than men with the needs and feelings of others. They pay more attention to others' 'face' (see Chapter 6 above), and for that reason prefer less confrontational styles of discourse. Once again, though, this finding lends itself to competing explanations in terms of 'difference' or 'dominance'. One could treat women's concern for others' face as a quasi-cultural preference, learnt through participation in female peer groups and networks, and perhaps related to the roles women play in the domestic sphere (e.g. as facilitators and peacemakers). Alternatively one could treat it as a consequence of women's subordinate position – for arguably subordinates have a particular interest in avoiding conflicts with the dominant group and building alliances with their own peers (Brown 1980).

But even if women's preference for particular ways of speaking does not arise directly or exclusively from their position as subordinates, the workings of power are still visible, Holmes suggests, in who ends up adjusting to whom. In institutional contexts, the style of speaking that typically prevails and is highly valued is also, to a large extent, the style preferred by men – or more exactly, perhaps, by the elite class of men who have dominated and still continue to dominate most institutions. To succeed in a given institution or profession, women (and other historical 'outsiders') must adjust to its preferred style of behaviour, including speech. Women MPs can either 'adjust', that is, learn to behave in competitive and adversarial ways that don't come easily to them (and of which in some cases they disapprove), or they can behave in accordance with their own habits and values, and risk being marginalized as a result. The women who decline to make illegal interventions in debates, for example, are marginalized to the extent that they are not getting their voices and views heard as often as the men who do this regularly, nor getting themselves noticed by the more senior politicians who are in a position to advance their careers.

This line of argument implies yet another view on what constitutes power in talk: the ability to define what counts as acceptable or valuable speech in accordance with your own values, interests and preferences. It is this kind of power, rather than the right to speak on equal terms with male colleagues, that eludes the women MPs. Women in Parliament are not subject to different rules from men in the way that defendants in court are subject to different rules from magistrates, but the rules themselves are based on assumptions which are not shared, it appears, by both genders equally. Of course, women do not have to play the game – as we have seen, some explicitly refuse to do so – but refusing to play is not the same as being able to change the rules so that the game itself is played differently by everyone.

Aki Uchida (1998 [1992]) makes a similar point about intercultural encounters. Here again, the workings of power are often seen in the fact that adjustment is not a two-way process: one group is expected to accommodate or assimilate to the norms of the other. In Chapter 8, for instance, I discussed examples of intercultural miscommunication that involved mismatches between the communicative practices of white Britons and African-Caribbean pupils or Asian workers. Although the researchers who analysed these cases located the problem in a clash of expectations which neither party was conscious of, outside academic discourse it is generally the minority party who is seen as having, or being, 'the problem'. Uchida points out that when contact between groups occurs in a context of unequal social relations, 'difference' is interpreted according to a pre-existing schema in which 'X is superior to Y', and thereby *becomes* 'dominance'.

As critical readers may have noticed already, in this discussion I have frequently referred to groups of people, such as 'women', 'men', 'African-Caribbean pupils', 'Asian workers', and so on, as if they were homogeneous masses, all behaving in the same ways and all sharing the same attitudes or values. This is problematic, since it tends to reproduce cultural stereotypes and to flatten out the internal variation that exists in every social group. For instance, it would be inaccurate to suggest that all women MPs in the British House of Commons are equally alienated by its style of debate, or that all men embrace that style with equal enthusiasm. There are women MPs who relish confrontation and excel in verbal duelling; there are men who do not. Generalizing about 'women' or 'Asians' also tends to suggest that attributes like gender and ethnicity work in isolation from one another, whereas every person in fact belongs to many social categories simultaneously. 'Women' are not just generic representatives of their gender, but have an ethnic identity, a class position, are members of particular generations, may be married or not, employed or not, mothers or not – the list could go on indefinitely. And every person also has their own individual history and their own network of relationships with others, which is not reducible to any list of social categories, though clearly people's membership in certain groups (and not others) must be among the factors that shape their life experiences.

In recent years, many social researchers have become interested in using discourse analysis to explore the ways in which social actors construct identities as (different kinds of) persons. In the next section I explore some of this work.

SOCIALLY CONSTRUCTED SELVES: IDENTITY IN DISCOURSE

Whatever else we do with words, when we speak we are always telling our listeners something about ourselves. It has long been axiomatic for students of language in society that language-using is an 'act of identity'. Traditionally, what that axiom was most often taken to mean was that language-users' ways of speaking 'reflected' or 'marked' the identities they already had. But this view of identity and its relationship to language has increasingly been challenged by poststructuralist and postmodernist theories. These theories, which have been influential in a number of disciplines where social research is undertaken (see Chapter 4), suggest that a person's identity is not something fixed, stable and unitary that they acquire early in life and possess forever afterwards. Rather identity is shifting and multiple, something people are continually constructing and reconstructing in their encounters with each other and the world. This way of understanding identity is *not* meant to imply that (most) people wake up every morning wondering who they are, or that they suffer from a version of what psychiatrists label 'multiple personality disorder'. What it is intended to challenge is the idea that our behaviour flows 'naturally' from some core or essence inside us: that we do A, B and C because we 'are' X, Y and Z. Some theorists would argue that what happens is actually the reverse – it is in doing X, Y and Z that we *become* or *construct ourselves as* A, B and C.

For example, in feminist theory in the 1980s and 1990s it became common to talk about 'doing gender' and/or 'performing gender'. The verb *doing* (or sometimes *accomplishing*) is favoured by ethnomethodologists[5] (cf. West and Zimmerman 1991), while *performing* is more often used by followers of the postmodernist theorist Judith Butler (cf. Butler 1990). There are differences between the two perspectives, but for the purposes of this discussion I will focus on what they share. Both suggest that gender is a property, not of persons themselves (though that is how we usually think of it and refer to it – in English we say that so-and-so 'is' a woman/a man) but of the *behaviours* to which members of a society ascribe a gendered meaning. 'Being a man/woman' involves appropriating gendered behaviours and making them part of the self that an individual presents to others. Repeated over time, these behaviours may be internalized as 'me' – that is, gender does not *feel* like a performance or an accomplishment to the actor, it just feels like her or his 'natural' way of behaving.

That gender is indeed a form of action, however, can become obvious in certain 'unusual' circumstances. An example is when you travel to a place where femininity or masculinity involves different behaviours from the ones you are used to. Suddenly you find that you are an anomaly: your 'foreign' behaviour is not intelligible to others, who are not sure whether to treat you as a woman or a man. Within a single society, too, there may be people who draw attention to the constructedness of gender by enacting it in anomalous ways: some 'transgendered' people, for instance, appropriate a combination of masculine and feminine styles and behaviours which make them appear to others as indeterminately gendered. Gender indeterminacy is something many people find disturbing. We do not even seem to be comfortable with not knowing whether an infant is a girl or a boy – very often this is the first question someone will ask about a baby they have not met before. The question arises because babies do not yet 'do gender'. Instead their carers do gender for them, referring to them by gendered names and pronouns and possibly dressing them in garments, or choosing objects for them, whose styles and colours are coded for gender.

For many contemporary theorists, then, gender, and other kinds of identity, involve continuous work: failure to do this work, or to do it in socially acceptable ways, can have a strong negative impact on social interaction (making people feel confused, uncomfortable or threatened). Spoken discourse is an important resource for researchers interested in the work of constructing identity, for in interactive talk one may observe both the construction of identities and their reception by participants. In addition, talk is a medium for 'meta' discussions *about* aspects of identity. This kind of metadiscussion is not rare in ordinary spontaneous interaction (one example appears below), but it is particularly common in social research data. It is the kind of talk that ensues when the researcher asks an interview subject or puts to a focus group a question like 'what do you consider typically English?' (inviting the respondent to bring up issues of national identity), or 'do you think of yourself as a "new man"?' (prompting reflection on issues of gender identity). Asking such questions is a convenient way of getting people to address the topic the researcher is interested in directly (the alternative, which is used alongside interviewing in ethnographic research, is to infer their notions of nationality or masculinity from observations of naturally occurring speech and other behaviour). But as I noted in Chapter 10, it is important to keep in mind that discourse data in the form of an interview or focus group discussion is not simply 'data' but also 'discourse'. When people talk about aspects of identity, they are not just operating at the 'meta' level; they may be reflecting on identity, but they are also *doing* identity at the same time. By analysing what they say in relation to what they are doing rather than focusing only on the former, a researcher may be able to get 'added value' from the data.

An example may help to clarify the point. The following piece of data is an extract from an interaction among four male college students (all white, straight, middle-class, unmarried and in their early 20s). It was recorded and transcribed by a student of mine in 1990; the three participants are his friends and housemates (he himself is also present, but does not speak in this extract). The talk took place while they were at home watching a basketball game on TV. It was not an interview, but spontaneous conversation: the original purpose of recording it was to find out (for a language and gender class) what men talk about in casual conversation with their friends.

Transcription conventions: [indicates onset of simultaneous speech (overlap); (.) indicates pause of less than 0.1 sec.; = indicates latching, i.e. turn transition with no gap and no overlap; ? indicates rising pitch; { } indicates sequence that is indecipherable or non-verbal; __ underline indicates emphatic stress

---

Bryan:	uh you know that really gay guy in our age of revolution class who sits in front of us? He wore shorts again by the way it's like 42 degrees out he wore shorts again {laughter}

_____1

Ed:	that [guy
Bryan:	[it's like a speedo he wears a speedo to class (.) he's got incredibly

_____2

Ed:	it's worse = you know like those shorts women volley
Bryan:	skinny legs you know=

_____3

Ed:	ball players wear? It's like those (.) it's l[ike
Bryan:	[you know what's even more

_____4

Ed:	[French cut spandex
Bryan:	ridicu[lous? when you wear those shorts and like a parka on

_____5

5 lines omitted

Bryan:	he's either got some condition that he's got to like have his legs exposed at all times or else he's got really good legs=
Ed:	= he's probably he'[s like
Carl:	[he really likes

_____6

Bryan:	=[he		=he doesn't have any leg hair
Ed:	=[he's like at home combing his leg hairs=		
Carl:	his legs=		

7

Bryan:	though	[yes and oh those ridiculous Reeboks that are always {*indeciph*}
Ed:	he real[ly likes his legs=	
Al:	=very long very white and very skinny

8

Bryan:	and goofy white socks always striped=	[tube socks
Ed:	=that's [right	he's the antithesis of
	man	

This conversation was not 'set up' for the men to engage in a discussion about gender, but in this sequence the subject comes up spontaneously. The four friends begin to talk about various other men they know, and about whom they use the label 'gay'. In this extract the subject is specifically 'that really gay guy in our age of revolution class', who is ultimately described by Ed (8) as 'the antithesis of man'. The talk that precedes this assessment provides information about how the participants define proper and improper masculinity. The 'really gay guy' is censured for the clothes he wears, which are overly revealing, too feminine, ridiculous and 'goofy'. He is also derided for taking a narcissistic interest in his body (combing the hairs on his skinny white legs). This inappropriate concern with bodily appearance and dress is what makes the object of criticism 'the antithesis of man' (it is also the only evidence provided for the guy being 'gay', which suggests that for these speakers, homosexuality has more to do with gender deviance than sexual preference per se).

A social researcher might well conclude that what is going on in this talk is essentially a kind of gender boundary policing. But that is not all that is going on. At the same time that they talk *about* masculinity – defining it by implication against its 'antithesis', the behaviour of the men they label 'gay' – these four speakers are also performing their own version of masculinity. As I have argued in a more extended analysis of this conversation (see Cameron 1997), the purpose of talking about 'what it is to be (or not to be) "a man"' for these speakers in this context is to bond with one another around a shared sense of themselves as men. They are doing identity – and also friendship – by implicitly emphasizing the difference between themselves and the objects of their criticism, 'gay' men. At the same time, it is striking that there is a kind of contradiction between what they are doing and saying, and the means they are using to do and say it. Though the speakers criticize, and define themselves against, people who deviate from their notion of proper masculinity, their conversation exemplifies a kind of talk which is itself popularly considered to be in conflict with proper masculinity: *gossip*. If gossip is defined as talk (often critical talk) about the personal qualities and private business of other people, then this sequence about 'the really gay guy' fits the definition. It also has some other supposedly 'feminine' characteristics: topically it focuses on details of clothing and appearance, for example, and stylistically it is co-operative rather than competitive or adversarial (the participants support and agree with each other).

Why would a group of men perform masculinity in a conversation about gender using the conventions of a 'feminine' speech genre? My answer would be that gossip is a form of bonding: collectively disparaging or 'trashing' people who are absent increases solidarity and intimacy among those who are actually present. Gossiping specifically about gay men allows these speakers to create intimacy ('doing friendship') without compromising their credentials as properly masculine straight men ('doing gender'). The form of the talk connotes intimacy, but the content makes clear this is not the kind of intimacy that might call a man's gender or (hetero)-sexuality into question.

My analysis of the 'antithesis of man' sequence belongs to a current of research, in sociolinguistics and other disciplines, where researchers are interested in the *different* ways identity is performed by different people, or indeed by the same person in different situations. (Obviously, gossiping about gay men is not the only way for young straight white men to perform masculinity; in other situations they would use other strategies.) However, while each 'performance' requires its own context-specific analysis, social researchers are also interested in delineating the more general cultural repertoire on which particular performers in particular situations draw. To say that selves are 'socially constructed' is also to say that there are limits on how they can be constructed. Individuals, if they are to be intelligible to others, cannot just construct identities any old way. A researcher working with a set of interviews or focus group discussions will be looking for recurring patterns in the way people talk about masculinity, or Englishness, or single parenthood, or whatever aspect of identity they have been invited to reflect upon. The question, in other words, is not only 'how do people do/talk about X?' but also 'from what range of culturally intelligible possibilities are they drawing their way of doing/talking about X?'

'CROSSING'

Above I suggested that '"Being a man/woman" involves appropriating gendered behaviours [i.e. ways of acting or speaking that are understood in a particular society as "feminine" or "masculine"] and making them part of the self that an individual presents to others'. Different people in different situations can do this in different ways: my self-presentation as a woman might be radically different from someone else's, because it draws on a different subset of what our culture defines as 'feminine' behaviours. I might also be appropriating some behaviours from the set that are defined culturally as 'masculine'. If identity is something you *do* rather than something you just 'are', then there is nothing to stop people appropriating ways of behaving (including, of course, ways of speaking) from a variety of different sources, including social groups to which they clearly do not belong.

This point is illustrated in a study by the anthropologist Kira Hall of the language used by telephone sex workers around San Francisco (Hall 1995). These workers' job is to provide sexually arousing talk on the phone for men who are paying for the service by the minute. Since the caller cannot see or touch them, the workers can use only the resources of spoken language to create a suitably erotic persona and scenario. Hall found that many of the sex workers she interviewed used a stereo-typical 'women's language', similar to the register described by Robin Lakoff (1975; see Chapter 8 above). They spoke in breathy or whispery voices, they asked lots of questions, they used rising intonation and 'feminine' vocabulary items (e.g. describing themselves as being dressed in 'peach' rather than 'orange' satin undergarments). They exploited the fact that this way of talking carries a particular cultural meaning, connoting a kind of femininity which many men find 'sexy'. This, however, was not the kind of femininity the workers generally performed outside their work. They appropriated it at work because they found it (economically) advantageous to do so.

Kira Hall discovered that one of the most experienced and successful workers in her sample was not only not the kind of woman conjured up by the use of 'women's language', the worker was not a woman at all. He was a man who was able to 'pass' as a woman by appropriating the gendered meaning of speaking in certain ways just as his female colleagues did. Hall also found that some workers had a repertoire of ethnically distinct 'characters'; according to the customer's preference they would 'do' a white woman, an African-American woman, an Asian woman, a Latina woman, and so on. Obviously, many of these linguistically constructed personas did not 'match' the performer's own ethnicity. In fact, several informants commented that women who were white in reality tended to make the best 'Black' women on the phone, and vice versa.

Hall uses the term 'cross-expressing' (on the analogy of 'cross-dressing') to refer to the behaviour of the sex workers who appropriate behaviours associated with groups they do not belong to. Other researchers have called it just 'crossing' (e.g. Rampton 1995), and have pointed out that it is both commoner than one might think, and used for a more complex set of purposes. The male sex worker in Kira Hall's sample was 'crossing' in order to 'pass' as a woman: he needed to conceal from heterosexual male callers that they were actually talking to a man. But in many cases, crossing is not done in order to pass. Rather it is done in order to 'index' – point to – certain characteristics which are culturally associated with the group whose behaviour is being appropriated, and which the speaker wants to claim as part of his or her own identity.

Cecilia Cutler (1999) studied the speech of a white adolescent boy from the affluent white neighbourhood of Yorkville in New York City. The boy identified with hip-hop culture, which originated in and is strongly associated with African American communities. In his discourse he used not only the vocabulary of hip-hop (e.g. the slang approbation term *phat*), as many white kids do, but also some elements of the phonology and grammar of African American Vernacular English (AAVE). Not surprisingly, he did not use these features in exactly the same way as African American speakers use them: it is difficult to master the nuances of a dialect one is not a native speaker of. But in any case, he was not trying to pass as Black, since it was obvious to anyone who met him that he was white. His crossing behaviour was meant to index, not race as such, but qualities such as toughness, street credibility, and intolerance of injustice, which are widely attributed to young urban working-class African Americans. Similarly, a woman who is accused of 'behaving like a man' because of the way she speaks (swearing or giving direct orders, for instance) is unlikely to be trying to pass as a man or even sound like one. Her behaviour is meant to index not masculinity but particular 'masculine' qualities such as toughness, decisiveness and authority.

CO-CONSTRUCTED SELVES

Of course, people who cross do run the risk of coming off as bad imitations or parodies, and their behaviour can cause controversy or resentment: the status of white hip-hoppers is a matter of some dispute among their Black peers, for example. Women who think they are performing authority may be understood by others as performing masculinity. Gay men's drag performances have been attacked by some feminists as offensive parodies that represent women as grotesque, while others argue that what drag expresses is not contempt for women but a particular gay male cultural sensibility. The meaning of crossing, then, is contested. And that raises a point which is relevant to all research on issues of language and identity: communication is not a one-way process. We have choices about the way we construct ourselves in talk, but the people with whom we talk may have their own ideas about what our choices mean.

Postmodernists have been criticized for neglecting the implications of this point. The notion of 'performing' identity puts the spotlight (to continue the theatrical metaphor) on the individual performer; but in everyday life, others are rarely just spectators at our performance. Since talk is interactive, and participants typically have the opportunity to be speakers as well as addressees, others have a role to play in the construction – or as some theorists (particularly ethnomethodologists) would prefer to call it, the *co-construction* – of the self. Discourse analysis carried out on spoken interaction is well suited to the task of showing how our performance is ongoingly affected by others' reception of it, and how our identities emerge not only from what we do ourselves, but also from the way others position us in what they say to and/or about us.

Consider, for example, the following extract from data collected by the researcher Cathryn Houghton, at a group therapy session in a US institution where young unemployed single mothers (mainly Latina) are involuntarily detained for their 'irresponsibility' in having had children they must depend on welfare payments to support. The institutional regime includes both vocational training to prepare inmates for the job market and group therapy to inculcate more 'responsible' attitudes. In this extract the subject under discussion is participants' experiences of wanting to have a baby (Houghton 1995:123–4).

Mirna:	you know how that is
	when you just want to have a baby
	just something that is yours
	and belongs to you . . .
Therapist:	no Mirna
	we don't know how it is
	please tell us
	but don't say 'you'
	it is your experience not ours
	so you need to say 'I' instead of 'you'
	this is how *I* feel when *I* see a baby.
Mirna:	OK. I.

This dispute over pronouns – *I* versus *you* – is at a deeper level about differing constructions of the self. Mirna constructs herself as part of a group of people who 'know how that is when you just want to have a baby'. The therapist, however, rejects this construction, and tries to position Mirna as a different kind of self: a unique individual with unique experiences, which must therefore be described in the first person – 'this is how *I* feel when *I* see a baby'. Mirna accepts this alternative positioning (though we might feel she does so under duress, a point I return to below). Cathryn Houghton analyses the exchange as a conflict between two ideological systems, collectivism (the self is defined in relation to others within a larger collectivity) and individualism (the self is defined as unique and independent of any collectivity). Individualism, Houghton adds, is the 'mainstream' orthodoxy of middle-class white America, and part of what the working-class Latina inmates are in the institution to learn.

As well as being an example of the process whereby selves are co-constructed in a process of interaction rather than just through the actions of the individual speaker, this is clearly a case of asymmetrical talk in which the asymmetry (re)produces social inequality. The therapist is powerful in all the ways discussed earlier in this chapter. First, she is privileged in terms of speaking rights. She has the right to issue orders ('you need to say "I"') and to respond to others' contributions with an evaluating move ('no Mirna we don't know how it is'), whereas they have no reciprocal right to evaluate her contributions. Second, she is apparently allowed to break the rules that apply to others. She has no hesitation in telling Mirna that 'we don't know how it is' – in the very act of telling Mirna that one should only speak for oneself, the therapist speaks for the whole group. Third, she is able to define what counts in general as acceptable talk, in accordance with the interests and values of the part of society she represents. 'Saying *I*' stands for a whole cluster of mainstream values (like independence, responsibility and self-sufficiency). Inmates of this institution are rewarded to the extent their speech signals conformity to those values.

Houghton's analysis makes clear, though, that the power of the institution does not go unchallenged by the inmates. They regularly fall into a discourse genre which Houghton calls 'girl talk', which emphasizes their collective shared experience and their solidarity with one another. The concerns of girl talk include relationships with men, roles within the family and feelings about children and motherhood. Since these are also the 'official' topics of therapeutic discourse, it is difficult for representatives of the institution to sanction girl talk as irrelevant – though they recognize, as do the inmates, that girl talk is not in fact therapeutic, but is a form of resistance to the institutional regime.

This example illustrates another point of general importance for researchers who work on issues of power and identity: that people may *resist* the way they are positioned by others, as subordinates or as members of a group they do not wish to be identified with. Research encounters too are asymmetrical, and it is not uncommon for research subjects to resist the way they are positioned by an interviewer's questions. In Chapter 10 we saw some examples of this: the youth subculture members who designed their talk to refute what they supposed were the interviewer's stereotypes of them, and the English people who displayed reluctance to speak positively about 'this country', suspecting that to do so would be taken as evidence of racism. Just as analysts must look systematically for the workings of power in discourse, so they must also look systematically for evidence of resistance to power. The two very often go together.

SUGGESTIONS FOR FURTHER READING ABOUT IDENTITY, DIFFERENCE AND POWER

Probably the best way to follow up on the points made in this chapter is to read some of the studies in which discourse analysis is used to shed light on the relevant issues. Asymmetry in institutional and professional discourse is discussed from a CA perspective by contributors to Drew and Heritage's *Talk at Work* (1992), and it is also a theme of Gunnarsson et al.'s *The Construction of Professional Discourse* (1997), while Teun van Dijk (1997) contains a shorter overview titled 'Institutional dialogue' by Paul Drew and Marja-Leena Sorjonen. A number of edited collections from the 1990s contain good examples of discourse analysis applied to issues of gender. Kira Hall and Mary Bucholtz's *Gender Articulated: Language and the Socially Constructed Self* (1995) has a 'postmodernist' orientation and includes various case studies of women and men performing different kinds of gender identity. Other collections which reflect the impact of postmodernism include Bergvall et al. (1996), Johnson and Meinhof (1997) and Livia and Hall (1997). Sue Wilkinson and Celia Kitzinger's collection *Feminism and Discourse* (1995) contains both a range of empirical studies and some valuable theoretical chapters in which the pros and cons of the 'turn to discourse' in psychology are debated. This volume touches on the argument about whether it is legitimate to make reference in data analysis to power structures or identity categories that are external to the data; a good short discussion of the points at issue in that debate can be found in Ian Hutchby's article on phone-in talk (Hutchby 1996). The phenomenon of 'crossing' is discussed in Ben Rampton's book *Crossing* (1995), and a range of examples are analysed by contributors to a special issue of the *Journal of Sociolinguistics* which Rampton edited in 1999 (Vol. 4.3).

NOTES

1   In many introductory textbooks, these complementary functions of language are illustrated by the Biblical story of the Ephraimites, who used the variable pronunciation of the word *shibboleth* to distinguish their own people from their enemies, the Gileadites. People who said *sibboleth* thereby revealed their status as members of the out-group, and were put to death.

2   Here it should be clarified that asymmetry can exist between people who are of equal social status. When a doctor consults a lawyer on a legal matter the lawyer is the institutionally powerful party; if the lawyer consults the doctor about a medical problem their positions are reversed. In both cases we are dealing with an asymmetrical encounter, though it is between two people who both have high status as members of a professional and social elite. In some contexts the institutionally powerful participant may have less power and status, globally speaking, than the other party: consider for instance the position of a journalist who interviews the US President on television.

3   Interestingly, Sylvia Shaw has found that powerful speakers have a tendency to grant requests to give way rather than using their position to hold on to the floor as long as possible. She suggests that refusal to give way is understood by experienced members of the House of Commons as a sign that the speaker is 'weak', unable or unwilling to face a direct challenge. Thus willingness to give up the floor on request is not in this context an expression of a co-operative, egalitarian ethos, but rather an aspect of the prevailing adversarial ethos.

4   MPs are in principle free to speak, and vote, against their own party, but such disloyalty is usually damaging to their political careers, and is therefore rare. On some issues the government allows a 'free vote', meaning the subject of the proposed law is deemed to be a matter of personal conscience rather than party politics. In this case the vote was not free.

5   Ethnomethodology is the school of sociology, founded by Harold Garfinkel, from which CA developed (see also Chapter 7).

12 Designing your own projects

This chapter is intended to help you think about designing and conducting a research project of your own. It is addressed primarily to students who will be doing this for an end-of-class assignment or a short dissertation of the kind required by many undergraduate and taught Masters degree programmes. Doctoral students may find some of the advice given here useful, but they should bear in mind that they are working on a larger scale and the requirements are more exacting.

Many teachers nowadays assess students at least partly on tasks which require them to show they can 'do it themselves', as opposed to just writing about what other analysts have done: that they can think of their own question, collect and transcribe their own data, do their own analysis, interpret and present their own findings. This sort of task develops not only skills which are specific to doing discourse analysis, but more general 'transferable' skills such as identifying and solving problems, gathering and synthesizing information, and presenting what has been done coherently in writing. Except in the case of a doctoral thesis, doing research is intended to provide a worthwhile educational experience for students rather than to produce ground-breaking results: PhDs apart, there is no requirement that a student research project must make an original and significant contribution to knowledge. It is useful for students to be clear about this, for a lot of anxiety about 'doing research' stems from imagining that the standard you have to meet is higher than it really is. That said, there is nothing wrong with aiming high. It is not unheard of for an undergraduate or Masters student to do a piece of research of sufficient quality to be presented at a professional conference, and/or published. All it takes is one good idea, pursued methodically and presented well. I will begin with the hardest part, which is having the good idea.

WHAT IS A GOOD IDEA?

There is a school of thought according to which an analyst should not approach spoken language data with any preconceived notions of what might be interesting about it. The conversation analyst Harvey Sacks once remarked:

> When we start out with a piece of data, the question of what we are going to end up with, what kind of findings it will give, should not be a consideration. We sit down

with a piece of data, make a bunch of observations, and see where they will go . . .
if we pick any data, without bringing any problems to it, we will find something.
(1984: 27)

Evidently this approach worked for Sacks, but I do not think his advice is very helpful
to the average student. Students often do not have the luxury of time to 'sit down
with a piece of data . . . and see where [their observations] will go'. They are also much
less experienced than Sacks in 'making observations'. A practised analyst like Sacks
may well find interesting patterns leaping out of any data they look at, but this is at
least partly because they have learned how to look. Student projects are usually
undertaken as part of that learning process, and students usually do need to 'bring
problems' to the data in order to know what to look for (and indeed, what kind
of data they need to obtain, since unlike experienced academics they are unlikely to
have built up an extensive corpus). Of course, if when they 'sit down with the data'
they notice some previously unsuspected pattern in it, there is nothing to stop them
pursuing that. But in general I would encourage student researchers to try to generate
a well-defined research question before they begin.

At a certain point in the courses I teach, I usually ask students to write down
a proposal for a research project in one sentence or less on a piece of paper. Invariably,
many of them write things like 'men's talk'. This is not a bad starting point, but as an
actual research plan it has two things wrong with it. First, it does not take the form
of a question. It is always a useful exercise to try to put a research idea in question
form. In the hypothetical case we are discussing, this produces something like 'how
do men talk?', which immediately draws attention to the second thing that is wrong
with it: it is vague. Putting it in question form makes this clearer, because asking a
question forces you to think about what the answer(s) might be. The question in this
case is so broad and general, it is hard to imagine how a single piece of analysis could
even begin to answer it.

A student who thinks 'I'd like to do something about men talking' has got the
germ of an idea, but it is not yet a 'proper' idea for a research project. Among the
questions it raises are: 'what kind of men?', 'what will they be talking about and what
setting will they be talking in?', 'what aspect of their talk will be analysed?'. Even more
fundamental is the question: why men? What has led you to suppose that there is
something interesting about men's talk, and what is it that might be interesting about
it? Do you have a *hypothesis*, a general claim about men's talk that you want to pursue
by examining some actual data?

I have chosen this example because I once had a student who began his project
in exactly this way, by declaring that he was interested in men talking. When I asked
him what had prompted his interest, it turned out he did have a hypothesis; he just
needed to make it explicit. Having read some of the scholarly literature on language
and gender, he had noticed that although most empirical research on same-sex talk
had been done on groups of *women*, analysts quite often made claims about the same-
sex talk of men. One claim that he found particularly questionable was that whereas
women talked a lot about people they knew, their feelings and relationships, men
talked more about 'impersonal' topics such as sport, cars and music. Feeling that this

was just a stereotype, the student wanted to show that it misrepresented men. With that in mind, he posed the question: 'what do men talk about in all-male groups?'. He started from the hypothesis proposed by earlier researchers on language and gender, that they talk about impersonal topics; but he was hoping his data would show this was simplistic.

'What do men talk about in all-male groups?' is a much better-defined question than just 'how do men talk?', because it makes clear what aspect of men's talk the researcher will focus on – in this case, *topic*. It still does not make clear what kind of all-male groups should be approached to provide data; but implicitly it does suggest certain possibilities. The student's question arose from his reading of previous research literature, and his aim was to find out whether the claims made in that literature were accurate or not. Therefore, it seemed logical to investigate a kind of all-male talk that paralleled the kind of all-female talk that had been investigated previously. Much of the literature he had read on women's talk was about female friends (as opposed to co-workers, say, or family members of different generations). So the student decided to examine the behaviour of male friends. His question became: 'what do men talk about in casual conversation with their friends?' Of course, he still had choices about what kind of men to approach (e.g. about their social class, ethnicity, age, marital status and sexual preference). In the event he chose to study his own friends – young, middle-class, single and straight white students – for practical reasons, because these were the men he had easiest access to. Another kind of project could have involved *comparing* what was talked about by different kinds of male friends. But this project was implicitly a comparison between men and women (the women other researchers had studied), and his choice of informants was appropriate for that purpose, always provided he was careful not to generalize the findings to 'all men'.

This example illustrates the point that most 'good ideas' for research do not just spring from the researcher's imagination, they are suggested by previous research (that is one reason why it is important to read widely). Knowledge on any subject is cumulative: people look at what is already known and notice gaps ('this claim about men's talk is being made without any real evidence'), or think of objections ('this might be true about middle-class men, but what about working-class ones?') or supplementary questions ('at what age does this difference between all-male and all-female talk appear?'). There are several ways in which previous research can be used to help design a new research project, and it may be helpful to set these out explicitly.

Replicate

The simplest kind of research project based on existing research involves *replicating* a previous study. You ask the same question(s) and use the same methods as a researcher whose work you have read, but you collect your own data: your question is whether your findings will resemble the original findings. This might sound dull, but in fact it is quite important to know whether patterns reported in research turn up consistently. Only when similar results have been obtained across a range of different studies can we make reliable generalizations about whatever is at issue. Another reason for replicating old studies is to find out if things have changed over time. In the case of studies concerned with gender, for instance, one might well ask whether patterns of male–female interaction have changed since the 1970s, or whether the idea that we now live in a much more equal world is just unsubstantiated hype.

A variant on straightforward replication is to undertake a study asking the same questions and using the same methods as a previous study, but deliberately altering one or more of the nonlinguistic variables (e.g. the social characteristics of the participants or the setting for their interaction). An example of this is my student Michael Higgins's analysis of his mother's knitting bee, referred to in Chapter 2. This project was inspired by Jennifer Coates's study of women friends' talk (Coates 1996). Michael looked at the same discourse features Coates did, but his informants were different from Coates's: hers were predominantly middle class whereas his were working-class women. His question, then, was 'do the patterns of friendly talk Coates discovered apply to women across classes, or are there differences?'. A similar example of 'replication with a twist' is a project undertaken by another student of mine, Kim Atherton, who took Pamela Fishman's study of married couples talking (Fishman 1983) and applied the same approach to cohabiting lesbian couples. Fishman had argued that among married couples, women ended up doing most of the 'work' of keeping conversation going (e.g. asking questions to 'draw their partners out'), while men reaped the benefits. Kim's question was: do couples observe a different (e.g. more egalitarian) division of labour when the partners are both women?

Compare and contrast

Another common type of research project compares two different kinds of talk. For example, Stuart May, who was a student in one of my classes, undertook a comparison between spontaneous casual conversation and soap opera dialogue – that is, casual conversation simulated for television. Here it should be remembered that in Britain, more than in the US or South America, say, soap opera is a 'naturalistic' genre, and the dialogue is designed to resemble 'real' talk as closely as possible. People often remark on how 'realistic' the dialogue on British soaps like *Coronation Street* is. Stuart's question was: how faithful an imitation of naturally occurring talk do the actors in soap operas deliver? Drawing on previous research, he identified features that are typical of spontaneous casual conversation, such as hesitation, repetition and false starts. He then collected a sample of casual conversation and a 'matching' sample of soap opera conversation (similar in length and number of participants), and compared the frequency of hesitation, repetition and false starts.

Marko Kukkonen's Internet Relay Chat study (1997) was also a kind of 'compare and contrast' project. Marko's question was whether the rules said by conversation analysts to govern turn-taking, opening and closing, topic shift, and so on, in face-to-face talk would also apply to IRC, where interaction takes place in writing between people who are distant in space. Unlike Stuart May, Marko did not collect a sample of face-to-face talk for purposes of comparison. This was a reasonable decision, because Marko, unlike Stuart, was not planning to compare the *frequency* with which a particular phenomenon would occur in his two data-types. Rather he was planning to compare the *rules* participants appeared to be following. In the case of face-to-face talk, these rules have been studied enough to be taken as given, so Marko could concentrate on trying to determine whether they were applied by people using IRC. Of course, any study that involves counting tokens to determine the frequency of something, as opposed to its mere existence, does require you to collect similar-sized samples of the data-types being compared.

Take issue with a previous claim

Marko Kukkonen got the idea for the IRC study from previous research – but not research in discourse analysis. He was interested in new communication media, and had read an article about IRC (not by a discourse analyst) which said it was a 'chaotic' medium, with thirty-odd people, unable to see one another, all trying to interact with each other at the same time. As an IRC user himself, Marko thought this was nonsense. It seemed to him that what users normally did was try to locate one other user to start a 'conversation' with, and then interact with that individual. He thought a close analysis of IRC discourse would show how people go about finding someone to interact with and how they manage the interaction; he wanted to show that far from being 'chaotic', their behaviour was highly organized and purposeful. His project thus exemplifies the strategy of 'taking issue', beginning from a claim you intuitively feel is misguided and trying to demonstrate empirically why it is misguided. The project on what male friends talk about, discussed above, also exemplifies 'taking issue', in this case with what the student felt were unwarranted stereotypes of men's talk.

Describe something new

You can also construct a worthwhile research project by focusing on a kind of data that has not been analysed before, and simply describing its discourse characteristics. (I will consider in a moment how previous research might be relevant to this kind of project.) Up to a point, Marko Kukkonen could be said to have done this; although Internet Relay Chat had been discussed extensively by academics, as far as he could tell, no one had applied the techniques of CA to it before.

Periodically, the broadcast media produce new genres whose language is interesting. For instance, Kay Richardson (1997) has analysed the talk that is heard on 'shopping channels', cable TV channels that work like mail order catalogues, offering goods that viewers can buy over the phone. Shopping channel presenters face a linguistic challenge: since viewers need to be able to inspect the object on offer for long enough to decide if they want to buy it, presenters have to talk about a single object, like a ring or a cardigan, for much longer than would be typical in other genres of talk. They have to describe the object, with particular attention to features the camera might distort (like its size – on the screen a small object will appear much larger, since it will be shot in close-up). They also have to make it sound attractive, and constantly repeat information like the price and the phone number to call if you wish to order. The resulting discourse is very distinctive.

Another way of describing something 'new' is to examine a familiar genre, but in a location that is less familiar. For instance, a student of mine once analysed radio DJ talk in Brunei. DJ talk has been studied by a number of researchers, but it is reasonable to suppose (and indeed, the student showed) that it has particular features in particular local contexts. Studying such local particularities contributes something new and valuable to our knowledge.

How is previous research relevant to a project that involves describing something new? In two ways. First, it is desirable to investigate whether anyone else actually has published a description of your chosen genre (if they have, that doesn't mean you should drop the idea, it just means reframing it slightly, e.g. as a replication), and that entails looking around in previous research (see below). Second, however, there may be a case for approaching a novel phenomenon on the model of something that has already been studied. Finding something to compare your data to gives you a handle on how to analyse it – what linguistic features might be worth looking at closely, for example – and a better idea of what makes it unique.

PURSUING THE IDEA

Having refined your question in such a way that it is possible to investigate it in a small-scale study, how do you pursue the investigation? An obvious initial step is to consider the practicalities of data collection. If you can't get the data you need (whether by collecting it yourself/via informants or taking it from an already available source), your idea may still be good, but in practice you can do nothing with it and you need to think of an alternative.

Assuming you can get the data, however, is the next step to collect and transcribe it? Not necessarily: in most cases I would advise doing some reading first. You will probably have done some already, in order to generate a research question, but having decided on your question you can extend your knowledge of previous work by searching library catalogues and databases (e.g. the abstracts of social science journals available on-line or on CD-ROM) using keywords to find out what else has been published on the topic you have chosen. If this produces an unmanageably long list of references, don't panic: no one expects you to read everything ever written for one assignment (though for a PhD they may expect something close). Also, do not begin your reading with the earliest references in your list; begin with the most recent references. That way you will quite quickly see which 'old' references are still being cited respectfully by researchers now. You can go back and read some of them if they seem relevant, and discard the ones that researchers no longer regard as important.

There are several reasons for reading around before you collect data, and none of them is the one many students worry about, i.e. getting a large number of references for their bibliography! The first is that by reading around you get a better idea of the field of enquiry where you want to locate your own project: what the questions are, what the arguments are about, what researchers currently believe they know about the subject. Knowing this helps you formulate better questions, and also gives you a clearer idea what findings you might expect, and what would be unexpected. The second advantage of reading is that it gives you some pointers on data collection. Published articles normally include a 'methods' section in which the author tells you, for instance, how many speakers and minutes/hours of tape s/he recorded. This provides a clue to how much data is thought to be needed for making generalizations. You may not be able to match the ideal: doctoral students and professional academics have more time and resources for collecting and transcribing data than you do. But if you cannot match it, at least you can present your own data with the appropriate disclaimer (i.e. this is not enough to generalize from). In assessing small-scale research done by students, teachers will not penalize you for falling short of the 'professional' standard, but generally they will give you credit for *recognizing* the inevitable limitations of your work. Finally, reading other people's work is one way to become familiar with the conventions for writing up a research project (a subject I will return to below).

The next stage is collecting and transcribing data, topics we have covered in earlier chapters. As I observed in Chapter 3, transcription is really the first stage of analysis/interpretation. But what do you do after that? The short answer is that it depends on the specifics of your project. Here it is useful to compare some of the student projects I have referred to in this book: Stuart May's study of soap opera conversation and naturally occurring conversation, Catriona Carson's study of the use of *oh* to introduce reported speech, and Marko Kukkonen's investigation of the discourse of Internet Relay Chat. What did these analysts do, and why?

Both Stuart May and Catriona Carson had asked questions that entailed working on a small number of linguistic variables: hesitations, repetitions and false starts in Stuart's case, *oh* following a quotative verb like *said, says, goes*, in Catriona's. For each of them, therefore, the first task was to *extract* every instance of the relevant variable and make a list of all the cases. Stuart, in fact, made several lists: two for each of his variables, one for each data sample, because his intention was to compare frequencies of each variable in soap opera talk and natural talk. So he made his lists and he counted how many items appeared in each. Catriona's analysis, by contrast, was qualitative; she did not need to *count* tokens of *oh*, rather she needed to *sort* them into sets based on their having a similar function. Catriona had made a general observation that when *oh* was used to introduce reported speech, it indicated that the person doing the reporting disagreed with or disapproved of some aspect of the quoted material. However, it was possible to be more specific. For instance, the speaker might disapprove either of the person whose words were quoted, or of something or someone alluded to in the quoted speech. Catriona needed to subdivide her examples to reflect this kind of difference, and propose a description for each subcategory, making sure that no examples were left out and that there were no counter-examples to her general claim.

Marko Kukkonen's study of IRC demanded a different approach. It focused on how people manage the 'floor' in a kind of interaction where they are not talking to each other face-to-face or by telephone, but typing their contributions on a computer keyboard and only then executing a command that transmits the message to other participants' screens. Analysis could not be a matter of extracting every token of a particular item, such as *um*, or of an item in a specified sequence such as 'quotative verb + *oh*', and then counting tokens or sorting them into sets. Marko was looking for general patterns across his whole corpus. More specifically, he was looking for evidence to show whether IRC users were orienting to the same principles described by CA for managing spoken interaction.

Marko had found that his data consisted to a large extent of fairly short question/answer sequences: no user in his sample embarked on a lengthy narrative or an elaborate description, and topics were seldom developed beyond a few turns. Just as he had predicted, then, IRC discourse was highly organized and tightly structured. In fact, the structure seemed to be 'tighter' and less variable than in most face-to-face interaction. That in itself called for comment: how did Marko explain it? He did so by relating it to the particular constraints of the medium. Participants in IRC do not receive messages continuously as they are being produced, as in speech, but are sent the whole message after the sender has finished typing it. Therefore, it is not advisable for anyone to 'hold the floor' for long turns. The addressee will experience the time spent by a sender composing a long message as 'dead' time, time when nothing is happening, and there is a risk they will leave the channel or initiate a new exchange with someone else. To maintain the interactive 'flow', then, users tend to keep their turns brief.

Analysts often look for points in their data where things seem to be going 'wrong'. Because of the production/reception conditions described above, Marko found a few places in his sample where the adjacency pair structure appeared to break down, when one user typed and sent a second message before receiving a reply to the first one, producing an 'out of synch' sequence of the form 'Question$_1$–Question$_2$–Answer$_1$'. (Though questions can follow questions in face-to-face interaction, this does not normally produce the kind of sequence just described, but 'Q$_1$–Q$_2$–A$_2$–A$_1$'. The participants have not got 'out of synch'; rather the answer to the first question has turned out to depend on the answer to a supplementary second question, as in 'Can I have a pint of Guinness?', 'Are you eighteen?'.) The 'getting behind' phenomenon may be one of the things underlying perceptions of IRC as 'chaotic'. But Marko was able both to explain *why* adjacency pairs sometimes became split (because of the 'lag' in sending/receiving messages in the IRC medium) and to show that users repaired the problem within a few turns, which suggested they were still orienting to the basic rule that pair-parts should be adjacent.

The basic elements of analysis are *description* (produce an account of general patterns in the data) and *explanation* (explain why the patterns occur). The balance of these elements varies in different cases, however. Catriona Carson's project, for instance, was descriptive. She proposed a function for *oh* that had not been described in detail before – signalling a negative attitude on the part of a speaker who uses it to introduce reported speech – and analysed/sorted a large number of examples to show that they all fulfilled some variant of that function. She did not need to explain *why* the item *oh* was used in this way: her claim was simply that it was. Marko Kukkonen on the other hand needed both to describe how participants in IRC managed the 'floor' and to explain why their interaction had certain characteristics (e.g. why it contained no long turns and consisted mainly of question/answer sequences). Stuart May, similarly, tried to propose some explanation for the comparative frequencies of repetition, hesitation and false starts in soap opera dialogue and naturally occurring talk. His frequency-counts showed that the soap opera dialogue contained far fewer hesitations and virtually no repetitions or false starts. He speculated that this was because repetitions and false starts are difficult for actors to perform convincingly, and potentially distracting for the TV viewer, who is an overhearer rather than a participant and cannot ask for clarification if s/he misses something. In other words there are good reasons why the 'naturalistic' dialogue heard in soap operas should not be an exact simulation of real spontaneous conversation. It might be pointed out here that both Stuart's project and Marko's were of the 'compare and contrast' type, whereas Catriona's was not. If a study involves comparing two things, analysts normally do not rest content with just describing the similarities and differences, but also feel the need to try and give reasons for them.

PUTTING IT IN WRITING

It is a common misconception that analysis and 'writing up' are totally separate stages of a research project, and that analysis has to be complete before the writing up can begin. But in reality, writing is *part* of the analytic process. I would advise beginning to write as soon as you have collected, transcribed and done the preliminary counting or sorting of your data (indeed, some parts of a long piece of writing – the review of previous relevant research, for example – can usefully be drafted even before that). It is by trying to organize your thoughts in written form that you clarify what you have actually discovered – and, equally important, what problems still remain to be solved by going back to the data and doing more analysis.

The writing you produce early on does not have to be, and probably will not be, the finished form of your project or dissertation; nevertheless it is useful to have some kind of skeleton structure to guide you. Although there is no single 'standard' way of presenting a research project in writing, certain basic conventions are very widely followed. Most written assignments or dissertations reporting research on spoken discourse will have some variant of the following structure:

1 *Introductory material* setting out the researcher's *question* and *why it is of interest* (it is never wise to neglect the reader's unspoken question, 'so what?').
2 A *literature review* surveying relevant previous work on the subject.
3 A *methods* section explaining in some detail what the researcher's data consist of, how they were collected, what approach was taken to analysing them (e.g. 'a CA approach' or 'an ethnography of speaking approach') and why that approach was chosen as most suitable for the purpose.
4 A section setting out the *results* of the project (e.g. listing and illustrating with

examples the variant uses of quotative + *oh* in Catriona Carson's case, or presenting the comparative real talk/soap opera dialogue frequencies of the three variables in Stuart May's).

5   A *discussion* section in which the researcher presents possible explanations for the results and discusses their meaning or significance.

6   A *conclusion* in which the researcher summarizes what has been learnt from the project, what its problems and limitations are, and what questions arise from it for future research.

7   A *bibliography* listing all the sources the researcher has consulted.

8   An appendix setting out *transcription conventions* used by the researcher.

9   An appendix containing transcribed *data* (how much of it is included depends on how large your corpus is, but samples should be sufficiently large to give the reader some sense of what your data 'look like')

10   If appropriate, an appendix containing a copy of your interview schedule or other research protocols.

When I say that most presentations will have 'some variant of' this structure, I am obviously implying that it does not have to be adhered to absolutely and without deviation. The organization of the text should reflect the logic of the material being organized: that might mean, for instance, that in a given project there is no real motivation for separating the results and discussion sections, or the introductory material and the literature review. Conversely, there might be a case for subdividing the analysis (i.e. results and discussion) into different sections dealing with different discourse variables or structures. For example, Marko Kukkonen's dissertation had separate sections for 'openings', 'closings', 'repair', etc. It may also be logical to subdivide the literature review. Again, Marko's project provides an example, since on one hand he needed to review research on computer-mediated communication, while on the other he also needed to summarize the findings of conversation analysts about the organization of face-to-face talk. Catriona Carson, similarly, reviewed both previous work on the various functions of *oh* and previous work on reported speech in conversation: her own project was at the interface between these two bodies of research, since it concerned the use of *oh* to introduce reported speech. A general point to bear in mind is that headings and subheadings do not just break up the text, they convey important information to the reader regarding both structure and subject-matter. While it is possible to use headings like 'Introduction', 'Literature Review', 'Methods', etc., more specific/descriptive headings will help your reader to follow what you are doing in your presentation.

When writing up small-scale research, there are some other general principles that should be considered throughout. One of them is to *use concrete examples*. Don't just *tell* the reader what is in your data, *show* the reader by choosing one or more examples of what you are discussing from your transcript and reproducing them in the text. Even if you have reproduced your whole transcript in an appendix for the reader's benefit, the point you are making will be clearer and more forceful if you provide at least one illustration actually in the text. A reference forward like 'see lines 30 and 47, Appendix B', does not have the same immediate clarifying effect. Examples can be used both in the analysis sections and in those parts of your text (e.g. the introduction or the method section) where you are defining your variables (a discussion of, say, the variable 'hesitation' should define it in general terms and then give examples from the data illustrating common hesitation phenomena such as silent and filled pauses). In analysis sections, do not be afraid to begin by reproducing a chunk of transcript, possibly quite a long one, which you can then discuss in detail. (This will be easier, by the way, if you number the lines when you reproduce it.)

There may be several chunks of talk in your data sample that illustrate the observation you are making (e.g. Marko Kukkonen's observation that IRC discourse sometimes gets 'out of synch'). If the pattern is the same in all of them, you only need to reproduce one instance in full: choose the case you think is most striking. In your discussion, however, make clear that this is not the only example in your data, and mention how many others you have. In a project like Catriona Carson's, where the aim is to sort all examples of one variable into categories, it may be desirable to reproduce *every* example of each type, because your aim is to show that all the examples you have put in the same category function in the same way. If you reproduce every case then the reader can judge this claim for her/himself. If your project involves counting, as Stuart May's did, your results will probably be best presented in the form of a table containing numbers;[1] but in discussion it is still worth illustrating your observations with examples from the data. Just as a picture is allegedly worth a thousand words, a concrete example will do much to enhance an abstract definition or claim in a written presentation of discourse analysis.

A second important general principle is to *be modest*. One way of being modest is to avoid making claims your project cannot support: you should qualify your claims to show you are aware of the limits on what conclusions can be drawn from any single piece of research, especially a relatively small-scale project. For instance, as I have already noted in passing, in a project on male friends' talk that uses only one group of (white, straight, middle-class and young) men friends as informants, it is important to remind the reader that your findings apply to that group and might not apply to others. Catriona Carson's project drew on quite a large corpus of data from more than one source, but still it was prudent for Catriona to point out that further research might reveal additional complexities in the use of *oh* to introduce reported speech, which were not apparent in her sample.

Another way of being modest is to acknowledge, in your writing up, any problems you perceive in the way you did your research. If, with hindsight, you would have taken a different approach to selecting informants and collecting spoken data, or if you think you should have looked at a different set of variables, it is perfectly OK to say so. An academic who submitted an article to a journal in which s/he said, 'I realize now that I did this, this and this completely wrong' would not get much credit: the reviewers would probably reply, 'well go back and do it right, then'. But if a student presents a flawed piece of research s/he will get credit for showing understanding of what went wrong. In the (rare) event that a student research project turns out disastrously, generating very small amounts of usable data and/or no clear results, it can be turned into a passable piece of work by focusing in the presentation on what caused the problems and how they might be addressed. I won't deny that a 'successful' research project is more likely to score high marks than a disastrous one, but it is not necessarily the case that a disastrous piece of research will fail because the results are worthless. Most student projects are assessed not on the interest or originality of their results but on the understanding they demonstrate of the research process and the issues addressed in the student's particular project.

Another principle that is important in writing up research is to *be scrupulous in using other people's work.* Your references to previous research (published or unpublished, accessed in print or on-line) must be full, clear, and made according to accepted scholarly conventions. I will not discuss those conventions in detail because they vary across different academic disciplines; in any case, this is one aspect of writing up which you will probably receive extended guidance on from your own teachers. But the principle underlying various conventions for citing or quoting other sources is always the same: if a researcher is using ideas or materials that are not her/his own, the reader must be aware of that, and moreover there must be enough detail about the source for the reader to check it for her or himself if s/he so wishes. Serious violations of that principle may be judged as plagiarism, even if (as is usually the case) the student had no thought of 'cheating' but was simply careless.

Let me emphasize again that the writing up of a project is not just an afterthought to research, but an integral part of the project, and whether it is done well matters a great deal. Until it is written up, a research project exists only for those directly involved, the researcher and the informants (and the supervisor/ course tutor, but remember, s/he may not be the only person assessing you). You may have a stunningly original methodology, argument or set of findings, you may have an impressively huge corpus of data and a fantastic interview technique, but you will get little credit for any of these things if they are so poorly presented in your report or dissertation that their significance cannot be appreciated by the reader. So you need to think as carefully about writing as about any other part of research, and you need to leave yourself the time to do it properly.

SUMMARY

In this chapter I have been trying not only to give helpful advice to students undertaking small-scale research but also to *demystify* the task by breaking it down into its components (e.g. formulating a question, collecting data, analysing the data, writing the project up), and then breaking some of those tasks down even further. In the end, how you organize these tasks in the time available to you will depend on your own judgement and circumstances. But having a clear understanding of what you have to do will enable you to plan, and thus to get the task under control. I hope this will help you to make the most of the opportunities a research project can provide to learn what working with spoken discourse is all about, and to appreciate from firsthand experience how fascinating and rewarding it can be.

SUGGESTIONS FOR FURTHER READING ABOUT DESIGNING YOUR OWN PROJECTS

For students of language and linguistics who are undertaking small-scale research, two useful resources are Barbara Johnstone's book *Qualitative Methods in Sociolinguistics* (2000) and Alison Wray et al.'s *Projects in Linguistics* (1998). Neither text is exclusively about discourse analysis, but both discuss it; both also include much good advice that is relevant to any kind of project involving the analysis of language data.

NOTE

1   The issue of doing statistical analysis and presenting the results is not discussed here, on the grounds that discourse analysis is essentially a non-quantitative approach to spoken language; where statistics are relevant they are generally of a simple and straightforward kind (e.g. Stuart May's frequencies).

Bibliography

Note: in most cases I have made reference to the source most easily accessible to a contemporary reader, which may not be the original source. But since readers should be aware of when something was written, in these cases the date of first publication is enclosed in square brackets.

Atkinson, [J.] Max (1984) *Our Masters' Voices.* London: Routledge.

Atkinson, J. Maxwell and Heritage, John (1999 [1984]) 'Jefferson's transcript notation', in Jaworski and Coupland. pp. 158–66.

Austin, J.L. (1962) *How To Do Things With Words.* Oxford: Clarendon Press.

Bakhtin, Mikhail (1999 [1935]) 'The problem of speech genres', trans. M. Holquist, in Jaworski and Coupland. pp. 121–32.

Barbour, Rosaline and Kitzinger, Jenny (eds) (1999) *Developing Focus Group Research: Politics, Theory and Practice.* London: Sage.

Barton, David and Ivanič, Roz (eds) (1991) *Writing in the Community.* London and Newbury Park, CA: Sage.

Barton, David, Hamilton, Mary and Ivanič, Roz (eds) (2000) *Situated Literacies: Reading and Writing in Context.* London: Routledge.

Bauman, Richard and Briggs, Charles (1990) 'Poetics and performance as critical perspectives on language and social life'. *Annual Review of Anthropology* 19: 59–88.

Bauman, Richard and Sherzer, Joel (eds) (1974) *Explorations in the Ethnography of Speaking.* Cambridge: Cambridge University Press.

Bergvall, Victoria, Bing, Janet and Freed, Alice (eds) (1996) *Rethinking Language and Gender Research: Theory and Practice.* London: Longman.

Biber, Douglas (1988) *Variation across Speech and Writing.* Cambridge: Cambridge University Press.

Billig, Michael (1992) *Talking of the Royal Family.* London: Routledge.

Blakemore, Diane (1992) *Understanding Utterances: An Introduction to Pragmatics.* Oxford: Basil Blackwell.

Blum-Kulka, Shoshana, House, Juliane and Kasper, Gabriele (eds) (1989) *Cross-cultural Pragmatics: Requests and Apologies.* Norwood, NJ: Ablex.

Boden, Deirdre (1994) *The Business of Talk: Organizations in Action.* Cambridge: Polity Press.

Briggs, Charles (1986) *Learning How To Ask: A Sociolinguistic Appraisal of the Role of the Interview in Social Science Research.* Cambridge: Cambridge University Press.

Brown, Gillian and Yule, George (1983) *Discourse Analysis.* Cambridge: Cambridge University Press.

Brown, Penelope (1980) 'How and why are women more polite?', in Sally McConnell-Ginet, Ruth Borker and Nelly Furman (eds), *Women and Language in Literature and Society.* New York: Praeger. pp. 111–35.

Brown, Penelope and Levinson, Stephen (1987) *Politeness: Some Universals in Language Usage.* Cambridge: Cambridge University Press.

Butler, Judith (1990) *Gender Trouble: Feminism and the Subversion of Identity.* New York: Routledge.

Caldas-Coulthard, Carmen Rosa and Coulthard, Malcolm (eds) (1996) *Texts and Practices: Readings in Critical Discourse Analysis.* London: Routledge.

Callender, Christine (1997) *Education for Empowerment.* Stoke on Trent: Trentham.

Callender, Christine and Cameron, Deborah (1990) 'Responsive listening as part of religious rhetoric: the case of Black Pentecostal preaching', in Graham McGregor and R.S. White (eds), *Reception and Response: Hearer Creativity in the Analysis of Spoken Discourse.* London: Routledge. pp. 160–78.

Cameron, Deborah (1997) 'Performing gender: young men's talk and the construction of heterosexual masculinity', in Sally Johnson and Ulrike Meinhof (eds), *Language and Masculinity.* Oxford: Blackwell. pp. 47–64.

Cameron, Deborah (ed.) (1998) *The Feminist Critique of Language: A Reader.* London: Routledge.

Cameron, Deborah (2000a) *Good to Talk? Living and Working in a Communication Culture.* London: Sage.

Cameron, Deborah (2000b) 'Styling the worker: gender and the commodification of language in the globalized service economy'. *Journal of Sociolinguistics* 4: 323–47.

Cameron, Deborah, McAlinden, Fiona and O'Leary, Kathy (1988) 'Lakoff in context: the form and function of tag questions', in Coates and Cameron. pp. 74–93.

Cameron, Deborah, Frazer, Elizabeth, Harvey, Penelope, Rampton, Ben and Richardson, Kay (1992) *Researching Language: Issues of Power and Method.* London: Routledge.

Carson, Catriona (1998) *Direct Speech and Attitude: The Relationship between the Formal Characteristics of Direct Speech and the Implication of Attitude.* Unpublished M.Litt dissertation, University of Strathclyde.

Clancy, Patricia (1986) 'The acquisition of communicative style in Japanese', in Bambi Schieffelin and Elinor Ochs (eds), *Language Socialization Across Cultures.* New York: Cambridge University Press. pp. 213–49.

Clyne, Michael (1996) *Intercultural Communication at Work.* Cambridge: Cambridge University Press.

Coates, Jennifer (1996) *Women Talk: Conversation Between Women Friends.* Oxford: Blackwell.

Coates, Jennifer and Cameron, Deborah (eds) (1988) *Women in their Speech Communities: New Perspectives on Language and Sex.* London: Longman.

Coates, Jennifer and Thornborrow, Joanna (1999) 'Myths, lies and audiotapes: some thoughts on data transcripts'. *Discourse & Society* 10(4): 594–7.

Condor, Susan (2000) 'Pride and prejudice: identity management in English people's talk about "this country"'. *Discourse & Society* 11(2): 175–205.

Coulmas, Florian (ed.) (1981) *Conversational Routine: Explorations in Standardized Communication Situations and Pre-patterned Speech.* Berlin: Mouton de Gruyter.

Coupland, Nikolas and Jaworski, Adam (eds) (1997) *Sociolinguistics: A Reader and Coursebook.* London: Macmillan.

Cutler, Cecilia (1999) 'Yorkville Crossing: White teens, hip hop and African American English'. *Journal of Sociolinguistics* 4: 428–42.

DeFrancisco, Victoria (1991) 'The sounds of silence: how men silence women in marital relations'. *Discourse & Society* 2(4): 413–23.

Drew, Paul and Heritage, John (1992) *Talk at Work: Interaction in Institutional Settings.* Cambridge: Cambridge University Press.

Drew, Paul and Sorjonen, Marja-Leena (1997) 'Institutional dialogue', in Teun van Dijk (ed.), *Discourse as Social Interaction: Discourse Studies Vol. II.* Newbury Park: Sage Publications. pp. 92–118.

Duranti, Alessandro (1997) *Linguistic Anthropology.* Cambridge: Cambridge University Press.

Edelsky, Carole (1981) 'Who's got the floor?' *Language in Society* 10: 383–421.

Ehrlich, Susan (1998) 'The discursive reconstruction of sexual consent'. *Discourse & Society* 9(2): 149–71.

Eldridge, John (ed.) (1995) *The Glasgow Media Group Reader, Vol. I: News Content, Language and Visuals*. London: Routledge.

Fabb, Nigel (1997) *Linguistics and Literature*. Oxford: Blackwell.

Fairclough, Norman (1989) *Language and Power*. London: Longman.

Fairclough, Norman (1992) *Discourse and Social Change*. Cambridge: Polity.

Fairclough, Norman (1995a) *Critical Discourse Analysis*. London: Longman.

Fairclough, Norman (1995b) *Media Discourse*. London: Arnold.

Fishman, Pamela (1983) 'Interaction: the work women do', in Barrie Thorne, Cheris Kramarae and Nancy Henley (eds), *Language, Gender and Society*. Rowley, MA: Newbury House. pp. 89–101.

Ford, Cecilia and Thompson, Sandra (1996) 'Interactional units in conversation: syntactic, intonational and pragmatic resources for the management of turns', in Ochs et al. pp. 134–84.

Foucault, Michel (1972) *The Archaeology of Knowledge and the Discourse on Language*. New York: Pantheon.

Foucault, Michel (1999 [1978]) 'The incitement to discourse', in Jaworski and Coupland. pp. 514–22.

Frazer, Elizabeth (1992) 'Talking about gender, race and class', in Cameron et al., pp. 90–112.

Gal, Susan (1979) *Language Shift*. New York: Academic Press.

Gee, James Paul (1999) *An Introduction to Discourse Analysis: Theory and Method*. London: Routledge.

Glasgow Media Group (1980) *More Bad News*. London: Routledge.

Goodwin, Marjorie H. (1990) *He-said-she-said: Talk as Social Organization among Black Children*. Bloomington: Indiana University Press.

Grice, H. Paul (1975) 'Logic and conversation', in P. Cole and J. Morgan (eds), *Syntax and Semantics 3: Speech Acts*. New York: Academic Press. pp. 41–58.

Gumperz, John (1982a) *Discourse Strategies*. Cambridge: Cambridge University Press.

Gumperz, John (ed.) (1982b) *Language and Social Identity*. Cambridge: Cambridge University Press.

Gumperz, John and Hymes, Dell (eds) (1972) *Directions in Sociolinguistics: The Ethnography of Communication*. Oxford: Blackwell.

Gumperz, John and Levinson, Stephen (eds) (1996) *Rethinking Linguistic Relativity*. Cambridge: Cambridge University Press.

Gumperz, John, Jupp, Tom and Roberts, Celia (1979) *Crosstalk*. Southall: National Centre for Industrial Language Training.

Gunnarsson, Britt-Louise, Linell, Per and Nordberg, Bengt (1997) *The Construction of Professional Discourse*. London: Longman.

Hall, Kira (1995) 'Lip service on the fantasy lines', in Hall and Bucholtz. pp. 183–216. (A shorter version is also reprinted in Cameron 1998.)

Hall, Kira and Bucholtz, Mary (eds) (1995) *Gender Articulated: Language and the Socially Constructed Self*. London: Routledge.

Hammersley, M. and Atkinson, P. (1995) *Ethnography*. London: Routledge.

Harding, Susan (1975) 'Women and words in a Spanish village', in Rayna Reiter (ed.), *Toward an Anthropology of Women*. New York: Monthly Review Press. pp. 283–308.

Harris, Sandra (1984) 'Questions as a mode of control in a magistrate's court'. *IJSL* 49: 5–27.

Harris, Zellig (1952) 'Discourse analysis'. *Language* 28: 1–30.

Harvey, Penelope (1992) 'Bilingualism in the Peruvian Andes', in Cameron et al. pp. 65–89.

Heath, Shirley Brice (1983) *Ways with Words: Language, Life, Work in Communities and Classrooms*. Cambridge: Cambridge University Press.

Heath, Shirley Brice (2000) 'Linguistics in the study of language in education'. *Harvard Educational Review* 70(1): 49–59.

Heritage, John (1984) *Garfinkel and Ethnomethodology*. Cambridge: Polity Press.

Holmes, Janet (1984) 'Hedging your bets and sitting on the fence: some evidence for tag questions as support structures'. *Te Reo* 27: 47–62.

Holmes, Janet (1995) *Women, Men and Politeness*. London: Longman.

Houghton, Cathryn (1995) 'Managing the body of labor: the treatment of reproduction and sexuality in a therapeutic institution', in Hall and Bucholtz. pp. 121–41.

Hutchby, Ian (1996) 'Power in discourse: the case of arguments on a British talk radio show'. *Discourse & Society* 7(4): 481–97.

Hutchby, Ian and Wooffitt, Robin (1998) *Conversation Analysis: An Introduction*. Cambridge: Polity Press.

Hymes, Dell (1972a) 'On Communicative Competence', in J.B. Pride and Janet Holmes (eds), *Sociolinguistics*. Harmondsworth: Penguin. pp. 269–93.

Hymes, Dell (1972b) 'Models of the interaction of language and social life', in John J. Gumperz and Dell Hymes (eds), *Directions in Sociolinguistics*. New York: Holt, Rinehart and Winston. pp. 35–71.

James, Deborah and Clarke, Sandra (1993) 'Women, men and interruptions: a critical review', in Deborah Tannen (ed.), *Gender and Conversational Interaction*. Oxford: Oxford University Press. pp. 231–74.

Jaworski, Adam and Coupland, Nikolas (eds) (1999) *The Discourse Reader*. London: Routledge.

Johnson, Sally and Meinhof, Ulrike (eds) (1997) *Language and Masculinity*. Oxford: Blackwell.

Johnstone, Barbara (2000) *Qualitative Methods in Sociolinguistics*. New York: Oxford University Press.

Kasper, Gabriele (1997) 'Linguistic etiquette', in Florian Coulmas (ed.), *The Handbook of Sociolinguistics*. Oxford: Basil Blackwell. pp. 374–85.

Kasper, Gabriele and Blum-Kulka, Shoshana (eds) (1993) *Interlanguage Pragmatics*. New York: Oxford University Press.

Kelly, John and Local, John (1988) 'On the use of general phonetic techniques in handling conversational material', in Roger and Bull. pp. 197–212.

Kitzinger, Celia (1998) 'Inaccuracies in quoting from data transcripts: *or* inaccuracy in quotations from data transcripts'. *Discourse & Society* 9(1): 136–43.

Kitzinger, Celia and Thomas, Alison (1995) 'Sexual harassment: a discursive approach', in Wilkinson and Kitzinger. pp. 32–48.

Kreckel, Marga (1981) *Communicative Acts and Shared Knowledge in Natural Discourse*. New York: Academic Press.

Kress, Gunther and van Leeuwen, Theo (1996) *Reading Images: The Grammar of Visual Design*. London: Routledge.

Kukkonen, Marko (1997) *Talk On The Screen: A Conversational Analysis of Internet Relay Chat*. Unpublished M.Litt dissertation, University of Strathclyde.

Kulick, Don (1992) *Language Shift and Cultural Reproduction: Socialization, Self and Syncretism in a Papua New Guinean Village*. Cambridge: Cambridge University Press.

Kulick, Don (1993) 'Speaking as a woman: structure and gender in domestic arguments in a New Guinea village'. *Cultural Anthropology* 8: 510–41.

Kulick, Don (1998) 'Anger, gender, language shift and the politics of revelation in a Papua New Guinean village', in Schieffelin et al. pp. 87–102.

Labov, William (1972a) 'The study of language in its social context', in Pier Paolo Giglioli (ed.), *Language and Social Context*. Harmondsworth: Penguin. pp. 283–307.

Labov, William (1972b) 'The transformation of experience in narrative syntax', *Language in the Inner City*. Philadelphia: University of Pennsylvania Press. pp. 354–96.

Labov, William (1997 [1972]) 'Rules for ritual insults', in Coupland and Jaworski. pp. 472–86.

Labov, William and Fanshel, David (1977) *Therapeutic Discourse: Therapy as Conversation*. New York: Academic Press.

Labov, William and Waletzsky, Joshua (1967) 'Narrative analysis', in J. Helm (ed.), *Essays on the Verbal and Visual Arts*. Seattle: University of Washington Press. pp. 12–44.

Lakoff, Robin (1975) *Language and Woman's Place*. New York: Harper & Row.

Leech, Geoffrey (1983) *Principles of Pragmatics*. London: Longman.

Lemke, Jay (1995) *Textual Politics: Discourse and Social Dynamics*. London: Taylor & Francis.

Levinson, Stephen (1983) *Pragmatics*. Cambridge: Cambridge University Press.

Livia, Anna and Hall, Kira (eds) (1997) *Queerly Phrased: Language, Gender and Sexuality*. New York: Oxford University Press.

Lucy, John (1992) *Language Diversity and Thought*. Cambridge: Cambridge University Press.

Macaulay, Ronald K.S. (1991) '"Coz it izny spelt when they say it": displaying dialect in writing'. *American Speech* 66: 280–91.

McConnell-Ginet, Sally (1988) 'Language and gender', in Frederick Newmeyer (ed.), *Linguistics: The Cambridge Survey, Vol IV*. Cambridge: Cambridge University Press. pp. 75–99.

McElhinny, Bonnie (1997) 'Ideologies of public and private language in sociolinguistics', in Ruth Wodak (ed.), *Gender and Discourse*. London: Sage. pp. 106–39.

McLemore, Cynthia (1991) *The Pragmatic Interpretation of English Intonation: Sorority Speech*. Unpublished PhD dissertation, University of Texas at Austin.

Maltz, Daniel and Borker, Ruth (1982) 'A cultural approach to male–female miscommunication', in Gumperz (ed.). pp. 195–216.

Maybin, Janet and Mercer, Neil (1996) *Using English: From Conversation to Canon*. London: Routledge.

Meinhof, Ulrike H. and Richardson, Kay (eds) (1994) *Text, Discourse and Context: Representations of Poverty in Britain*. London: Routledge.

Merritt, Marilyn (1976) 'On questions following questions in service encounters'. *Language in Society* 5: 315–57.

Mills, Sara (1997) *Discourse*. London: Routledge.

Milroy, Lesley (1987) *Observing and Analysing Natural Language*. Oxford: Blackwell.

Moerman, Michael (1988) *Talking Culture: Ethnography and Conversation Analysis*. Philadelphia: University of Pennsylvania Press.

Montgomery, Martin (1999) 'Speaking sincerely: public reactions to the death of Diana'. *Language and Literature* 8(1): 5–33.

Myers, Greg and Macnaghten, Phil (1999) 'Can focus groups be analysed as talk?', in Barbour and Kitzinger. pp. 173–85.

Ochs [Keenan], Elinor (1976) 'The universality of conversational postulates'. *Language in Society* 5: 67–80.

Ochs, Elinor (1988) *Culture and Language Development: Language Acquisition and Language Socialization in a Samoan Village*. Cambridge: Cambridge University Press.

Ochs, Elinor (1999 [1979]) 'Transcription as theory', in Jaworski and Coupland. pp. 167–82.

Ochs, Elinor and Schieffelin, Bambi (eds) (1983) *Acquiring Conversational Competence*. London: Routledge and Kegan Paul.

Ochs, Elinor and Taylor, Carolyn (1995) 'The "Father knows best" dynamic in dinner time narratives', in Hall and Bucholtz. pp. 97–120.

Ochs, Elinor, Schegloff, Emmanuel and Thompson, Sandra (eds) (1996) *Interaction and Grammar*. Cambridge: Cambridge University Press.

Olsen, David (1994) *The World On Paper: The Conceptual and Cognitive Implications of Writing and Reading*. Cambridge: Cambridge University Press.

Owen, Marion (1983) *Apologies and Remedial Interchanges*. Cambridge: Cambridge University Press.

Philips, Susan, Steele, Susan and Tanz, Christine (eds) (1987) *Language, Gender and Sex in Comparative Perspective*. Cambridge: Cambridge University Press.

Potter, Jonathan and Wetherell, Margaret (1987) *Discourse and Social Psychology*. London: Sage.

Preston, Dennis (1985) 'The Li'l Abner Syndrome: written representations of speech'. *American Speech* 60(4): 328–36.

Rampton, Ben (1995) *Crossing: Language and Ethnicity among Adolescents.* London: Longman.

Rampton, Ben (ed.) (1999) 'Styling the Other'. Theme issue of *Journal of Sociolinguistics,* Vol. 4(3).

Reid-Thomas, Helen (1993) *The Use and Interpretation by Men and Women of Minimal Responses in Informal Conversation.* Unpublished M.Litt dissertation, University of Strathclyde.

Reinharz, Shulamit (1992) *Feminist Methods in Social Research.* New York: Oxford University Press.

Reisman, Karl (1974) 'Contrapuntal conversation in an Antiguan village', in Bauman and Sherzer. pp. 110–24.

Richardson, Kay (1997) 'Twenty first century commerce: the case of QVC'. *Text* 2(2): 199–223.

Roberts, Celia, Davies, Evelyn and Jupp, Tom (1992) *Language and Discrimination: A Study of Multiethnic Workplaces.* London: Longman.

Roger, Derek and Bull, Peter (1988) *Conversation: An Interdisciplinary Perspective.* Clevedon, Avon: Multilingual Matters.

Sacks, Harvey (1972) 'On the analyzability of stories by children', in John J. Gumperz and Dell Hymes (eds), *Directions in Sociolinguistics.* New York: Holt, Rinehart Winston. pp. 325–45.

Sacks, Harvey (1984) 'Notes on methodology', in J.M. Atkinson and John Heritage (eds), *Structures of Social Action: Studies in Conversation Analysis.* Cambridge: Cambridge University Press. pp. 21–7.

Sacks, Harvey (1995) *Lectures on Conversation Vols I and II.* Oxford: Blackwell.

Sacks, Harvey, Schegloff, Emmanuel A. and Jefferson, Gail (1974) 'A simplest systematics for the organization of turn-taking for conversation'. *Language* 50: 696–735.

Saville-Troike, Muriel (1989) *The Ethnography of Communication: An Introduction.* Oxford and New York: Oxford University Press.

Scannell, Paddy (ed.) (1991) *Broadcast Talk.* London: Sage.

Schegloff, Emmanuel (1972) 'Sequencing in conversational openings', in John Gumperz and Dell Hymes (eds), *Directions in Sociolinguistics,* New York: Holt, Rinehart and Winston.

Schegloff, Emmanuel and Sacks, Harvey (1973) 'Opening up closings'. *Semiotica* 7: 289–327. (Also reprinted in Jaworski and Coupland.)

Scheinkein, James (1978) *Studies in the Organization of Conversational Interaction.* New York: Academic Press.

Schieffelin, Bambi (1990) *The Give and Take of Everyday Life: Language Socialization of Kaluli Children.* Cambridge: Cambridge University Press.

Schieffelin, Bambi, Woolard, Kathryn and Kroskrity, Paul (eds) (1998) *Language Ideologies: Practice and Theory.* New York and London: Oxford University Press.

Schiffrin, Deborah (1987) *Discourse Markers.* Cambridge: Cambridge University Press.

Schiffrin, Deborah (1994) *Approaches to Discourse.* Oxford: Blackwell.

Searle, John (1969) *Speech Acts: An Essay in the Philosophy of Language.* Cambridge: Cambridge University Press.

Shaw, Sylvia (2000) 'Language, gender and floor apportionment in political debates'. *Discourse & Society* 11(3): 401–18.

Shuy, Roger (1993) *Language Crimes: The Use and Abuse of Language Evidence in the Courtroom.* Oxford: Blackwell.

Silverman, David (1993) *Interpreting Qualitative Data: Methods for Analysing Talk, Text and Interaction.* London: Sage.

Silverman, David (1997) *Qualitative Research: Theory, Method and Practice.* London: Sage.

Silverstein, Michael and Urban, Greg (eds) (1996) *Natural Histories of Discourse.* Chicago: University of Chicago Press.

Sinclair, John and Coulthard, Malcolm (1975) *Toward an Analysis of Spoken Discourse: The English Used by Teachers and Pupils.* Oxford: Oxford University Press.

Stubbs, Michael (1983) *Discourse Analysis: The Sociolinguistic Analysis of Natural Language.* Oxford: Blackwell.

Stubbs, Michael (1996) *Text and Corpus Analysis: Computer-assisted Studies of Language and Culture.* Oxford: Blackwell.

Stubbs, Michael (1997) 'Whorf's children: critical comments on Critical Discourse Analysis (CDA)', in Ann Ryan and Alison Wray (eds), *Evolving Models of Language.* British Studies in Applied Linguistics Vol.12. Clevedon: Multilingual Matters. pp. 100–16.

Swann, Joan (1988) 'Talk control: an illustration from the classroom of problems in analysing male dominance in conversation', in Coates and Cameron. pp. 122–40.

Tannen, Deborah (1982) 'Ethnic style in male–female conversation', in John Gumperz (ed.), *Language and Social Identity.* Cambridge: Cambridge University Press. pp. 217–31.

Tannen, Deborah (1984) *Conversational Style: Analyzing Talk Among Friends.* Norwood, NJ: Ablex.

Tannen, Deborah (1989) *Talking Voices: Repetition, Dialogue and Imagery in Conversational Discourse.* Cambridge: Cambridge University Press.

Tannen, Deborah (1990) *You Just Don't Understand.* New York: William Morrow.

Tannen, Deborah (1994a) *Gender and Discourse.* New York and Oxford: Oxford University Press.

Tannen, Deborah (1994b) 'The relativity of linguistic strategies', in Tannen (1994a). pp. 19–52.

Tannen, Deborah and Saville-Troike, Muriel (eds) (1985) *Perspectives on Silence.* Norwood, NJ: Ablex.

Taylor, Talbot and Cameron, Deborah (1987) *Analysing Conversation: Rules and Units in the Structure of Talk.* Oxford: Pergamon Press.

Thomas, Jenny (1995) *Meaning in Interaction: An Introduction to Pragmatics.* London: Longman.

Thornton, Sarah (1999) 'An academic Alice in Adland: Ethnography and the commercial world'. *Critical Quarterly* 41(1): 58–68.

Ting-Toomey, Stella (1999) *Communicating Across Cultures.* New York: Guilford Press.

Turner, Roy (ed.) (1974) *Ethnomethodology.* Harmondsworth: Penguin.

Uchida, Aki (1998 [1992]) 'When "difference" is "dominance": a critique of the "anti-power based" cultural approach to sex differences', in Cameron. pp. 280–92.

van Dijk, Teun (1987) *Communicating Racism.* London: Academic Press.

van Dijk, Teun (1991) *Racism and the Press.* London: Routledge.

van Dijk, Teun (1993) 'Principles of critical discourse analysis', *Discourse & Society* 4: 249–83.

van Dijk, Teun (1996) 'Discourse, power and access', in Caldas-Coulthard and Coulthard. pp. 84–104.

van Dijk, Teun (ed.) (1997) *Discourse Studies: A Multidisciplinary Introduction (Vols I and II).* Thousand Oaks, CA: Sage.

Webb, Christine (1984) 'Feminist methodology in nursing research'. *Journal of Advanced Nursing* 9: 249–56.

West, Candace and Zimmerman, Don (1991) 'Doing gender'. *Gender and Society* 1: 125–51.

Widdicombe, Sue and Wooffitt, Robin (1995) *The Language of Youth Subcultures.* Hemel Hempstead: Harvester Wheatsheaf.

Widdowson, Henry (1995) 'Discourse analysis: a critical view'. *Language and Literature* 4(3): 157–72.

Wilkinson, Sue and Kitzinger, Celia (eds) (1995) *Feminism and Discourse: Psychological Perspectives.* London: Sage.

Wolfson, Nessa (1976) 'Speech events and natural speech: some implications for socio-linguistic methodology'. *Language in Society* 5(2): 189–209. (A shortened version appears in Coupland and Jaworski. pp. 116–25.)

Wooffitt, Robin (1992) *Telling Tales of the Unexpected: Accounts of Paranormal Experiences.* Hemel Hempstead: Harvester.

Woolard, Kathryn (1989) *Double Talk: Bilingualism and the Politics of Ethnicity in Catalonia.* Stanford, CA: Stanford University Press.

Wray, Alison, Trott, Kate and Bloomer, Aileen (1998) *Projects in Linguistics: A Practical Guide to Researching Language.* London: Arnold.

Yule, George (1996) *Pragmatics.* Oxford: Oxford University Press.

Zimmerman, Don and West, Candace (1975) 'Sex roles, interruptions and silences in conversation', in Barrie Thorne and Nancy Henley (eds), *Language and Sex: Difference and Dominance.* Rowley, MA: Newbury House. pp. 105–29.

Index

adjacency pairs, 94–7, 187
adult-child talk, 21, 40, 146
advertising, 54, 130
African American Vernacular English, 41, 42, 175–6
African Caribbeans, 58–62, 107, 169, 170
African diaspora, cultural/linguistic heritage of, 62
anthropology, 47–8, 53, 54
apologies, 69, 70, 71, 74, 86n
applause, 62, 104–5
Argentina, 94
Asians, British, 108–11
asymmetrical talk, 102, 133, 159, 161–4, 177, 178, 179n
Atherton, Kim, 183
Atkinson, Max, 38, 44, 87, 105
Atkinson, Paul, 30
audience studies, 65, 139–40
Austin, J.L., 48, 69–70, 85, 86n
Australia, 86n, 114

Bakhtin, Mikhail, 67n
Barbour, Rosaline, 160
Barthes, Roland, 50
Barton, David, 1, 67
Bauman, Richard, 66, 67n
BBC [British Broadcasting Corporation], 124
Bergvall, Victoria, 178
Biber, Douglas, 1
bilingualism, 4, 64–5, 108
Billig, Michael, 18n
Bing, Janet, 178
Blakemore, Diane, 86
Bloomer, Aileen, 192
Blum-Kulka, Shoshana, 85
Borker, Ruth, 117
Briggs, Charles, 67, 67n, 146, 147, 155, 160
British Telecom, 7

Broadcast talk, 21, 25–6, 76–8
    see also radio, television
Brown, Gillian, 1
Brown, Penelope, 79–81, 85, 97, 169
Bucholtz, Mary, 178
Bull, Peter, 44
Butler, Judith, 50

CA, see conversation analysis
Caldas-Coulthard, Carmen, 140
call centres, 103–4
Callender, Christine, 58, 62, 88
Cameron, Deborah, 30, 52, 62, 74, 93, 132
Carson, Catriona, 27, 29, 186–8, 189, 190
CDA, see critical discourse analysis
chat rooms, see computer-mediated communication
Chomsky, Noam, 55
Clarke, Sandra, 86n
class, 157–9
classroom talk, 38, 107, 162
closings, 99–100
Clyne, Michael, 86, 121
Coates, Jennifer, 22, 24, 28, 30, 39, 183
code-switching, 4
cohesion, 11
communicative competence, 55
    acquisition of by children, 21, 100
compliments, 73, 81–3
computer-mediated communication, 2, 9, 26, 27, 183–4, 186–8
Condor, Susan, 148–50
conflict talk, 62–5, 168–9
consent, see informed consent
content analysis, 139, 147
contextualization cues, 109, 113
    cultural differences in use of, 109–111
    in narratives, 154
    methods for investigating, 111, 112–19
conversation, 8–10

conversation analysis, 18n, 40, 48–9, 87–105
    and interview data, 148–52, 160
    and power, 88, 162, 163–4
co-operative principle, 75–8, 155
corpus linguistics, 1–2, 27, 39
Coulmas, Florian, 74
Coulthard, Malcolm, 49, 140
Coupland, Nikolas, 18, 44, 67n
courtroom discourse, 74, 101–103, 120,
    125–6, 161, 162
Critical Discourse Analysis, 50–51, 123–141
    criticisms of, 137–40, 162
critical theory, 50–51, 123
cross-cultural communication, see
    intercultural communication
'crossing', 174–6
'Crosstalk', 108–112
cultural studies, 8, 53
Cutler, Cecilia, 175–6

data
    coding of, 27
    collection of, 18–30, 185–6
    'naturalness' of, 20
    procedures for analysis of, 186–8
    quantity of, 28–9
    recording of, 19, 20, 22, 38–9, 44n
Davies, Evelyn, 109–110, 111, 121
DeFrancisco, Victoria, 21
Derrida, Jacques, 50
discourse
    definitions of, 10–17
    social change and, 129–34
discourse analysis
    as qualitative research method, 1,13–17,
        145–60
    designing research projects in, 180–92
    interdisciplinarity of, 7–8, 47–52
    key terms in, 8–10
discourse markers, 114–15, 121, 122n, 156,
    186–7
discursive construction of reality, 15–16, 50,
    51, 123, 124–9
dominance
    versus 'difference', 167–9, see also
        asymmetrical talk, power
Drew, Paul, 21, 87, 100–101, 102, 105, 178
Duranti, Alessandro, 66

Edelsky, Carole, 93, 165
education, discourse analysis in research on,
    8, 159–60
Ehrlich, Susan, 125–6, 128

Eldridge, John, 124
elicitation tasks, 116, 117–19
emotion, 133, 135–6
England, 148–50
English, 4
    African American, 41, 42
    African Caribbean, 58–62, 107
    American, 113–14
    Anglo-American, 116
    Australian, 114
    British, 108–12, 114
    Indian, 108–12
    transcribing nonstandard varieties of,
        41–3
    see also Scots
ethics, 4, 19, 22–7
ethnic minorities, 108–12, 127, 161
ethnic styles, 116–17, 175–6
    see also contextualization cues,
        intercultural communication
ethnography, 47, 53–4, 171–2
ethnography of speaking, 47–8, 65–67, 87,
    169
ethnomethodology, 48–9, 88, 171, 179n
eye-dialect, 40–43

Fabb, Nigel, 67n
face, 79, 147, 168
face-threatening acts, 79–83, 147
Fairclough, Norman, 129, 130, 131, 140,
    141n
Fanshel, David, 49, 51, 75
fascism, 126–7
felicity conditions, 69, 71
feminism, 88, 126, 159, 171
fillers, 33, 114, 155–6
Fishman, Pamela, 21, 88, 162, 183
floor, 90, see also turn-taking
fluency/disfluency, see hesitation
focus groups, 139, 160, 171, 174
Ford, Cecilia, 105n
forensic linguistics, 119–20
formality, see discourse, social change and,
    sincerity, synthetic personalization
form/function relationships, 13, 72–5
Foucault, Michel, 15–17, 18, 50, 157
Frazer, Elizabeth, 157–9
Freed, Alice, 178

Gal, Susan, 67
Garfinkel, Harold, 48, 179n
gay men, 165–7, 173, 176
gaze, see nonverbal communication

Gee, John Paul, 140
gender
    as cultural difference, 117–19, 167–9
    class and, 157
    ethnic style and, 117
    indirectness and, 116
    interruption and, 86n, 88, 165–7
    minimal responses and, 117–19
    performance of, 171–4, 175
    politeness and, 86
    see also gay men, heterosexuals, kros,
        lesbians
genre, 55, 66, 67n
given v. new information, 113–14
Glasgow Media Group, 124
Goffman, Erving, 149
Goodwin, Marjorie Harness, 67
gossip, 56, 57, 65, 173–4
grammar, 61
    and ideology, 125–6
    of spoken discourse, 35, 90–1, 105n
Greek, 116
greetings, 96, 98
Grice, H. Paul, 48, 75–8, 85, 94
Gumperz, John, 105, 108–12, 121, 141
Gunnarsson, Britt-Louise, 178

Hall, Kira, 175, 178
Hamilton, Mary, 1, 67
Hammersley, Martin, 30
Harding, Susan, 65
Harris, Sandra, 101–103, 161, 162
Harris, Zellig, 11, 49
Heath, Shirley Brice, 21, 67, 159
Heritage, John, 21, 38, 44, 87, 100–101, 102,
    105, 178
hesitation, 33, 38, 135–6, 152, 186, 188
heterosexuals, 162–3, 172, 183
Higgins, Michael, 24, 43, 183
'high vs. low context' cultures, 84–5
Holmes, Janet, 74, 86, 168–9
Houghton, Cathryn, 176–8
House, Juliane, 85
House of Commons debates, 164–9, 170,
    179n
Hutchby, Ian, 44, 87, 88, 105, 145, 160,
    163–4, 178
Hymes, Dell, 55–7, 66, 105, 115

identity 159, 161, 170–8
ideology, 123, 124, 125–6, 132–3, 136–7
illocution, 70
implicature, 76–8

indexicality, 175–6
Indian languages, 108, see also English,
    Indian
indirectness, 110–11, 116–17
    see also implicature, politeness, speech
        acts
informed consent, 22–3
institutional talk, 20–22, 100–103, 123
    collecting samples of, 24–5
    'conversationalization' of, 129–32
    see also asymmetrical talk, power
insults, 64, 67n
intention, 71
interactional sociolinguistics, 50, 106–22,
    162
intercultural (mis)communication, 84–5,
    107–8, 108–112, 161, 169
International Phonetic Alphabet, 41
internet, see computer mediated
    communication
interpretation, variation in, 72, 77–8,
    137–40
interruption, 74, 86n, 88, 92, see also
    simultaneous speech
intertextuality, 130, 141n
interviews
    as data collection method, 19–20
    as type of speech event, 20, 66, 146
    contradictions in, 156–9
    conventions of, 66, 130, 146
    narratives in, 151–2, 154
    self-presentation in, 145, 147–151, 171
    'unstructured', 146
intonation, 35
    rising v. falling, 109, 110, 112–14, see also
        prosodic and paralinguistic features
Ivanič, Roz, 1, 67

James, Deborah, 86n
Japanese, 74, 85, 119–20
Jaworski, Adam, 18, 44, 67n
Jefferson, Gail, 37, 44, 90–2
Johnson, Sally, 178
Johnstone, Barbara, 25, 30, 192
judicial discourse, see courtroom discourse,
    forensic linguistics
Jupp, Tom, 109–110, 111, 121

Kasper, Gabriele, 85–6
Kelly, John, 44
Kitzinger, Celia, 18n, 39, 159, 178
Kitzinger, Jenny, 160
Kreckel, Marga, 26, 72

Kress, Gunther, 7
Kristeva, Julia, 50
kros, 62–5
Kroskrity, Paul, 67
Kukkonen, Marko, 26, 183–4, 186–8, 189, 190
Kulick, Don, 21, 62–5, 67, 84

laboratory research, 20
Labov, William, 20, 49, 51, 67n, 75, 94, 152–4, 155
Lacan, Jacques, 50
Lakoff, Robin, 73, 112, 175
Leech, Geoffrey, 78–9, 85
Lemke, Jay, 15, 156
lesbians, 183
Levinson, Stephen, 21, 52, 55, 79–81, 85, 97, 141
Linell, Per, 178
linguistic relativity, 141
linguistics, 49–51
    see also phonetics, phonology, sociolinguistics, syntax
Livia, Anna, 178
Local, John, 44
local management of talk, 90, 103
Lucy, John, 141

McAlinden, Fiona, 74
Macaulay, Ronald, 37, 42–3, 44
McConnell-Ginet, Sally, 126
McElhinny, Bonnie, 21
McLemore, Cynthia, 113–14
Macnaghten, Phil, 160
Malagasy, 83–5
Maltz, Daniel, 117
masculinity, *see* gay men, gender, heterosexuals
May, Stuart, 183, 186–8, 190
Maybin, Janet, 1
media discourse, 25–27, 123, 137
    see also broadcast talk, computer mediated communication, news reporting, radio, television
Meinhof, Ulrike, 139, 178
Mercer, Neil, 1
Merritt, Marilyn, 28, 95
metalanguage, 8, 10, 56
metaphor, 128
Mexicano, 146
Mills, Sara, 18
Milroy, Lesley, 30
minimal responses, 107, 116–120

Moerman, Michael, 67
Montgomery, Martin, 133–7
multimedia texts, 2
Myers, Greg, 160

narrative, 11, 37, 42, 49, 87, 145, 151–4
national identity, 148–50, 171
news reporting, 19, 124, 127–8, 137–9
nonstandard English, *see* English
nonverbal communication, 38, 53, 90, 107
Nordberg, Bengt, 178

Observer's Paradox, 20, 24
Ochs, Elinor, 21, 40, 44, 65, 67, 83–4, 105n
O'Leary, Kathy, 74
Olsen, David, 32
oral history, 145
oral performance, 67n
'ordinary talk', 20–21, 100
overlap, 92, *see also* simultaneous speech
Owen, Marion, 98

Papua New Guinea, 62–5, 84–5
parallelism, 136
participant observation, 19, 47, 53–4
pauses, *see* hesitation
Pentecostalism, 58, 59–62, 133
performatives, 69–70
Philips, Susan, 67
philosophy of language, 48
phonetics, 27, 41, 44
phonology, 49, 50
poetics, 67n
politeness, 78, 79–83, 86, 97–8, 132, 155
    see also face
political discourse, 133–7, 164–9
postmodernism, 50–51, 170, 171, 176, 178
poststructuralism, 50–51, 170
Potter, Jonathan, 159
power, 16–17, 88, 132–3, 161–9, 177–8
    see also asymmetrical talk
pragmatics, 47, 48, 68–86
    see also co-operative principle, speech acts, politeness
preference systems, 96–8
    and politeness, 97–8
Preston, Dennis, 41, 44
privacy, 23–4
promises, 70–71
prosodic and paralinguistic features, 37–8, 41, 90, 107, 109, 110
psychology, discourse analysis in, 159
punctuation, 34–5, 38

qualitative research methodology, 13–17, 30, 159

quantitative methods, 14–15, 192n

questionnaires, 14–15

questions, 87, 95–6, 101–3, 155
  see also tag questions

quotative verbs, 27, 186

race, 157, 175–6

racism, 107, 126–8, 149–50, 161, 162, 178

radio
  DJ talk, 185
  phone-in programmes, 25, 26, 163–4

Rampton, Ben, 175, 178

Reid-Thomas, Helen, 117–19

Reinharz, Shulamit, 159

Reisman, Karl, 93

religious discourse, 58–62

repair, 19, 89

repetition, 33–4

replication studies, 182–3

reported speech, 27, 29, 186, 187–8

resistance, 177–8

Richardson, Kay, 44n, 139–40, 184

Roberts, Celia, 109–10, 111, 121

Roger, Derek, 44

Sacks, Harvey, 11, 89–90, 90–2, 99, 105, 180–1

Said, Edward, 50

sales talk, 131–2

sampling, 28

Saville-Troike, Muriel, 66, 93–4

Scannell, Paddy, 21, 29

Scargill, Arthur, 76

Schegloff, Emanuel, 90–2, 99, 105n

Scheinkein, James, 105

Schieffelin, Bambi, 21, 67

Schiffrin, Deborah, 13, 18, 30, 52, 57, 66, 114, 121, 122n

Scots, 41, 42–3

scripted talk, 103–104

Searle, John, 48, 70–72, 85

sentences, 12, 18n, 34–5

service encounters, 28, 103–4, 132

sexuality, see gay men, heterosexuals, lesbians

Shaw, Sylvia, 164–8, 179n

Sherzer, Joel, 66

Shuy, Roger, 119–20, 121

sign languages, 7

silence, 19, 49, 89, 92

Silverman, David, 30, 159

Silverstein, Michael, 67

simultaneous speech, 89, 92–3

sincerity
  as felicity condition for speech acts, 71
  in public speaking, 133–7

Sinclair, John, 49

social constructionism, 50, 170–8

sociolinguistics, 20, 48, 49, 50–51

sociology, 48, 53, see also ethnomethodology

Sorjonen, Marja-Leena, 178

sororities, 112–114, 121n

Spanish, 146

'Speaking' grid, 56, 57, 115

speech acts, 52, 56, 69–75

speech events, 52, 55, 58–66, 111

speech-writing differences, 31–6, 108, 187

spelling, see eye-dialect

Steele, Susan, 67

stress, see prosodic and paralinguistic features

Stubbs, Michael, 11, 141, 141n

subcultures, 53–4, 150–1, 175–6, 178

Swann, Joan, 38–9

Sweden, 94

syntax, 49, 73, 102

synthetic personalization, 131–3

tag questions, 73–4, 102

Taiap, 64–5

Tannen, Deborah, 28, 44, 74, 93–4, 116–17, 121, 162

Tanz, Christine, 67

Tarantino, Quentin, 141n

Taylor, Carolyn, 21, 65

Taylor, Talbot, 52

telephone
  conventions of talk on, 98–100, 104, 105n
  sex work, 175
  see also radio phone-in programmes

television
  documentary, 26, 139–40,
  shopping channels, 184–5
  sincerity and, 134
  soap opera, 65, 183, 188
  talk shows, 25
  see also broadcast talk

therapeutic discourse, 49, 94, 95–6, 130, 176–8

Thomas, Alison, 18n

Thomas, Jenny, 68–9, 70, 85

Thompson, Sandra, 105n

Thornborrow, Joanna, 39

Thornton, Sarah, 54

Ting-Toomey, Stella, 85
Tok Pisin, 62–5
transcription, 4, 19, 31–44, 186
  accuracy of, 39–40
  conventions for, 36–9
  theoretical issues in, 40–43
Trott, Kate, 192
Turner, Roy, 105
turn-taking, 61, 87, 89–94
  computer mediated communication and,
    183–4, 186–8
  cultural differences in, 93–4
  simplest systematics for, 90–2

Uchida, Aki, 121n, 169
universals, 48, 83–5
'uptalk', 112–14,
  see also intonation, rising v. falling
Urban, Greg, 67

Van Dijk, Teun, 18, 127–8, 138, 139, 140,
    178
Van Leeuwen, Theo, 7
verbal art, 37, 67n, 152
videotape, 38–9, 44n

Waletzsky, Joshua, 49, 151–4, 155
Webb, Christine, 154
West, Candace, 74, 86n, 88, 92
Wetherell, Margaret, 159
Widdicombe, Sue, 18n, 67, 150–1
Widdowson, Henry, 12, 18n, 141n, 162
Wilkinson, Sue, 159, 178
Wolfson, Nessa, 30, 146
Wooffitt, Robin, 18n, 44, 67, 105, 145,
    150–1, 153, 160
Woolard, Kathryn, 67
workplace talk, 65, 110, 111
  see also classroom talk, institutional talk,
    political discourse, sales talk, service
    encounters
Wray, Alison, 192
writing up research, 188–91
written discourse, 1–2, 8, 33, 123, *see also*
  speech writing differences

xenophobia, 149–50, *see also* racism

Yule, George, 1, 85

Zimmerman, Don, 74, 86n, 88, 92